Timetabling

A timetabler's cook-book

by

Keith Johnson

with

Mervyn Wakefield
and Chris Johnson

First published in 1980 by Hutchinson Education.
Reprinted 1980, 1981 (twice) 1982, 1983, 1985, 1993, 1995, 2002, 2003, 2004, 2005, 2006, 2007, 2008
This edition published in 2009 by:
October ReSolutions Limited, 3 Crown Green, Lymm, WA13 9JG, UK.
Reprinted 2009 (twice).

ISBN : 978-0-9561161-0-9

Designed and typeset by Keith Johnson

Cartoons by David Summerville, Chris Johnson, Adrian Downie, Simon Wrafter and Ann Johnson.

Printed and bound by : Lightning Source

I timetable — therefore I am!

Everything should be made as simple as possible, but not simpler.
Albert Einstein

There are no such things as 'problems', only solutions.
Jacques Cabanat

Acknowledgements

In the first edition I acknowledged the help that had been provided by people that I knew at that time, including: Mike Zarraga, formerly of the School Timetabling Applications Group; Peter Thompson, formerly Senior Secondary Inspector in Manchester; Donald Moore, formerly Head of Wilbraham High School; I.B. Butterworth, HMI and Fred Tye, Director of the North-West Educational Management Centre; Paul Murphy and Steve Bates, members of the Manchester Schools Timetabling Group.

In the years since then I have exchanged emails with thousands of timetablers (as part of the HelpLine service for *TimeTabler* software) and this has been enormously helpful in giving me a wide view of the huge range of problems facing timetablers today. I have always enjoyed solving these timetabling problems - it's much more fun than Sudoku!

This second edition has benefitted enormously from the expertise and wisdom of Mervyn Wakefield. His long experience of UK schools and timetabling, and his light-hearted approach to the many timetabling courses that he provides have added significantly to this new edition, and his spreadsheets (provided on the CD) can save you many hours.

Chris Johnson is the chief programmer for the *TimeTabler* range of software and his insight into the logic of timetabling has been invaluable in suggesting improvements and in proof-reading and checking this new edition.

Paul Murphy has been involved in timetabling for over thirty years and I am grateful for his comments on the draft.

Thanks also to Rachel Johnson and Janet Woodhouse for proof-reading.

David Summerville, Chris Johnson, Adrian Downie, Si Wrafter and Ann Johnson have provided the cartoons to show the lighter side of this serious subject.

My thanks to everyone for their help and support.

If you have any suggestions, comments or criticisms while reading this book, please send them to me at: keith@timetabler.com

Keith Johnson

*You're right — it **is** last year's, turned upside-down!*

Foreword to the First Edition

We are in the thick of discussing the school curriculum. Political and professional attention has swung from the structure of the schools to the content and process. What should be taught? In what mix? How should it be taught? Who should decide all this, and how much or which aspects should be decided nationally, by the Local Authority, or by the school? This is a healthy and necessary development and will, no doubt, take some years to reach any coherence.

Meanwhile, and indeed after any kind of agreement is reached, schools will have to make timetables. The timetable is the practical embodiment of the curriculum. All the fine talk about skills, knowledge, concepts, areas of human experience, the interrelationship of subjects and the totality of the curriculum is set at naught if the school does not have an efficient engine for changing the theory into practice. At the end of the day, teachers (as individuals and teams) have to be allocated to spend time (in differing spans) with the children (divided into groups appropriate for the purpose in hand), and it all has to be done with the constraints imposed by the building (or buildings) and the balance of practical and general accommodation available.

If the translation is done well, the intentions for an integrated curriculum, the sum of whose parts adds up to the intended whole, is achieved. Done badly, the timetable actually inhibits the intentions of those who planned the curriculum and committed themselves to its value system.
As in all human organisations, therefore, the most mechanical-seeming process needs as much care and thought as the more obviously profound.
Those who neglect the detailed and the arduous (or, even worse, regard it as beneath their concern) find their grand designs frustrated.

I welcome this book because it approaches its task in what seems to be exactly the right spirit. Get your philosophy of the curriculum and teaching method clear first. Then take pains and devise the best timetable circumstances allow.

This practical and sometimes humorous guide will help and sustain those who use it and indirectly benefit generations of pupils.

John Tomlinson CBE

Chairman of the Schools Council
Director of Education for Cheshire
Professor of Education, Warwick University

Foreword to this Second Edition

In the years since John Tomlinson wrote his foreword for the first edition of this book, there have not been many changes to the timetabler's task.
There are many 'eternal truths' in timetabling.

However in two areas things have altered: two counter-acting changes have been at work.

On the one hand, the timetable in most schools has become more complex. There are a number of reasons for this: the increase in part-time teaching and job-shares; a trend towards fortnightly cycles; options patterns have generally become more complex with the introduction of double-option courses and off-site learning; the introduction of consortium arrangements between schools (and not just at 'sixth form' level) has required joint timetabling (or, at least, compatible timetabling).

On the other hand, it is now normal to enlist the aid of computer software. Modern technology can relieve you of much of the donkey-work of timetabling, leaving you with more time to apply your skill and judgement where they are needed, in order to produce a timetable of the highest quality.
This 'symbiotic' approach, a joint effort between the electronic computer and the 'computer between your ears' is the key to getting a quality timetable. However, for this approach to work well it is essential to understand the principles of timetabling, even if the software is doing most of the work.
This book covers those principles.

Timetabling has a powerful effect on the life of a school or college, and as the timetabler you carry a heavy responsibility. We hope this book will help to give you the skills to achieve the highest quality timetable, for the benefit of your colleagues and students.

Keith Johnson

Mervyn Wakefield

Chris Johnson

Contents

5   Staff Deployment Analysis

6   Collecting the data

7   Timetable test 1   The Combing Chart

8   Timetable test 2   The Conflict Matrix

13 Block timetabling

14 Scheduling in Primary Schools

15 Timetabling by Computer

16 Doing the daily Cover for absent staff

Appendices

It's like the buses — you wait all week for a free period, and then 3 come all at once!

I've heard that timetablers have 70 ways of saying "It can't be done"!

1 Timetabling

Timetabling is probably the most important single event in the school year. The completed timetable may well rule the lives of a thousand pupils and 70 staff for the 190 days in the school year, period by period, bell by bell. Such a powerful tool may easily make or break teachers and teaching situations, and may easily distort or destroy the curricular philosophy of the school.

Timetabling has been called the art of compromise. From a given set of data there are likely to be many possible solutions, each involving compromises which detract from the ideal. Clearly we wish to obtain the solution with the fewest, least important compromises. This solution will give a timetable with the best quality — a timetable which is *enabling*, not restrictive, so that the teaching staff may develop to the full the curricular aims of the school.

The aim of this book is to describe ways of achieving a quality timetable by methods which are as logical and painless as possible.
If you are already a timetabler yourself, we hope you will find it of interest to compare our methods with your own.
If you have yet to try your first timetable, we hope this book will help to launch you gently, at the shallow end.
And even if you intend never to do any timetabling at all, we hope you will find these pages helpful in reducing the mystique surrounding timetabling — the mystique which too often allows a timetabler to end a discussion by saying, without reasons, 'It can't be done'.

We feel sure that all schools can only benefit by a more widespread understanding of the language and the unique problems of timetabling, so that discussions — whether in the Head's Room, the Staff Room or in Staff Meetings — can take place within a framework of informed opinion.

A FlowChart of Timetabling

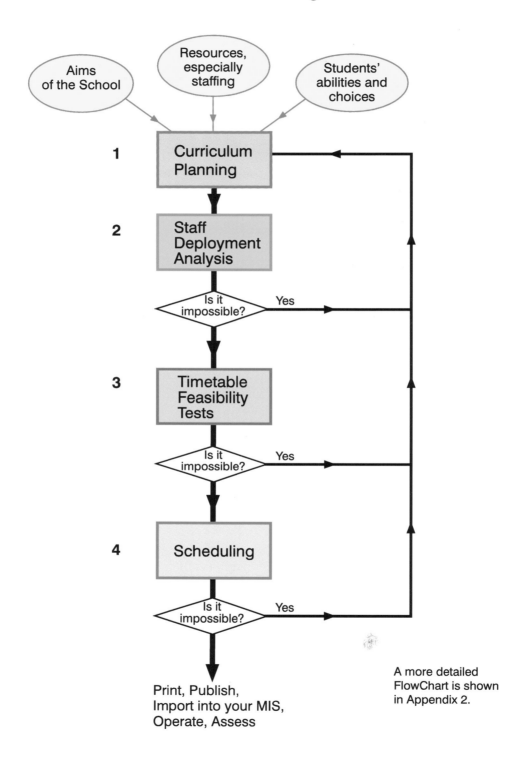

Aims of the School

Resources, especially staffing

Students' abilities and choices

1 Curriculum Planning

2 Staff Deployment Analysis

Is it impossible? — Yes

3 Timetable Feasibility Tests

Is it impossible? — Yes

4 Scheduling

Is it impossible? — Yes

Print, Publish, Import into your MIS, Operate, Assess

A more detailed FlowChart is shown in Appendix 2.

1.2   A Flow Chart of Timetabling

The activity which is usually called 'timetabling' (the fitting of classes, teachers, rooms into particular times of the week) should more properly be called scheduling.

Scheduling is only a part of the overall process, as the flow chart (opposite) shows.

The flow chart has four main parts:

1   Curriculum Planning

By considering the aims of the school (preferably laid down in writing and available to all members of staff, including part-time, supply, temporary staff and teaching assistants) and the available resources (particularly staffing and accommodation) a 'curriculum diagram' is produced.

This curriculum diagram is a key planning document. This is discussed in detail in Chapter 2.

This curriculum diagram will show, unambiguously, the subjects and numbers of periods to be provided for each group of pupils throughout the school.

The greatest attention is likely to be given to upper secondary years when students are given some choice in the subjects that they will study. Most schools take some account of their students' preferences when deciding the blocks or 'pools' of options. This is discussed in more detail in Chapter 3.

A useful test at this stage is to look at a Schematic Diagram of problematical parts of the curricular structure. This is discussed in Chapter 4.

2   Analysis

In order to see whether this curriculum diagram is feasible with the staffing that you have, some staffing analysis should take place. This may be done by counting the number of periods required for each subject area.

Another method is that originated by T.I. Davies and called 'staff deployment analysis'. This method allows us to compare classes and year-groups in order to see the distribution throughout the school of our most important resource, staffing. It also allows you to see, year on year, how your school is changing its allocation of staffing resources.

In some cases (for example, when newly joining a school or when the size of the intake is changing) it may be more useful to consider this analysis as the first step in the flow chart, to be completed before deciding the detailed curriculum diagram. The method is discussed in Chapter 5.

The events covered by steps 1 and 2 normally take place during the Autumn and Spring terms.

3 Timetable tests

Later, during the scheduling stage, problems will arise and the assigning of a class or a teacher will appear to be impossible. But is it really impossible? Is there a mathematical impossibility in the data or is it merely the timetabler's inability to see the solution? Clearly, it helps if most or all of the mathematical impossibilities have been removed earlier — the timetabler is then more likely to persevere in the hope of finding a solution with little or no compromise.

There is no known test for showing whether a given set of data will produce a timetable. However there are tests for showing whether a timetable is *im*possible. These feasibility tests are described in chapters 7–10.

Despite the temptation to rush to the final stage, it is essential to apply some or all of the tests if you are to achieve a timetable of the highest quality. These tests will normally be completed in April or May (in the northern hemisphere).

4 Scheduling

This is the integration of the 5 variables — teachers, classes (students), rooms, time, subjects — into a viable pattern. It is a kind of 5-dimensional jigsaw, built up with the aid of a timetable 'model' by following certain rules.

These days a computer is normally used, because of the speed and efficiency that it provides. However it is the skill of the *human* timetabler that determines the **quality** of the final timetable.

The many aspects of scheduling are discussed in chapters 11-15.
The scheduling is normally completed in June or July.

1.3   A timetable of timetabling — The Timetabler's Year

The diagram on the opposite page outlines the sequence of events during the school year.
A more detailed timetable of timetabling is given in Appendix 1.

A brief timetable of timetabling

Evaluating
   Distribute timetables and details of option groups to students.
   Interview students who now wish to change options or courses.

   Discuss and evaluate the new timetable in operation, including
   via Heads of Departments/Subjects and the Staff Room.

   Use Staff Deployment Analysis?
   Review of curriculum policy (by Senior Leadership Group?)
   Consider reports from any curriculum working groups?

Options
   Careers advice to Year 9.
   Produce an Options Booklet, and Options Choice Form.
   Parents Evening for Year 9; perhaps a careers convention?

   Option forms vetted; Choices analysed; Counselling begins.
   Option Blocks pattern determined.

Data
   Staffing checks - Staff Deployment Analysis?
   Draw up the agreed Curriculum Diagram; Curriculum audit.
   Staffing forms to Heads of Department / Heads of Subject.
   Staffing forms vetted.
   Staff Loading Chart completed.

Feasibility Tests
   Timetable Test 1 - Combing Chart.
   Timetable Test 2 - Conflict Matrix.
   Timetable Test 3 - Rooming.
   Other timetable tests.
   Consultation and negotiation with staff as necessary.

Scheduling
   Scheduling; compromise and consultation as necessary.

Publishing
   Printing and distributing timetables.
   Importing the timetable into the school's MIS (admin) system.
   Setting up the system used to cover staff absences.

(Left margin, top to bottom: Autumn Term | Spring Term | Summer Term)

1.4 Summary

'Scheduling' is only part of the overall timetabling process. The timetabler's year includes a number of activities which eventually lead up to the key scheduling stage.

Throughout this book timetabling terms are usually explained as they are used, but in any case a full **Glossary** of timetabling terms is shown in Appendix 5.

Year numbers

The Year numbers (Grade numbers) on the diagrams in this book are the National Curriculum Year-numbers used in England & Wales, where Year 7 is the First Year in secondary education (pupils aged 11–12).

Year 8 in this system (pupils aged 12–13) is Year 9 in Northern Ireland and S1 in Scotland, and Year 2 in many independent schools.

Years (Grades) 12/13 (ages 16–19) are still often called the 'Sixth Form'.

*But I thought **you** were doing the timetable...*

2   Planning the Curriculum

When planning changes to the curricular structure of your school, it is very important to describe this structure unambiguously.

A **Curriculum Diagram** is a way of showing the curricular structure of your school graphically. It shows clearly and unambiguously the Subject Teaching Groups that you are going to offer to each cohort of students, and whether any of these groups are to be 'blocked' together on the timetable.

A Curriculum Diagram is an essential planning tool. It is the only way to show your curricular structure unambiguously.
To have meaningful staff discussions about the curriculum or the timetable, each member of staff should be familiar with it. A copy will normally be required by visiting inspectors.

The simplest way to draw a Curriculum Diagram is to use a spreadsheet (such as Excel) because the diagram is essentially a grouping of rectangular boxes, and the spreadsheet makes it easy to draw the boxes and align the items.
An example of a Curriculum Diagram drawn this way can be downloaded from:
http://www.timetabler.com/SupportCentre/CurriculumDiagram.xls

The next 12 pages show a series of Curriculum Diagrams, of varying complexity. You may find them useful when discussing the development of the curricular structure in your school.

The second part of the chapter discusses the management of changes to the curricular structure, the effects of innovation, and ways for the Timetabler to look at the feasibility of changes. One common change, changing the timetable cycle, is looked at in detail.

2.2 Curriculum Notation

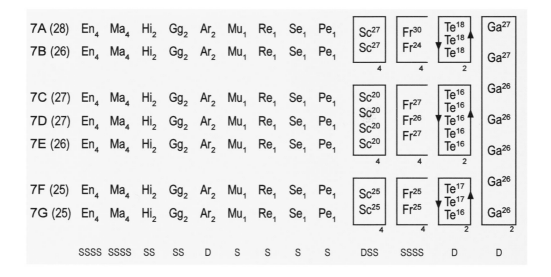

The Curriculum Diagram above is shown with full 'Curriculum Notation'.
Normally you will not need this level of detail.
It is decribed in detail, step by step, below.

It shows a Year which has 7 basic groupings, labelled 7A to 7G. These are usually called '**Registration Groups**' or '**Tutor Groups**' or '**Forms**'.
Such a year is often called '7 f.e.' (7 form entry), though this term may also mean a school designed to accept an intake of 7 x 30 = 210 students.

The number (28) shows the number of students in TutorGroup 7A.

In this school Year 7 is divided into 3 curriculum-populations or '**bands**', 7AB, 7CDE, 7FG.

Against each TutorGroup the **Subjects** are shown. See also the blue box on the opposite page.
The subscripts show the number of periods of teaching time for each subject (in each timetable cycle, normally per week or per fortnight).
So En_4 means the students have access to 4 periods of English.

The diagram also shows the '**period-breakdown**' for each subject.
English is to be taught as 4 Single lessons (SSSS), whereas Art is to be timetabled as a Double-period (D). (If the period-breakdowns were different for each band they would be shown in a row under each band.)

The subjects En, Ma, Hi, ...Pe are 'pure class' activities, and for each of these subjects the students are taught in their Tutor Groups.

Let's look now at the **Science** part of the curriculum, which is 'blocked'.
The students in 7AB are *re-grouped* into 2 Science groups, with 27 students in each. (The superscript Sc^{27} shows the number of students in each group.)
Similarly the students in 7CDE are re-divided into 4 Science groups.

If we look at the **French** blocks, the box-line is shown only on 3 sides of the rectangle. This is the convention for groups that are 'setted', in this case by their attainment (or ability) in French. On a timetable they will normally be labelled Set 1, Set 2.

The box round the **Technology** groups has arrows on it. This is the convention for a rotating 'circus' or 'carousel' or 'rota', when the students change groups according to a calendar. Perhaps the students study a different technology each term.

The box for whole-year **Games** shows that all the groups for this subject take place simultaneously. They may be divided by sex or some other criterion.

In fact, for *scheduling* purposes, the distinction between these types of blocks is irrelevant and will be ignored in the diagrams on the following pages.
In each case the block shows Teaching Groups in parallel and so we just have to schedule a team of teachers *at the same time*.

Even for the 'rota' block, the arrows are irrelevant for scheduling purposes. They are only needed for the calendar aspect of the rota when you put the timetable into your MIS (admin) system.

In looking at the Curriculum Diagrams on the following pages, you may wish to evaluate your existing curricular structure, to consider to what extent it fulfils the requirements of your students.

Too often a school's structure may reflect the idiosyncrasies of a previous timetabler or the particular enthusiasm of a previous Head; the intransigence of an influential Head of Department or the advice of an inspection from eight years ago. Is it still fit for purpose?

Subject Codes
Traditionally, subjects have been shown with 2-letter codes, like **En** (English), **Ma** (Maths), **Sc** (Science), etc, with the only surprises being **Se** (for PSHE), **De** (for German) and **Gg** (for Geography) .
However there is currently a move by the government to standardise on 3-character codes, using upper-case only.
For example, ENG, MAT, SCI, PSH, GER, GEO for these 6 subjects.
However in the following diagrams we have kept to the traditional labels (which are more legible and more compact).

2.3   2-form-entry school   All 'pure-class' activities

7A	En	Ma	Sc	Fr	Hi	Gg	Ar	Mu	Re	Se	Te	Pe
7B	En	Ma	Sc	Fr	Hi	Gg	Ar	Mu	Re	Se	Te	Pe

In this simple example of a Curriculum Diagram all the students in 7A follow a series of lessons as class 7A, and without ever mixing with 7B.
As in all timetabling diagrams, time runs horizontally.

2.4   2-form-entry school   With some joint activities

7A	En	Ma	Sc	Fr	Hi	Gg	Ar	Mu	Re	Se	Te	Pe
7B	En	Ma	Sc	Fr	Hi	Gg	Ar	Mu	Re	Se	Te	Pe

7A and 7B students now join together for one subject (Pe), with two teachers, who may divide them up in any way they wish.
While scheduling we have to ensure that these two Pe teachers are teaching at the same time, whereas for all the other subjects there is not the same restriction. In mixed schools it is normal for two classes to be paired for Pe, so as to allow a girls group and a boys group.

2.5   2-form-entry school   With more joint activities

7A	En	Ma	Sc	Fr	Hi	Gg	Ar	Mu	Re	Se	Te	Pe
											Te	
7B	En	Ma	Sc	Fr	Hi	Gg	Ar	Mu	Re	Se	Te	Pe

In this example, 7A and 7B also join together for Technology, with three teachers (teaching at the same time).
The composition of the Technology groups can be decided by the Technology staff, independently of any other subject, and they can also rotate the groups during the course of the year, if and when they wish.

2.6   4-f.e. school   With more joint activities

In this example the school is bigger, with 4 tutor groups, and most subjects are still taught in those tutor groups, with all the flexibility that that gives.

Technology is taught with 3 groups across each half-year-band ...probably the school cannot afford Technology to go across the whole year because of a shortage of Technology teachers and/or Technology rooms.

As well as Pe across the whole year, PSHE ('Se') is also taught across the whole year ...and perhaps at the same time of the week for the *whole* school, not just Year 8.

2.7   4-f.e. school   Varied groupings

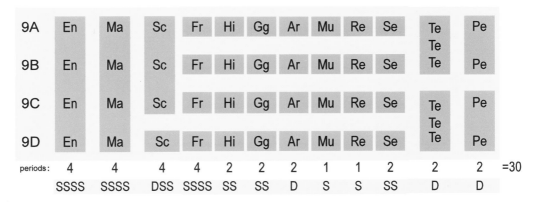

In this example, the English and Maths are setted across the Year, giving more flexibility to those departments (but less flexibility to the timetabler).

Science is setted across only 3 TutorGroups. This may be because the school has only 3 Science teachers (or labs).

As timetabler you will find it essential to always show the number of periods for each subject, and also the period-breakdown (into S=Single, D=Double), as shown above. It is ***vital*** to check that the total (eg. 30) is correct for your cycle.

2.8 Half-year Bands for Core Subjects

	En	Ma	Sc	Fr	Sp	Hi	IT	Te
10A	En	Ma	Sc	Fr	Sp	Hi	IT	Te
	En	Ma	Sc	Fr	Te	Hi	Te	Dr
10B	En	Ma	Sc	Fr	Mu	Ar	Fo	Pe
					Gg	Gg	Gr	Ar
10C	En	Ma	Sc	Fr	Hi	Dr	Ar	IT
	En	Ma	Sc	Fr	Ss	Te	Hi	Bs
10D	En	Ma	Sc	Fr	Pe	Tx	Bs	Re

←——— core subjects ———→   ←——— optional subjects ———→

The core subjects are setted across the half-year bands ...often because of the difficulty of getting enough teachers of the same subject to go across the full year.

The blocks of 'optional' or 'elective' subjects go across the full year. The varied subjects mean there is no difficulty in staffing the groups, but as we shall see later the varied teacher-team for each block can cause difficulty in scheduling (as the mixed teams interact with any single-subject setted blocks in lower school with the same teachers).

Some schools will have fewer core blocks and more option blocks.

Some schools may have (some) option-blocks across the half-year band.

2.9 Blocks across the year

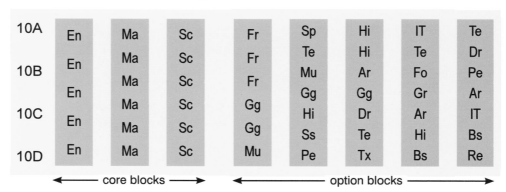

←——— core blocks ———→   ←——— option blocks ———→

A scheme like this depends on having sufficient teachers (and labs) for the whole year at once. Its value lies in having more groups to differentiate teaching in the core subjects (eg. a Maths set 1 for the most able mathematicians).

Option blocks can include 'sets' (see French in the diagram above).

Options are discussed in more detail in Chapter 3.

2.10 'Consistent setting'

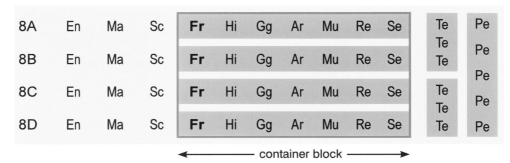

8A	En	Ma	Sc	**Fr**	Hi	Gg	Ar	Mu	Re	Se	Te	Pe
8B	En	Ma	Sc	**Fr**	Hi	Gg	Ar	Mu	Re	Se	Te Te	Pe
8C	En	Ma	Sc	**Fr**	Hi	Gg	Ar	Mu	Re	Se	Te	Pe Pe
8D	En	Ma	Sc	**Fr**	Hi	Gg	Ar	Mu	Re	Se	Te Te	Pe Pe

◄─────── container block ───────►

In this school they would like to have French setted by attainment (ability) but they do not have 4 French teachers. So the curricular structure above, which implies 4 French groups scheduled at the same time, would appear at first sight to be impossible. It also implies that the school would need 4 Music teachers and 4 Re teachers, which may be even more impossible!

However, if several subject departments can agree between themselves on how to group the students, then a '**consistent setting**' arrangement can give a solution, as explained here.

In the diagram above, the French, History, Geography, Art, Music, Re and PSHE teachers have agreed to divide all the students in 8ABCD into 4 consistent groups. The criterion may be their ability (attainment) in French, or it could be based on some other factor(s).

From a scheduling perspective we then have to ensure that these seven subjects are treated as though they are in a **Container Block**, which isolates them and ensures that these 7 subjects do not get mixed up with the other subjects, which are grouped using different criteria.

(Dealing with a Container Block is difficult in manual scheduling, but it is much easier using timetabler software, see chapter 15).

Within the Container Block (which of course is spread out across the timetable cycle) the subjects can slide against each other, so that there is never a need for more than one French (or Music or Re) teacher.

The diagram below shows one solution but there are others:

8A	En	Ma	Sc	**Fr**	Hi	Gg	Ar	Mu	Re	Se	Te	Pe
8B	En	Ma	Sc	Hi	**Fr**	Mu	Gg	Ar	Se	Re	Te Te	Pe
8C	En	Ma	Sc	Gg	Se	**Fr**	Hi	Re	Ar	Mu	Te	Pe Pe
8D	En	Ma	Sc	Se	Re	Hi	**Fr**	Gg	Mu	Ar	Te Te	Pe Pe

2.11 Consistent setting in Science

9A	En	Ma	Ph-1	Ch-1	Bi-1	Fr	Hi	Gg	...
9B	En	Ma	Ph-1	Ch-2	Bi-2	Fr	Hi	Gg	...
9C	En	Ma	Ph-1	Ch-1	Bi-2	Fr	Hi	Gg	...
9D	En	Ma	Ph-2	Ch-2	Bi-1	Fr	Hi	Gg	...
			Ph-2	Ch-1	Bi-3				

A common requirement for teaching Coordinated Science is that the same group of students should be taught by a Physicist, a Chemist and a Biologist.

In the Year 9 shown above, the 4 Tutor Groups (9A, 9B, 9C, 9D) are re-divided into 5 Science groups (shown by the 5 rows) ...but the school has only 2 Physics teachers, 2 Chemistry teachers and 3 Biology teachers!

Note: the labelling on this diagram is a little different ...as well as the subject (Ph, Ch, Bi) it also shows the teacher that is required for each of the 5 Science groups (Ph-1, Ph-2, etc).

The top strip in the diagram shows that the 'top' Science group should be taught by teachers Ph-1, Ch-1 and Bi-1 (but in any order).

At first sight (in the diagram above) this seems an impossible situation as it appears that Ph-1 must be in 3 places at the same time!

However, using a Container Block (as in section 2.10) allows the Science groups to slide against each other (but only within the Container Block).

This gives several solutions, one of which is shown below:

9A	En	Ma	Ph-1	Ch-1	Bi-1	Fr	Hi	Gg	...
9B	En	Ma	Ch-2	Ph-1	Bi-2	Fr	Hi	Gg	...
9C	En	Ma	Ch-1	Bi-2	Ph-1	Fr	Hi	Gg	...
9D	En	Ma	Ph-2	Bi-1	Ch-2	Fr	Hi	Gg	...
			Bi-3	Ph-2	Ch-1				

← container block →

2.12　Consistent setting, in several container blocks

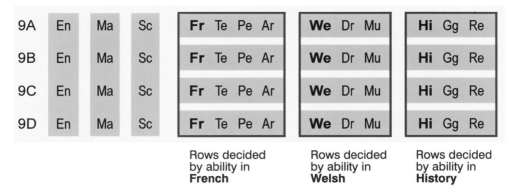

				Rows decided by ability in **French**	Rows decided by ability in **Welsh**	Rows decided by ability in **History**
9A	En	Ma	Sc	**Fr** Te Pe Ar	**We** Dr Mu	**Hi** Gg Re
9B	En	Ma	Sc	**Fr** Te Pe Ar	**We** Dr Mu	**Hi** Gg Re
9C	En	Ma	Sc	**Fr** Te Pe Ar	**We** Dr Mu	**Hi** Gg Re
9D	En	Ma	Sc	**Fr** Te Pe Ar	**We** Dr Mu	**Hi** Gg Re

In this example, from a school in Wales, there are 3 container blocks, each of which has rows of subjects which can slide against each other (horizontally) within the same block (as shown in sections 2.10, 2.11).
The students from 9ABCD are re-divided in different ways for each block.

In order to decide whether each block has enough subjects & periods in it to be feasible, you will need to apply the ideas discussed in the chapter on Schematic Diagrams (see Chapter 4).

2.13　Blocks within blocks

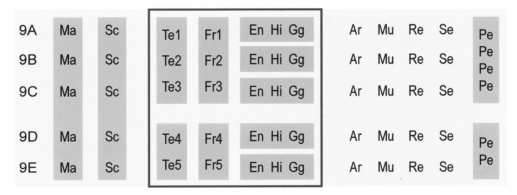

A container block can have other blocks within it.
In this example the Te1/Te2/Te3 block can be scheduled at the same time as the Fr4/Fr5 block, or at the same time as the lower En, Hi, Gg groups (which are each consistently setted).

As Curriculum Diagrams get more complicated, a key question to ask is "What is the benefit to the students?".

2.14 Blocks within blocks, varying populations

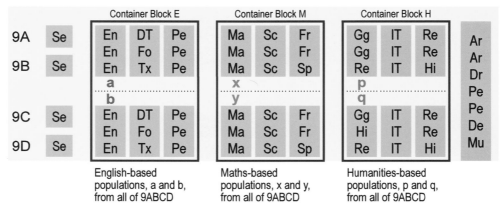

English-based populations, a and b, from all of 9ABCD

Maths-based populations, x and y, from all of 9ABCD

Humanities-based populations, p and q, from all of 9ABCD

In this curriculum the yeargroup is sometimes divided into two populations (called 'sub-bands' a and b) based on their attainment in English.

At other times the yeargroup is divided by their attainment in Maths (sub-bands x and y) or their attainment in Humanities (sub-bands p and q).

Because the populations are separate, within any container block, the subject blocks can slide against each other. For example the 'x' Maths block can be scheduled at the same time as the 'y' blocks for Ma or Sc or Fr/Sp.

2.15 Incompatible structures

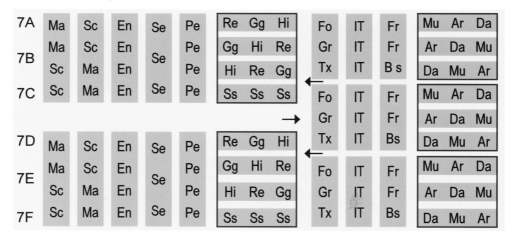

A school in Manchester has this very complicated curricular structure even in Year 7. From a scheduling perspective, probably the worst part is that the right-hand parts (combined as 7AB, 7CD, 7EF) cannot slide or be scheduled at the same times as any of the left-hand parts (which are combined as 7ABC, 7DEF) ...a very serious difficulty for the timetabler (see also section 2.16).

A loss of scheduling flexibility — for what curricular gain?

2.16   Other features of Curriculum Diagrams

The last example (diagram 2.15) shows a 'trick' (sometimes called '**cross-setting**') that is often used if the school does not have sufficient Science or Maths teachers to construct a single-subject block across the full year:

Ma	Sc		Hum	Lang
Ma	Sc		Hum	Lang
Ma	Sc	or perhaps:	Hum	Lang
Sc	Ma		Lang	Hum
Sc	Ma		Lang	Hum
Sc	Ma		Lang	Hum

The linked subjects must have the same period allocation.
However the individual sets in each subject do not have to be 'consistent'.
Only the populations, 'upper' and 'lower', have to agree. Within these 2 populations each subject can 'set' unilaterally.

Consistent setting was shown across the year in examples 2.10, 2.11, 2.12, and across parts of the year in example 2.15.

If you have, for example, only one Music teacher in a structure like 2.15 then great care is needed to ensure that the structure is logically possible. This is discussed in Chapter 4, on Schematic Diagrams.

The more subjects involved in a consistently-setted block, the more flexibility you are likely to have when scheduling it.

If a school has only 3 French teachers but needs 4 sets across the year, then a simplified consistent-setting arrangement is often used, shown here by mixing Re with the French:

	Fr	Fr	Fr	Re
Set 1:	Fr	Fr	Fr	Re
Set 2:	Fr	Fr	Re	Fr
Set 3:	Fr	Re	Fr	Fr
Set 4:	Re	Fr	Fr	Fr

'**Incompatible structures**' like the one shown in diagram 2.15 may or may not be serious. For example:

impossible

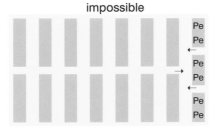

probably possible, perhaps tight

⟵ A ⟶   ⟵ B ⟶

If there is only one 'triplet' (of Pe in this example) then clearly all 3 parts of the triplet can only occur at the same time.
If they have a teacher (or specialist room) in common then the timetable is impossible.

If there are several 'doublets' (A) they can slide against each other; and if there are several 'triplets' (B) they can slide against each other.
But the 'A' blocks cannot slide against the 'B' blocks, so the solution space is restricted, but probably not impossible.

2.17 Vertical Curriculum Design

Traditionally students have been taught all their subjects with their peers. That is, they are taught with students in the same age cohort. The students are not the same age (between youngest—oldest there may be an age difference of 364 days), and they are not at the same stage of development, but for school organisation purposes they are treated as being at the same age and stage.

For some students this is clearly limiting for their education. For example, a student aged 11, in Year 7, may have a mathematical ability as good as any student in Year 8.

Some schools are devising ways to allow such students to learn within an older group of students, with 'vertical grouping'.

Consider the two diagrams below:

In diagram **A** the students in Year 7 are in 2 mixed-ability half-year Bands. For Maths they are taught together and divided into 6 sets by their ability/attainment in Maths.

In diagram **B**, the 2 bands in Year 7 may still be broadly mixed-ability, but the generally more-able or higher-attaining students are in Band 7A. And on the timetable, higher Band 7A is scheduled with lower Band 8B in Year 8, and the combination divided into 6 Maths sets. It is likely that these 6 sets will each have a narrower range of ability/attainment than the sets in diagram **A**.

In diagram **B** a student could be working with others who are up to (almost) two years older or two years younger. The Maths Department can decide whether or not only a few students are working outside their normal age cohort, but the possibility exists for the school to offer some 'acceleration' to an able mathematician.

There are further possibilities raised by the idea of an under-achieving student in Band 7A being transferred to Band 8B in the following year. Or a late-developing student could be transferred from Band 7B to Band 8A, effectively moving up two years.

If you are thinking of introducing a similar scheme in your school you will need to try some 'What if...?' experiments as discussed in chapter 15.

'School within a school'

In some schools the pupils are grouped vertically into sub-schools, (rather like an old 'House' system).

For example, a 6-form-entry school might divide all its Key Stage 3 pupils into 3 vertical 'schools', each one with a curricular structure as shown. Instead of 6 Maths sets across a Year, they are across the Key Stage.

Year 9	Ma	En	
+	Ma	En	
Year 8	Ma	En	etc
	Ma	En	
+	Ma	En	
Year 7	Ma	En	

Vertical options in Years 9, 10, 11

Some schools, perhaps within a consortium, have devised vertical options across Years 9, 10, 11. In the following example the consortium of schools has agreed that the 'consortium days' are Tuesday and Thursday.

	Mon	Tues	Wed	Thurs	Fri
Year 11	core	option groups for all students	core	option groups for all students	core
Year 10	core		core		core
Year 9	core		core		core

Within each option block there are usually at least 2 groups for each subject, which might act as Set 1 and Set 2.

Set 1 can be a faster group of more-able students who finish GCSE early (eg. in Year 10) and then continue with an AS-level course. Set 2 may need the full 3 years to gain GCSE.

Tues
French Set 1
French Set 2

Other vertical structures

Some schools are looking to develop 'consistent setting' (see sections 2.10–2.12) across two or more year-groups. And others are attempting to use 'consistent blocking' across years, see section 12.7 and section 13.3.

Diplomas (see also section 2.18)

With the development of Diplomas there may be more pressure for Year 10 and Year 11 options to be aligned, so that students from each year can be taught together on one-year courses. Obviously it makes scheduling more difficult.

Two basic patterns for 14–19 Diplomas, provided by a consortium of schools, with fixed consortium days (often Tuesdays and Thursdays), are shown here each with 3 possible 'lines of learning':

ASL = "Additional & Specialist Learning" to support the Diploma 'lines of learning'

2.18 Managing Change : the effect of innovations

Recent innovations
Over the last few years, there have been curricular initiatives for some parts of the secondary school curriculum which may have had a detrimental effect on the timetable quality for the rest of the students in the school.

These initiatives include features like 'Sixth Form' cooperation in Years 12-13 (which range from 'Consortium Days' to 'Joint Sixth Forms' or 'Federated' Sixth Forms), see also Chapter 12.   Or, perhaps in Key Stage 4, they are under the heading of 'Work-related Curriculum' and perhaps involve local companies and one or more local colleges.

Because they involve more than one institution, they have to be scheduled at agreed fixed times. So each of these is a 'glued down' piece of the jigsaw that the timetabler has to complete each year.

As the number of these glued-down pieces increases, so the compromises necessary to get a working timetable increase.

For every curriculum action there is a timetabling consequence.

Diplomas in Key Stage 4
One of the problems facing schools now is the pressure to introduce Diplomas in KS4. Schools are encouraged to cooperate with other schools in the locality in order to provide a wide range of diploma courses in an area, rather than each school trying to provide all of these choices internally.

The result of this approach is to require the schools involved to synchronise their timetables with those of neighbouring schools. Many of them are already trying to synchronise their timetables with their partners in the 'Joint Sixth Form' or the local Sixth Form College and with the local providers of a 'Work-related Curriculum'.

The result of this increasing number of external constraints is that the school will probably have to cut back, perhaps severely, on the quality of provision for the rest of the school. This is simply due to the increased logistical complexity caused by linking timetables with other groups of establishments.

This is exacerbated by :

- Institutions having different start times, break and lunch times, and lesson lengths,

- Some having 1-week timetables, with others having 2-week timetables,

- Travel time between institutions may also be a significant factor, depending on the distance apart.

Changes in Year 7

There is a move (again) to try to present the Year 7 curriculum (ie. for pupils in the first year of secondary schooling) more on the Primary model, with subjects interwoven into 'projects' or 'themes', resulting in Year 7 pupils being taught by fewer teachers than the traditional 'new-start' secondary approach.

One teacher could perhaps provide all the History, Geography, PSHE, RE and maybe even some Art and Music, while another might perhaps provide the Science, Maths, Technology and even PE.

The potential social and pastoral benefits for many Year 7 students are clear, even if the academic benefits are less obvious. Secondary schools see their role as providing specialist teaching by experts in the usual subject disciplines. In order to do this effectively, secondary schools usually have their subject specialists working together *in teams*.

For example, a team of Science teachers can deal with half of Year 9 at one time, dividing them up into groups so that the appropriate specialist can deliver their own specialist area of Science to that group.

In Maths or English it is often the case that as children move through secondary schools they are put into teaching groups according to their achievement in that subject (ie. 'setted' according to attainment levels).

This again needs a team of specialist teachers to be scheduled at the same time so that the half-year or full-year can be divided into their attainment-level groups for that subject and be taught the subject at the same time.

And here we have the basic dilemma.

Secondary schools need their teachers working in subject teams most of the time, while the need for 'generalist' teachers for 'themes' in Year 7 is taking people out of the specialist teams for a great proportion of their week.

The obvious consequence is that :

- either these 'generalists' should relinquish their role in their specialist team (a few may be willing to do this),

- or the specialist teams have to limp along with one of their key players missing on occasions (causing 'split classes', with the subject group taught by a different teacher at different times of the week),

- or both.

In any case there are pedagogical and curricular implications.

In recent years, because of the emphasis on examination performance, most secondary schools have attempted to increase the opportunities for subject departments to 'set' groups by attainment.

Moving to a 'primary' Year 7 will necessarily reduce the opportunity for ability 'setting' across Years 8 to 11.

What effect will this have on the exam results in your school?

2.19 Managing Change :
Practical ways forward for the Timetabler

If a new curricular structure is put forward, what can you do to test whether it is feasible?

1. If you are sharing your curricular ideas with colleagues in your school or in other (linked) schools, the only non-ambiguous way is to use a **Curriculum Diagram** as described earlier in this chapter.

2. A **Schematic Diagram** can help to clarify impossibilities in the structure and the staffing of that structure. See Chapter 4.
    It is often not necessary to draw a schematic diagram of the whole year. For example if you are investigating whether you have enough Music teachers to schedule the section involving Music, then you may only need to draw the schematic diagram for that part of the curriculum.

3. A **Combing Chart** (see Chapter 7) is a useful pre-scheduling test which can indicate if a schedule will be impossible to schedule, and it may help you to identify the exact reason for scheduling impossibilities. It is best done for each department (or faculty) initially, and then extended to pairs of departments which have a member of staff in common, or are otherwise linked (for example by the option blocks in years 10–11).

4. A **Conflict Matrix** (see Chapter 8) is another pre-scheduling test which can help you to identify clashes which may make a schedule impossible.

5. One of the tensions caused by new curricular structures is the interaction between teachers 'in parallel' in Upper school (ie. a teacher-team all teaching at the same time) and teachers 'in series' in Lower school (ie. a team of teachers teaching the same population at different times).
    This interaction can be examined and improved by using **Zarraga's Rule** (see Chapter 10), but the results are not always easy to interpret.

6. **'What if...?' investigations**
    With modern timetabler software it is easy to do 'What if...?' trial runs, to see how difficult any new curricular proposals may be.
    If you have Keith Johnson's **TimeTabler** software then get the full details of how to do some 'What if...?' investigations by clicking on:
    http://www.timetabler.com/SupportCentre/What-if-investigations.pdf

2.20　New challenges for Schools

As well as 14-19 Diplomas, thematic approaches in Year 7 and joint 'Sixth Forms', other developments under active consideration in England are shown in the list below, roughly in order of increasing difficulty for the timetabler:

● Different finishing times for different Key Stages;

● Moving the start of the school year from September to June, for all year groups;

● Staggered lunch breaks, or schools starting early enough to abandon lunch;

● 4-term, 5-term or 6-term years; fixed-length terms;

● Allowing non-teaching study time in Key Stage 4, and replacing 'attendance in school' with 'learning attendance', using new technologies for remote learning;

● 'Schools-within-a-school' learning communities, vertically grouped by age, rather like the old 'house' system (see section 2.17) but for learning as well as social purposes (see section 2.17);

● Using school buildings for 50 weeks of the year, instead of the current 38 weeks;

● Having 3 sessions per day, and allowing students to take a permutation of two from three across the calendar year to obtain the legal 380 sessions per year;

● Two cohorts of students using the same building at different times, with the staff working shifts.

More details of some of these at: www.innovation-unit.co.uk

2.21   Changing the time-frame : what are the factors involved?

The Law of Novelty : *Quite often, about one year after the appointment of a new Head, there is a major change in the school's curricular structure.*

Quite often this involves a change of the time-frame (ie. changing the number of lessons in the week/fortnight or the length of lessons).
For example, this may be necessary in order to align schools that are joining together in a consortium (eg. for the delivery of a range of 14-19 diplomas). Or there may be other reasons (see below).

However, changing the timetable cycle is not something to be undertaken lightly or in a hurry! It is always best to plan for the September after next! Everyone needs to be consulted.
Parents in particular may react angrily to your plans if the start/end times of schooling are affected.

If start-time or end-time are to be changed then the local bus/taxi companies will need to be consulted as well as parents. The local transport authority may not be able to cope if several schools are synchronised.
If lunch time is to be moved then the caterers and lunch-time supervisors will need to be involved. Some extra-curricular activities may happen at lunch time and the new arrangements will possibly affect them.

Other reasons for changing the timetable cycle

Most often the change has been from a 1-week cycle to a 2-week cycle.

If the number of periods in the 2-week cycle is exactly double that of the one-week cycle, then:
Scenario A is that the pattern of lessons in Week-1 is very different from Week-2,
Scenario B is that Week-1 and Week-2 are almost identical,

Scenario C is that the number of periods in the 2-week cycle is more or less than double the one-week cycle.

1. Pedagogical reason:
Scenario A might be used to reduce the "Friday afternoon is bad" effect. Instead of the same class having an uninspiring teacher on Friday afternoon every week, it is reduced to once a fortnight ...thus possibly improving learning, and behaviour?
(Monitoring absences for each class by odd/even Friday afternoons might show a pattern.)
Also, to reduce the effect of public holidays if they tend to be the same day (eg. Mondays in the UK).

2. Managerial reason:

Same as 1, but intended to reduce staff grumbling about the same difficult class every Friday. It may improve staff morale. It may reduce staff absence.

3. Curricular reason:

Scenario B (and scenario A) allow some time-slots to alternate (eg. Monday-period-3 is ICT in week 1, but Spanish in week 2).
So it may be expanding the curricular experiences of the students, giving two subjects instead of one.

4. Managerial reason:

As in (3) scenario B (and A) allows some time-slots to alternate (eg. ICT in week 1, Spanish in week 2). In effect this is giving a half-period of IT to the class (by giving them one period per fortnight).

Another example: 2 hours per week is too much for History (say) in KS3 and 1 hour per week is not enough, so we go for 3 (hour) lessons per fortnight. So this method is sometimes used when the 'robber-barons' of the Heads of Department can't agree to give up any periods for a new or expanding subject, and the Head avoids a confrontation by this device (typically going from a 25-period-week to a 50-period-fortnight).

5. Managerial & curricular reasons:

Scenario C is an extension of reason 4. If (for example) a 25-period week is changed to a 60-period fortnight, then the main reason for the change to a 2-week cycle may be to disguise that fact that the amount of curriculum-time for a subject often cannot remain the same.

For example, if Maths had 4 periods in a 25-period week (16%) then if it has double the number (8 periods) in a 2-week 60-period cycle its curriculum-time has been reduced (to 13.3%) ...or if it has 9 periods it has 15% ...etc. See also the box on the next page.

The result is that no-one can have the same as before (so no department is being obviously singled out) and the Head can then adjust the balance of time in the direction s/he wants, and/or which is more appropriate to the students' needs (if the staffing and their specialisms allow a change of direction like this). Machiavellian? Or pragmatic?

(As a further refinement, a school already with a 50-period fortnight may change to a 60-period fortnight for the same reason.)

Schools have different tactics for remembering whether this week is Week-A or Week-B. On the whole the students remember better than the staff!
In one school in Manchester the Head wore a red tie in Weeks-A and a blue tie in Weeks-B, so he knew by looking down!

2.22   Changing the timetable cycle : Sharing out the time

('ppw' = periods per week, 'ppf' = periods per fortnight)

40 ppw	1 lesson = 2.5%	60 ppf	1 lesson = 1.7%
35 ppw	1 lesson = 2.9%	50 ppf	1 lesson = 2%
30 ppw	1 lesson = 3.3%		
25 ppw	1 lesson = 4%		

100 modules pw (eg. on a 15-minute grid)   1 module = 1%
75 modules pw (eg. on a 20-minute grid)   1 module = 1.3%

The effect of any changes:
Of course when you change the timeframe, individual subjects gain or lose time in each year and may gain or lose time overall.
Some subjects are taught to small groups, others are taught to large, ...so any changes can affect your staffing levels.

Taking a Year focus: If small-group subjects increase their time, average teaching group size goes down in that year, the number of staff used will go up. Check what the Staff Deployment Analysis looks like!

Looking at the Whole School: If small-group subjects gain time overall, then the overall average group size goes down, and so the Contact Ratio goes up *or* more staff are needed. Check the budget!

Length of lessons
You will need to consult with your colleagues, but typical reactions from different subject areas are:

35 mins	MFL (languages) prefer 1 period, Maths may like 2, Science and Technology like 2, 3 or 4 periods.
40 mins	MFL like 1 period, Maths like 1 or 2, Science/Tech like 2, 3 or 4.
50 mins	MFL cope with 1 period, Maths like 1, Science/Tech like 2 or 3.
60 mins	MFL want 0.5, Maths like 1, Science/Technology want 1 or 2 (depending on the age of the students).
15 mins	MFL like 2 units, Maths like 3, Science/Technology like 5 units.

2.23   Summary

A vital tool for the Timetabler is a clear Curriculum Diagram, because it allows focussed discussion about the school's curricular structure, in an unambiguous way.   The curricular structure needs to respond to the needs of the students, and to innovations urged on the school by external factors, while at the same time remaining a logically feasible structure.

One of the commonest changes, changing the timetable cycle, can cause difficulties for staff and for parents, and needs careful management.

3   Option Schemes

In most British-style secondary schools, the students are allowed some choice in their curriculum for the last two or three years of compulsory schooling. There may be some element of choice earlier (for example in the introduction of a second foreign language), but this chapter is concerned with the option 'pools' usually offered to students for years/grades 10 and 11.

An option pool is a set of subjects or teaching groups which are timetabled to occur simultaneously and in which a student must study one subject.
On the curriculum diagram and the timetable it forms a block, with a team of teachers, teaching simultaneously.
In Scotland the pool or block is often called a 'column'; in other countries the subjects may be called 'electives', and the block called an 'elective line'.

In some schools, option blocks may account for 70% of the school week. In other schools there has been a move towards a larger common core and a reduced number of option blocks. However few schools are likely to remove options entirely and so the problems associated with option blocks and their timetabling remain with us. Option blocks are the main reason for the complexity of UK school timetabling.

The three main types of option schemes are shown on the next page.

3.2   Option Block structures

The diagrams show the 3 main types of option block structures:

A   'Free Choice' structure (heterogeneous blocks)

block:	1	2	3	4
	Hi	Gg	Hi	Re
	Dr	Ar	Fr	Mu
	Fr	Sp	Tx	Fo
	Te	Bs	IT	Ms

B   'Faculty' structure (homogeneous blocks)

block:	1	2	3	4
	Hi	Fr	Te	Ar
	Hi	Fr	Tx	Dr
	Gg	Sp	Fo	Mu
	Gg	De	IT	Ms
	Humanities	Languages	Technology	Creative

C   'Courses' structure

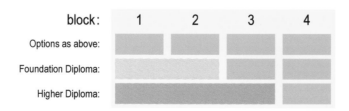

Each student studies one subject in each block
(except in the 'sixth form', when a student may have a study period instead).

3.3 Types of option blocks

Option pool structures may be classified into three types. These are shown on the opposite page.

They don't show the compulsory core curriculum (English, Science, Maths, etc).

A 'Free choice' structure (heterogeneous blocks)

In this type of structure, the subjects are arranged so as to try to accommodate the students' requests – the school is trying to provide 'customer satisfaction'.

In the example shown, the numbers of groups imply that the scheme is being offered to a 'band' of about 90 students (perhaps a half-year group or one-third of a year-group). However the blocks could easily be extended in depth to be applied to a whole year-group, because none of the blocks is likely to demand all the school's resources. (For example, none of the blocks shown needs more than one Technology room.)

However there are some disadvantages with this type of option block. Philosophically, it looks rather odd. For example, block 1: 'History or Drama or French or Technology' presents a strange choice to the student.

In conjunction with the other pools, it allows students to select an unbalanced curriculum (for example: Drama, Art, Pe and Music).

The school must then devise rules, sometimes quite complicated, to ensure that students select a balanced curriculum (for example, at least one 'creative' subject, at least one of the 'humanities'). All the choices will need to be checked (by the Director of Studies, Year-Tutor, or Form-Tutor) or checked by **Options** software that allows you to specify the rules that have to be followed.

When it comes to scheduling these heterogeneous pools, difficulties will arise. Elsewhere you may wish to timetable some French 'sets' in Year 8 (ie. two or more French groups timetabled to occur 'in parallel', at the same time). This means a group of French teachers must be free to teach Year 8 as a team. This is less likely to happen if you have a heterogeneous structure in Year 10 because the Language groups are dispersed throughout the option blocks and so the French teachers are neither teaching nor free as a team.

If the option blocks are changed from year to year to satisfy the students' choices then the number of timetable conflicts is likely to increase and limit any setting in the lower school (unless several members of staff teach lower school classes only). The heterogeneous nature of the pools almost certainly prevents the timetabling of departmental conference periods and precludes the possibility of attempting 'block' timetabling (chapter 13).

In this context it is essential to remember that it is **teachers** who cause conflicts on the timetable, **not subjects**. Until the curriculum diagram shows staffing as well as subjects, one cannot be sure about where the conflicts will occur (and this is more difficult when some staff teach more than one subject in the pools).

A further disadvantage of heterogeneous pools arises in the teaching groups. In the example shown in section 3.2 (A), there are two groups for French but the groups are in different pools. This implies that each French group will include the full range of ability of the band. This may lead to a difficult teaching situation. A tactic sometimes adopted is to pair subjects in the way shown by History and French in that diagram (pools 1 and 3). The aim is to have a better French group paired with a poorer History group and vice versa.

Such tactics may not work well in practice because there may be a poor correlation between abilities in the subjects concerned. Of course, each French group shown in the diagram could really be two Fr teaching groups or 'sets'.

Another problem that applies to all blocks (but particularly to 'hetero' pools) is that the period-breakdown of all subjects in the block **must be the same**.

In example A above, French and Technology (block 1) must *both* have single periods or must *both* have Double periods. Neither case is ideal for both subjects.

Summary of heterogeneous blocks

Advantages
1 Students' satisfaction rate is high.
2 Blocks can be applied across a whole year-group (but see disadvantage 3).

Disadvantages
1 Rules and vetting may be needed to ensure a balanced curriculum for each student (this may affect advantage 1).
2 Timetabling difficulties: setting in lower school, departmental meetings, block timetabling are limited or impossible.
3 Blocks may enforce mixed-ability teaching in most or all subjects.

B   'Faculty' structure (homogeneous blocks)

The word 'Faculty' here is not meant to imply that the school must be staffed, administered or accommodated in true faculties; only that similar subjects are grouped together in the curriculum (and thus on the timetable).

Diagram B shown in section 3.2 shows a Humanities block, a Languages block, a Technology block and a Creative block.

In this type of structure, the educational philosophy is explicit: subjects within a block have a similar methodology, content or skill. 'French or Spanish' is a valid option and is allowed: 'French or Art' is not.

The curriculum diagram forces students to make a balanced choice and no extra rules are needed (although the students' choices still may need to be vetted with a view to career prospects).

With the blocks shown in diagram B, there is no opportunity for a student to take two languages or two humanities. However we shall see later how these can be accommodated with a 'bias' pool.

A disadvantage of homogeneous blocks is that the satisfaction rate for fitting the students' choices is unlikely to be as high as with heterogeneous blocks.

A further disadvantage may arise: most schools will probably not have sufficient resources to timetable homogeneous option blocks across a full year-group (eg. schools may not have the necessary number of Technology rooms).

If homogeneous option blocks are timetabled across half-year groups, then within each block or 'faculty' most schools can offer a range of courses, perhaps aimed at different examination levels and thus reducing the spread of ability within each group.

If it is argued that the 'hump' of the normal distribution curve is the wrong place at which to divide a population, then the blocks and the courses for the two half-years may be identical.

Alternatively, in a large school, the year-group may be divided into three ability-bands at Key Stage 4 (and of course some bands may be more homogeneous, some more heterogeneous in structure).

The more homogeneous the option blocks, the more likely that the timetable will benefit. If the languages teachers are scheduled as a team to teach a languages block in Year 10, then it is likely that at other times they will be free as a team to teach languages sets in Year 9. Similarly with other departments.

In the same way, there is a greater likelihood that departmental conference periods can be scheduled and that 'block' timetabling could be used.

Summary of homogeneous blocks

Advantages
1   The blocks force a balanced curriculum.
2   Timetabling of sets (in other years) and departmental periods is easier.
3   Parallel sets in each 'faculty' can reduce the spread of ability within a group.

Disadvantages
1   The students' satisfaction rate is likely to be lower than with 'hetero' pools.
2   Homogeneous blocks often cannot be timetabled across a full Year.

C   'Courses' structure

Diagram C shown in section 3.2 shows a simple 'courses' structure.

This structure may be straightforward to timetable because each group in course A is independent of each group in courses B and C (unless the same teacher or room is involved).

There are disadvantages: the satisfaction rate may be low (because in the simplest case a student choosing course A must study *all* of course A).

As a variation, within each course there may be some option pools of either the homogeneous or heterogeneous type.

Summary of the 'courses' structure

Advantages
1 Timetabling may be easier, with fewer problems scheduling lower school.
2 They can be applied to a full year-group.

Disadvantages
1 The students' satisfaction rate is likely to be lower than with 'hetero' pools.
2 The curriculum is likely to be less balanced.
3 There may be a wide range of ability within a group unless students are persuaded into certain courses.
4 Exam targets for students may be more restricted than in other structures.

So far we have looked at the three types of structure in their 'pure' form.
In practice they are often combined in ways which reduce their individual disadvantages.

D Combinations of homogeneous and heterogeneous pools

There is often a debate about the need for a balanced curriculum. One way of achieving this is to give less choice to the students: increase the compulsory common core of the curriculum to 80% (or more) of the school week and allow only two (or fewer) option blocks, probably of the heterogeneous type.

An alternative which is likely to be more acceptable in most schools, is to adopt a homogeneous pool structure with an addition: since the 'pure' homogeneous blocks do not allow a student to follow his/her special interests by taking two humanities or two languages, we may add one (or two) heterogeneous 'bias' pools:

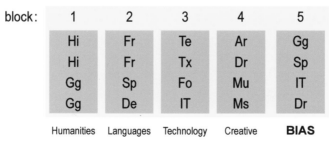

block:	1	2	3	4	5
	Hi	Fr	Te	Ar	Gg
	Hi	Fr	Tx	Dr	Sp
	Gg	Sp	Fo	Mu	IT
	Gg	De	IT	Ms	Dr
	Humanities	Languages	Technology	Creative	**BIAS**

This example would allow students to study two humanities, two languages etc depending on each student's personal bias. Obviously the students' satisfaction rate will depend upon the care with which the bias pool is determined.
For a band of less academic students, two bias pools may be more appropriate (for example, blocks 4 and 5 above may be mixed up).

With care in choosing the number of groups and the contents of the bias block (as explained in section 3.7), a combination like this can preserve the advantages of both the homogeneous and heterogeneous types.

3.4 Methods of determining the option pools

Once the type of pool structure is decided by a school, the precise contents of each pool have to be determined. The method varies from school to school. For example:

School A

1 The Head or the Senior Leadership Group decides the number of teaching groups for each subject and the arrangement of those groups in the blocks on a philosophical basis (but with due regard to the limitations of staffing and accommodation).

2 The students (and their parents) are given information on the courses and relevant careers and then asked to choose one subject from each block (possibly with a second choice as reserve).

School B

1 The students (with or without their parents) are asked in a preliminary survey to indicate five choices from a full list of subjects (with a warning that this is only a survey).

2 Using this information, the school (the Head or the Senior Team) decides the number of groups for each subject (for example, 'one more History group this year, one fewer Geography group').

3 The school decides the arrangement of these groups within the blocks without directly consulting the students' individual choices.

4 The students and their parents are given information about the courses and careers and then asked to choose one subject from each block.

5 The Director of Studies, the relevant Year-Tutor, the Careers Tutor or Heads of Subject Departments vet the replies for suitability.

School C

1 The students (and their parents) are given information about the examination courses and relevant careers.

2 If the blocks are to be heterogeneous, students are given advice about a balanced curriculum.

3 The students are asked to choose five subjects, in order of preference, from a full list (with one other subject as a reserve) with a warning that the school cannot guarantee to offer the student all of his/her choices.

4 Replies are vetted for balance and, for some subjects, ability to take the course.

5 Using the students' replies, the school decides the number of groups for each subject.

6 The school uses the students' choices (and their order of preference) to decide the subjects in the bias pool (or all the pools in a 'hetero' structure).

7 Students who do not fit into the final arrangement of pools are interviewed, counselled and reassigned (preferably using their Reserve subject).

Other permutations of events are possible, but of the three given here School C would seem to offer the best approach, in that it tries to respond as the needs of the school's population change from year to year.

It may be difficult to make a response that requires much less Art and much more French, but it is relatively easy to make small changes in the grouping of subjects so as to increase the satisfaction of the students.

Even a small increase in the motivation of the students and a consequent decrease in disruptive behaviour ought to make the effort worthwhile.

To illustrate the sort of simple change we are suggesting, consider these two examples of parts of a 'homogeneous + bias' structure:

Scheme 1 block:	1	5		Scheme 2 block:	1	5
	Hi	Gg			Hi	Hi
	Hi	Sp			Gg	Sp
	Gg	IT			Gg	IT
	Re	Dr			Re	Dr
	Humanities	BIAS			Humanities	BIAS

The numbers of groups, rooms and teachers (staffing cost) are the same in each case; simply a History and a Geography group are interchanged.

There is no clear preference on a philosophical basis. The better scheme cannot be determined until the choices of this particular group of students have been inspected to determine the satisfaction rates and the sizes of the teaching groups in each case. One scheme should give a better motivation and a better teaching atmosphere than the other.

There are two disadvantages to the procedure outlined under School C above. One is that students and parents may be upset, despite the warning in step 3, if they do not receive all of their first choices and have to be re-assigned (step 7). Explaining the reasons for the procedure helps to solve this problem.

The second disadvantage is the length of time involved in analysing the students' choices. However this is mostly a routine task, ideally suited to a computer. Later in this chapter we'll see how computers can help us to analyse our students' requests in order to provide the best possible option scheme.

The remainder of this chapter follows the steps listed earlier under School C.

3.5   Obtaining the students' choices

Whether they are asked to choose a few subjects from a full list, or one subject from each option pool, the students and their parents can expect to receive more than a single sheet of notes from the school.

The decisions to be made are so important that parents can surely expect to receive comprehensive details in the form of an Options Booklet.

An outline of such an Options Booklet is given on the opposite page.

Outline of an Options Booklet

(perhaps 30 pages long, in A5 format)

Students' Questions and Answers
Why choose? Why choose now? Can I change my mind later? Can I take
any subject? Which subjects are compulsory? How many do I choose?
How should I choose? - do's and don'ts   What is a good balance?
How can I get careers advice? Will I definitely get the subjects I ask for?

Careers advice
Availability of a Careers Teacher or Advisor, reference to any literature or
web-sites giving advice.
Details of Parents' Evening (or Careers Convention, if provided).

Assessment
Details of assessments made during the next two years – times of reports
and examinations, relevance of any 'mock' examinations, course work, the
times expected for homework, etc.

At the end of Year 11/12
The alternatives, including arrangements for further study in a 'Sixth Form'
or further education college, and courses offered at present.
Possibly an ideal Leaving Certificate, if you provide them.

Examinations
The distinctions between the various qualifications being offered.
The letters and numbers used in the grades and their meanings.

The Subjects or Courses being offered at present
Perhaps 200 words on each, including:
- the aims, relevance and importance of the subject
- an outline of the course to be followed
- any special facilities that are available
- the style of the examination assessments, perhaps including the
  proportion of marks for each part.

Final questions
How do I fill in the Options Form?
What do I do if I need help?

The Options Form

When you give out the Options Booklet to the students, you also need to give them an Options Form, detailing either the option pools (as in Schools A and B) or the list of subjects from which a few are to be chosen (as in School C).

In the latter case, it helps if the subjects are grouped into humanities, languages, creative, etc so that a balanced curriculum can be first chosen and later vetted more easily.

Since large numbers of Options Forms will have to be inspected later, it helps (for right-handed people) if the subjects are shown in a vertical list to the right of the page with the spaces for the student to indicate his/her choices near the right hand edge.

The instructions for the students (and their parents) should be clear and concise — it helps to have a practice in school before the Options Forms go home. The instructions should explain how to mark a '1' next to their first choice, a '2' for their second choice and so on. They can also be told to mark a reserve subject (perhaps with an 'R').

If you are going to use computer software to analyse the students' choices, it may help to include a subject code next to each subject to save time and obviate mistakes later.

The Options Form might appear like this:

Laura Norder High School			
Year 10 Options Choice Form			

Name: ....   Class: ....

How to complete
the Option Form
....
(detailed step-by-step
instructions, with any
rules to be followed)
....
....
....
....
....

History	(Hi)	......
Geography	(Gg)	.**1**..
French	(Fr)	**2**..
German	(De)	......
Spanish	(Sp)	.**R**.
Art	(Ar)	......
Drama	(Dr)	**4**..
Music	(MU)	......
Media Studies	(Ms)	......
D&T : Food Technology	(Fo)	.**3**..
D&T : Textiles	(Tx)	......
D&T : Graphic Products	(Gr)	......

The distribution of the Options Booklet and the Options Form will normally take place during the Spring Term — the earlier the better, although some schools may be limited by the wish to hold Year 9 examinations either before the choices are made or before the choices are vetted.

A Parents' Evening (perhaps with a Careers Convention) ought to occur before the Options Forms are returned to school.

When all the Forms are received, they ought to be vetted, either manually (by the Director of Studies, Careers Tutor, Year-Tutor, House-Tutor, Form-Tutor or Subject Leaders), or using software, to check the following points:

1   Does each Option Form have different numbers clearly written against the correct number of subjects?

2   Has the student followed your rules in choosing a balanced curriculum and is the choice of subjects a sensible one?

3   If the student has a particular career in mind, do the chosen subjects allow for that career?

4   In each of their chosen subjects, does the student have sufficient ability to cope with the work? To assist in this, the Director of Studies might request Subject Teachers to provide class lists with two groups of students marked as follows:

(a) The top quarter of the class or those with a particular aptitude for that subject marked with a + sign.

(b) The bottom quarter of the class or those with a distinct weakness in that subject marked with a – sign.

Or the subject teacher may be asked to give a projected exam grade.

If you are using options software (eg. like the tutorial version of the **Options** software, which is on the CD provided with this book) then there is no need to do the first two of these checks manually – the computer will do it for you.

You can tell the program which Rules you wish it to use to check the students' Choices:

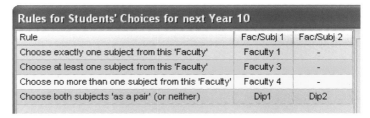

Rules for Students' Choices for next Year 10		
Rule	Fac/Subj 1	Fac/Subj 2
Choose exactly one subject from this 'Faculty'	Faculty 1	-
Choose at least one subject from this 'Faculty'	Faculty 3	-
Choose no more than one subject from this 'Faculty'	Faculty 4	-
Choose both subjects 'as a pair' (or neither)	Dip1	Dip2

'Faculty' in this context is not a real faculty but could correspond to the groupings shown on the Options Form.

If any student does not make their choices in accordance with these Rules, then they will be flagged up by the software.

You can then interview them and counsel them as necessary.

3.6 Analysing the students' choices – part 1: The Clash Table

Having received the students' information and vetted it, how can we analyse it in the most convenient way? This can be done manually but using a computer is much more efficient and time-saving.

In order to see the number of students requesting each subject (and hence the number of groups for each subject), and to see the ways in which these subjects might fit together into option blocks, we need a **Clash Table**.

This consists of a list of the subjects along two sides of a square, with the number of clashes at each intersection of a row and a column.

Consider this example of a Clash Table:

Clash Table for Year 10													
	Hi	Gg	Fr	De	Sp	Ar	Dr	Mu	Ms	Fo	Tx	Gr	Grp
Hi	62	22	30	15	16	21	14	12	15	10	15	16	3
Gg	22	40	24	3	5	12	9	4	15	9	10	7	2
Fr	30	24	41	3	8	14	14	7	6	16	0	1	2
De	15	3	3	18	0	7	4	4	3	0	7	8	1
Sp	16	5	8	0	21	10	4	3	4	1	5	7	1
Ar	21	12	14	7	10	27	0	0	0	4	5	8	1
Dr	14	9	14	4	4	0	18	0	0	5	2	2	1
Mu	12	4	7	4	3	0	0	14	0	5	4	3	1
Ms	15	15	6	3	4	0	0	0	21	5	8	7	1
Fo	10	9	16	0	1	4	5	5	5	19	1	1	1
Tx	15	10	0	7	5	5	2	4	8	1	19	0	1
Gr	16	7	1	8	7	8	2	3	7	1	0	20	1

The table shows the results of 12 subjects offered to a band of 80 students. The students were asked to choose 4 subjects each, with a view to providing 4 option blocks.

The figures along the diagonal show the total numbers of students choosing each subject. For example, 62 have chosen History (Hi), 40 have chosen Geography (Gg), 41 French (Fr), etc.

The two triangles forming the two halves on either side of the diagonal are mirror images of each other (reflected in the diagonal). The number of students requesting both History and French is 30 (as shown at the intersection of the Hi column and the Fr row, or the Hi row and the Fr column).

The number of students requesting both Geography and German (De) is 3, etc.

The Clash Table can be obtained manually by going repeatedly through the returned Option Forms, and counting the number of students for each pair of subjects.

In practice, this is best done using computer software. The students' names can be imported from your school admin system (or 'MIS'), and their choices added very quickly with your mouse (about 10 minutes for 100 students).

Having got the Clash Table, how then do we use it to decide the option pools? To illustrate this, we can use the Clash Table shown opposite to obtain one possible solution.

3.7   Deciding the subjects in the blocks

First let us emphasize that this is a simplified example using only 4 option blocks and the numbers shown in the Clash Table. Your real situation will be both larger (perhaps 20+ subjects) and more particular to your own school.

The first step is to decide **the number of groups** to be provided in each subject, using the numbers along the diagonal of the Clash Table.

In the diagram shown opposite the software is suggesting how many groups you need (in the final column), but clearly it is your decision, depending on your staffing.

With 62 students, History (Hi) is popular enough for 3 groups to be provided; 2 groups would seem right for Geography (Gg); 2 for French (Fr); 1 for German (De): 1 for Spanish (Sp); 1 rather large group for Art (Ar); 1 for Drama (Dr); 1 rather small group for Music (M); 1 for Media Studies (Ms); and 1 group for each of the Design & Technology groups (Food Technology, Textiles, Graphic Products). This would give 16 groups for 4 option blocks and so 4 groups per block.

If you have a borderline case (e.g. Art has 27 students requesting it) then you can investigate the effect of the students' Reserve choices. This can be done manually (and tediously) by looking at all the Art Option Forms to count how many students (say 9) have put Art as their *last* main choice. Subtracting this number from 27 gives 18 as a lower limit. Then look through all the other Option Forms to see how many students (say 2) have put Art as their first Reserve. Adding this to 27 gives 29 as an upper limit.
We can write this as: Art 18-**27**-29   This shows that Art is much more likely to shrink and remain as one group than grow to 2 groups.
Considering other subjects in the same way can sometimes make a dramatic difference to a subject's claim for a place in the pools.
For example: Music 2-**14**-14 This suggests that you might have to be rather careful in the placing of Music in the blocks in order to preserve it as a viable group.

Having looked at the desirable numbers of groups for each subject, reality must decide how many can be afforded (see also chapter 6). Perhaps the first way to view this is by comparing these desirable numbers with the numbers of groups in the present Year 11 curriculum which is about to disappear.

You may have to try 'musical chairs' moves. For example, if one more French group is needed but one fewer Spanish group, then this can often be achieved by adjustments in the Languages department.

It often helps to ask *different* members of staff to take Games lessons in the coming year. Alternatively you might ask all members of staff to tell you which other subjects they are able to teach.

The solutions will vary from school to school. Let us assume for this example that a solution can be found, so that we have the 16 groups decided earlier.

The following sections describe how you can procede manually, but in practice most schools use options software to do these steps.

Let us now suppose that the school's policy is to have at least two homogeneous groups. The popularity of History suggests a humanities pool. For example:

A	B	C	D
Hi			
Hi			
Hi			
Gg			

In our example Clash Table, the Creative subjects (Ar, Dr, Mu, Ms) are showing zeros between any pairs of these subjects (perhaps because the students were told that they could only choose *one* of these subjects). This means that we can make them into an option pool without disadvantaging any student:

A	B	C	D
Hi	Ar		
Hi	Dr		
Hi	Mu		
Gg	Ms		

The Languages department would prefer the two French groups to be in parallel for setting purposes; German must be in a different pool from French to allow two languages to be studied; similarly for Spanish. Hence:

A	B	C	D
Hi	Ar	Fr	De
Hi	Dr	Fr	Sp
Hi	Mu		
Gg	Ms		

There are 4 groups (Gg, Fo, Tx, Gr) yet to be fitted. If there is no clear philosophical preference for their arrangement then the Clash Table will help us.

Consider the subjects that have only one group (Fo, Tx, Gr).

The Clash Table shows that no one wants to do Fr and Tx, so clearly Tx can go into block C. Such zeros (or low numbers) in the Clash Table always indicate possible pairings of subjects in the blocks.

Putting Fo also into block C would cause difficulties because 16 people want to do Fo and Fr, while the clashes between Fo and the subjects in block D are low. Thus:

A	B	C	D
Hi	Ar	Fr	De
Hi	Dr	Fr	Sp
Hi	Mu	Tx	Fo
Gg	Ms		

Throughout these stages it is important to remember 3 constraints that apply:

1   Subjects in the same block must have the same '**period-breakdown**'.
    That is, if one subject is taught in double periods, all the subjects in that block must be taught in double periods. If one subject demands single periods, all subjects in the block must be timetabled as singles. In our example, there is a problem between German/Spanish (who will prefer Singles) and Food Technology (who will want longer lessons). Unless the Subject Leaders agree or accept this, this option pool is not viable.

2   Subjects taken in Technology rooms can't have more than 20 students in the group. If you can't balance Technology groups with bigger classroom subjects in the same block, you may have to provide more groups.

3   In mixed schools, despite encouragement for boys and girls to cross traditional barriers in certain subjects, there remains some bias. Subjects with such a bias should be balanced in each block.

Returning to our example, there are 2 groups unfitted (Gr, Graphics and Gg, Geography), leading to 2 possible solutions.

We can put Gr in block C and Gg in block D, or vice versa.

In this way we arrive at two possible schemes:

A	B	C	D		A	B	C	D
Hi	Ar	Fr	De	**or**	Hi	Ar	Fr	De
Hi	Dr	Fr	Sp		Hi	Dr	Fr	Sp
Hi	Mu	Tx	Fo		Hi	Mu	Tx	Fo
Gg	Ms	Gr	Gg		Gg	Ms	Gg	Gr

To decide on the better of the these two schemes we need to look at the choices of each individual student.

3.8 Part 2 : comparing the blocks with the students' choices

To see which of these two option schemes will be best *for this particular population of students*, we should try each student's choice of subjects against the proposed option blocks to see which students will not fit.

The choices for these 'unfitted' students can then be inspected by considering some or all of the following points:

1 Has the student lost a subject which he/she thought was of high priority, or is the lost subject his/her last choice (i.e. the least-wanted subject)?

2 Did the student choose the lost subject for valid reasons or perhaps because his/her friends intended to take that subject?

3 Is the lost subject necessary either for a balanced curriculum or for a particular careers intention?

4 Is this particular student (and his/her parents) well motivated?

5 Is this student likely to be particularly upset by losing this subject?

6 Will the student be able to take his/her first reserve subject instead?

7 Can the situation be improved by changing one of the other subjects originally chosen by the student?

Taking each student's choices and comparing them with each of the proposed schemes can take a long time. It is possible to ask the students to do it, but even the more able students (and their parents) are not very reliable when given two or three alternative schemes, even after a practice session.

However, this routine task is ideal for a computer. Whether you do it manually or by computer, the results should look something like this:

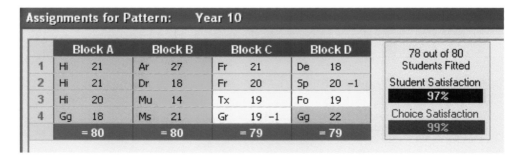

Assignments for Pattern:		Year 10						
	Block A		Block B		Block C		Block D	
1	Hi	21	Ar	27	Fr	21	De	18
2	Hi	21	Dr	18	Fr	20	Sp	20 −1
3	Hi	20	Mu	14	Tx	19	Fo	19
4	Gg	18	Ms	21	Gr	19 −1	Gg	22
	= 80		= 80		= 79		= 79	

78 out of 80
Students Fitted

Student Satisfaction
97%

Choice Satisfaction
99%

This corresponds to the *first* option scheme developed earlier (in section 3.7).

It shows, for example, that of the 21 students requesting Spanish (see the Clash Table), 20 students have fitted into the group in pool D (bearing in mind the order of preference of the choices of each student), but that 1 student could not fit (perhaps they had put Fo as a higher priority or they wished to study a combination like Hi-Ar-Gg-Sp). It also shows that, of the 40 students requesting Geography, 18 will fit into pool A and 22 into pool D.

The table also shows, underneath each pool, the total number fitted to that pool (ideally all these numbers would balance out at 80 since there are 80 students). It also shows the number and percentage of students fitted.

In addition, the computer will give a display to show which students are fitted or not fitted. For example:

Johnson Keith 9A

Student's Choices:				Allocated to blocks:			
1	2	3	4	A	B	C	D
Fr	Sp	Hi	Ar	Hi	Ar	Fr	Sp

This shows that Keith Johnson in class 9A had chosen, in order, Fr-Sp-Hi-Ar. He would be able to study all of these subjects by taking Hi in block A, Ar in block B, Fr in block C, and Sp in block D.

If the student's choices do not fit into the blocks, the display is slightly different:

Johnson Chris 9A

Student's Choices:				Allocated to blocks:			
1	2	3	4	A	B	C	D
Hi	Sp	Ar	Gg	Hi	Ar		Sp

This shows that the student chose, in order, Hi-Sp-Ar-Gg. The display shows that he would **not** get his last choice, Gg. He was fitted to Hi in block A, Ar in block B, and Sp in block D. The display shows he could only get Gg if a Geography group was added to block C.

Using all this information, the Head, the Senior Leadership Group or a meeting of Subject Leaders can decide on the best option scheme **for this particular group of students**. For a different population, it would be a different pattern.

Alternatively, if the **other** scheme at the end of section 3.7 had been used, then the results would have looked like this:

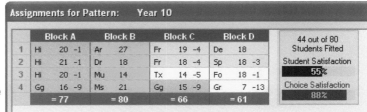

This shows that even a minor tweaking to the options scheme can make a huge difference to the lives of your students. Only 44 are satisfied this time!

We have looked here at the gradual building up of an options scheme manually, but of course modern software can do the whole thing for you, automatically. (In the Tutorial software on the CD, look for the 'AutoCreate' feature.)

3.9   Part 3 : unfitted students

There are two possibilities for the next step.

If the students were asked to provide a Reserve Choice, then this can be swapped-in to replace their last main choice, to see if this solves the problem. Software allows you to try this, and undo it, at the click of your mouse.
Often it solves the problem. If so, students and parents need to be informed.

Alternatively (or in addition) individual 'unfitted' students should be interviewed, either by the Director of Studies, the Careers Tutor or perhaps by someone who knows the student better. Consideration can be given to the seven points listed at the beginning of section 3.8.
When the student has modified his/her choices to fit the option blocks, the parents should be informed (and invited to discuss the situation if necessary). The student's Option Form (and/or the computer data and printout) can be updated.

3.10   Part 4 : option group lists

The lists of students in each option group will need to be ready for September, preferably earlier. The groups should be headed by the name of the subject and the teacher's name. The groups should be in alphabetical order. It can help distribution if the lists for different bands of students are printed on different colours of paper.
Individual sheets can be given to the staff teaching the groups. Booklets of complete sets can be provided to the Head, Deputies, Year-Learning-Managers, Office Staff, Staff noticeboard etc.

If you have been using a computer then the software will give you these lists at the push of a button:

(The scheduled lesson times are received from the timetabler software, after the timetable is completed.)

Laura Norder High School

Group Lists for Block A

History Group (A):

Monday, periods 3-4 : Mr J Smith in Room 32
Thursday, periods 1-2 : Mr J Smith in Room 32

Patrick Horne 10C
Laura Howarth 10C
Calum Johnson 10C
Jack Marland 10L

3.11 Part 5 : Individual Student Timetable printouts

It helps enormously to get a clean start to the new school year if you can hand out individual student timetables, particularly where the students have optional subjects.

You can get these individual timetables (after the timetable has been completed) either from your school admin system, the timetabling software that you use, or the Options software:

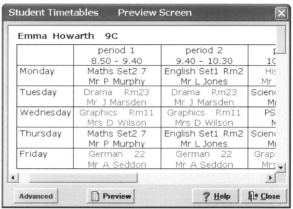

3.12 Sixth Form options : Years 12 and 13

If you have a 'Sixth Form' (Years 12 and 13) you may decide to take a survey of Year 11 before they leave, in order to see how many are likely to return and which subjects they might be considering. Such surveys are not very reliable.

If you do take such a survey then, of course, you can analyse it in the same way as for the Year 10 options, drawing up a Clash Table and seeing how the students fit the proposed options. The problem is likely to be simpler than with the Year 10 options (because of the number of students and the number of subjects).

How valid the results will be when the students return in September may be decided by experience, but the individual attention you give your students in this way may well help to keep them from drifting away to another institution.

3.13 Summary

Of the different types of option schemes, the one with the most advantages appears to be a combination of homogeneous blocks with one or more heterogeneous bias blocks. Whatever type of option scheme is chosen by a school, information must be given to the students (Options Booklet) and information must be obtained from the students (Options Form).

The exact contents of each option block can be decided by looking at a Clash Table and at students' individual choices. Software can save a lot of time and allow staff to spend more time advising and motivating individual students.

4 Schematic Diagrams

Whenever a new curriculum diagram is proposed, or structural changes are made to an existing curriculum, it is essential to look at the viability of the new **structure**, to see if it is logically and practically possible.

This involves drawing a simplified timetable grid called a Schematic Diagram, to see if it shows us any impossibilities.

It is valuable to draw a Schematic Diagram for all, or part, of the curricular structure whenever the curriculum diagram changes, or whenever the constraints on the curriculum change.

It is far better to discover any problems at this stage, when you can see the underlying reasons, and find solutions, than later when you are deep in the complexities of scheduling.

And it was going so well, until I started to try to put lessons on the timetable...

4.2 Looking at the logic of the curricular structure

An 11-16 school in Derbyshire had only one Re teacher, so they teamed Re with Careers (Ca) and proposed a Curriculum Diagram like this:

Year 11	En	Ma	Sc	Fr	Fr	It	Pe	Hs	Ar	Hi	Re Ca	Se
	En	Ma	Sc	Fr	Fr	It	Pe	Pe	It	Hi		Se
	En	Ma	Sc	Fr	Fr	It	Pe	Dr	Hi	Ms	Re Ca	Se
	En	Ma	Sc	Te	Te	Pe	Pe	Mu	Dr	Gg		Se
	En	Ma	Sc	Te	Te	Pe	It	Gg	Sp	Hs	Re Ca	Se
	En	Ma	Sc	Te	Te	Pe	It	Ms	Gg	Ar		Se

Look at the Re + Ca blocks in the diagram. Is this feasible?
To staff each of these small blocks needs only 1 Re teacher + 1 Ca teacher.
But because everything else is blocked across the Year, all these Re+Ca blocks have to occur *at the same time!* And with only 1 Re teacher it means that this curriculum is not possible.

4.3 Looking at the spread that is available

A 2-form-entry school in Staffordshire proposed the following:

6A	Se_2	Pe_1	Re_2	En_5	Te_4	Ma_6	Ga_2	Mu_2	Ar_2	Sc_6 Fr_4 Hi_2 Gg_2
						Ma_6				Sc_6 Fr_4 Hi_2 Gg_2
6B	Se_2	Pe_1	Re_2	En_5	Te_4	Ma_6	Ga_2	Mu_2	Ar_2	Sc_6 Fr_4 Hi_2 Gg_2

$\longleftarrow$ 14 periods $\longrightarrow$

The Sc, Fr, Hi, Gg are in a Container Block, to provide 3 groups for each of these subjects, consistently-setted (see section 2.10), because the school has only one French teacher and only one Science lab.
Ignoring the oddness of consistently-setting Science-with-French, is this structure possible?

In fact the last block is mathematically impossible.
For Sc_6 to be taught to 3 groups non-simultaneously needs $6 + 6 + 6 = 18$ periods:
But there are only $6 + 4 + 2 + 2 = 14$ periods included in the block. It cannot be done.

Sc_6		
	Sc_6	
		Sc_6

$\longleftarrow$ 18 periods $\longrightarrow$

The solution is to add *at least* 4 more periods to the block, so it is *at least* 18 periods wide.
For example, bring Music and Art into the block:

Sc_6	Fr_4	Hi_2	Gg_2	Mu_2	Ar_2
Sc_6	Fr_4	Hi_2	Gg_2	Mu_2	Ar_2
Sc_6	Fr_4	Hi_2	Gg_2	Mu_2	Ar_2

4.4   Drawing a Schematic Diagram

A Schematic Diagram is like a simplified school timetable.
It plots **classes** against **time** but it ignores (at least initially) some of the essential features of the final timetable.

A Schematic Diagram completely ignores the effects of period-breakdown (singles or doubles, etc), the effects of part-time teachers, the effects of fixed times for PSHE or swimming, or the requirement for the distribution of lessons over the timetable cycle.

Instead it focusses on **constraints**, to see whether these make the proposed Curriculum Diagram impossible.

Schematic Diagrams can be useful in answering "What if . . .?" questions, particularly when a major change in the curricular structure is being considered, or if the constraints on the curriculum change.

An 11-16 6-f.e. school in London proposed this Curriculum Diagram:

9A	Ma	En	Sc	Hu	Fr	Te	Pe	Ga	Re	Mu
9B	Ma	En	Sc	Hu	Fr	Te	Pe	Ga	Re	Mu
9C	Ma	En	Sc	Hu	Fr	Te	Pe	Ga	Re	Mu
9D	Ma	En	Sc	Hu	Fr	It	Pe	Ga	Re	Mu
9E	Ma	En	Sc	Hu	Fr	Ar	Pe	Ga	Re	Mu
9F	Ma	En	Sc	Hu	Fr	Ar	Pe	Ga	Re	Mu
periods:	3	3	3	3	3	4	2	2	1	1 = 25 pds

So far so good. But (like all schools) this school has some **constraints**:

1. Maths is shown in half-year blocks because the school does not have enough Maths teachers to teach both halves together.
    The same applies to En, Sc, Hu and Fr.
2. There is only 1 Re teacher.
3. There is only 1 Music room.
4. There are only 2 teaching-spaces for Pe (the Gym and the Hall).

Question : Is the Curriculum Diagram still feasible with these constraints?

The answer is to draw a Schematic Diagram, as shown on the next page.

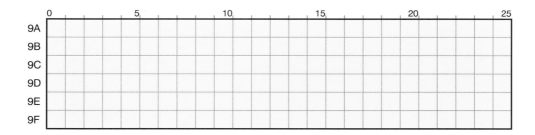

The grid shows **classes** vertically, and **time** horizontally.

(Time is always 'horizontal' on all the diagrams in this book.)

In drawing a Schematic Diagram it is often best to use a pencil, on squared paper. This school has a 25-period cycle.

Start with the biggest teams (Te, Ga in this case), and mark them on the grid for the correct number of periods (4 for Te, 2 for Ga).

Then add the next-size teams (Ma, En, Sc, Hu, Fr, for 3 periods each) for one half of this Year 9.

At this stage the Schematic Diagram shows:

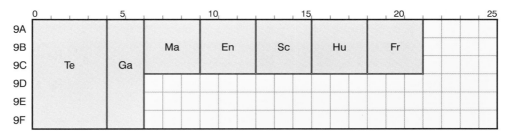

Now add Ma, En, Sc, Hu, Fr for the other half-year, remembering that because of Constraint No. 1 (on the opposite page), you cannot add Maths under Maths, or English under English, etc.

Then add Pe for classes 9AB (see below).

We can then complete the diagram for 9AB by adding Re and Mu, as Re-Mu above Mu-Re, remembering Constraints 2 and 3 (that there is only 1 Re teacher and only 1 Mu room):

We can then do the reverse (with Pe, and Re-Mu) to complete the diagram for 9CD, like this:

	0		5		10		15		20		25
9A									Pe	Re	Mu
9B			Ma	En	Sc	Hu	Fr		Pe	Mu	Re
9C	Te	Ga							Re Mu	Pe	
9D									Mu Re	Pe	
9E			En	Sc	Hu	Fr	Ma		?	?	
9F											

But what can now go into the 2 spaces marked '?' Nothing can fit there, because of the constraints.

This curriculum diagram fails in practice, because of:

a) The unfortunate pairing of classes for Pe (because of the shortage of Pe teaching-spaces) while the rest of the blocks are triplets, and

b) The fact that there is only a single resource for Re (only 1 teacher) and only a single resource for Music (only 1 Music room).

The consequences of (a) and (b) need to be resolved before continuing.

Note that there is more than one way to build the Schematic Diagram, but they all lead to the same result.

Schematic diagrams are useful to draw whenever (part of) a curriculum diagram changes, or when the constraints on the curriculum change.

If you have timetabler software it will draw a schematic diagram for you.

4.5   Limitations

Be aware that a Schematic Diagram is not a timetable (see the start of section 4.4), and just because it is possible to draw a Schematic Diagram doesn't mean that it can be scheduled in a working timetable.

For example, here is a fragment of a Schematic Diagram: Sc for 7A has been fitted against Fr for 7B.

But if Sc requires a double-period, while Fr requires 2 singles, then you cannot schedule this part of the Schematic Diagram as it stands.

If the Schematic Diagram allows this:
then all is well. Fr can be followed by Gg for 7B (or Gg followed by Fr) while Sc is taught to 7A.

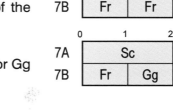

Here is another potentially impossible situation:

If the subjects can *only* be arranged like this then they interlock to form a triple period – and you may not have space for this in your day.

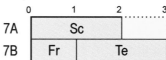

4.6   Worked Example 4

You may wish to try drawing a Schematic Diagram for the curriculum shown here, yourself, before reading the comments below.

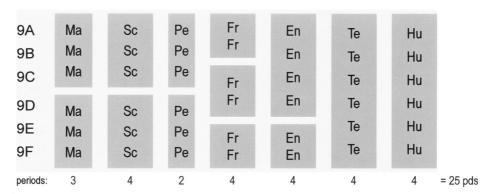

| periods: | 3 | 4 | 2 | 4 | 4 | 4 | 4 | = 25 pds |

The constraints here are that only Te and Hu have enough staff to cover the whole year.
Can this work in practice?

Because of the way that this Year 9 has been 'banded' (some subjects in pairs, some in triplets), only Fr can go against En, and vice versa, like this:

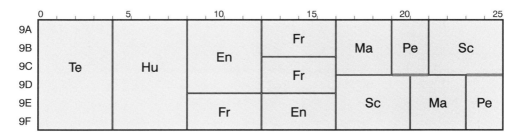

This diagram assumes that the two Fr teachers taking 9AB are *different* teachers from the two Fr teachers taking the 9CD pair.
In practice you'd need to check this with the Head of French, early on.

The Ma/Sc/Pe part will only work if *none* of the Ma and Sc staff also teach Pe to Year 9.   See the coloured boundaries on the diagram above.

Depending on the period-breakdown (into Singles/Doubles) of Ma/Sc/Pe there may also be a problem of the kind discussed in section 4.5.

4.7 Worked Example 5

You may like to try sketching a Schematic Diagram for the curriculum shown here, yourself, before reading the discussion below.

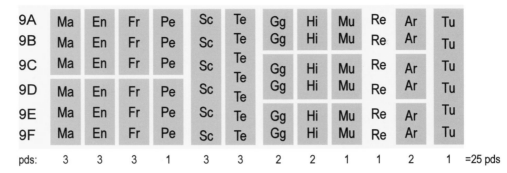

9A	Ma	En	Fr	Pe	Sc	Te	Gg	Hi	Mu	Re	Ar	Tu
9B	Ma	En	Fr	Pe	Sc	Te	Gg	Hi	Mu	Re	Ar	Tu
9C	Ma	En	Fr	Pe	Sc	Te	Gg	Hi	Mu	Re	Ar	Tu
9D	Ma	En	Fr	Pe	Sc	Te	Gg	Hi	Mu	Re	Ar	Tu
9E	Ma	En	Fr	Pe	Sc	Te	Gg	Hi	Mu	Re	Ar	Tu
9F	Ma	En	Fr	Pe	Sc	Te	Gg	Hi	Mu	Re	Ar	Tu
pds:	3	3	3	1	3	3	2	2	1	1	2	1 =25 pds

Constraints: there are only 2 Gg teachers, only 2 Hi teachers, only 2 Music rooms, only 2 Art rooms, and only 1 Re teacher.
There are also fewer than 6 teachers for each of Ma, En, Fr, Pe.

Is this possible? If not, what are the possible solutions?

The main problem here is that there is only 1 Re teacher.
See the '?' space below - who can teach there?
The same problem arises with the 9CD and 9EF parts.

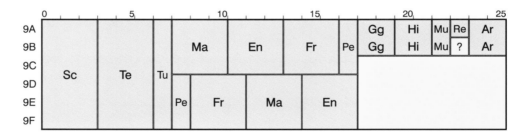

There are 3 possible solutions:

Solution 1:

Find an extra Re teacher.
The final section can then look like this:

(There are other possible permutations.)

In this solution, the Gg, Hi, Ar and Mu can still be taught in paired upper-lower sets.

	20				25
9A	Gg	Hi	Mu	Re	Ar
9B	Gg	Hi	Mu	Re	Ar
9C	Ar	Gg	Re	Mu	Hi
9D	Ar	Gg	Re	Mu	Hi
9E	Hi	Ar	Gg	Mu	Re
9F	Hi	Ar	Gg	Mu	Re

Solution 2:

Unpick some of the setting in other subjects.

eg. unpick the setting/pairing in Art or Music or Hi or Gg, sufficiently to allow it to work with only 1 Re teacher.

Here's the solution if you just unpick the Music pair. It only needs 1 Mu teacher.

There can still be an upper/lower group in Mu (and Re) if the two teachers agree between them.

	20			25
9A	Gg	Hi	Mu Re	Ar
9B	Gg	Hi	Re Mu	Ar
9C	Ar	Gg	Hi	Mu Re
9D	Ar	Gg	Hi	Re Mu
9E	Mu Re	Ar	Gg	Hi
9F	Re Mu	Ar	Gg	Hi

Solution 3:

Use consistent setting based on attainment in one of the subjects (see 'consistent setting' in section 2.10).

All the students in 9ABCDEF are re-grouped into 6 sets, based on some agreed criterion.

In this particular solution (one of many) the subjects are taught in double-periods except for Mu, Re:

	20			25
set 1	Gg	Hi	Mu Re	Ar
set 2	Gg	Ar	Hi	Re Mu
set 3	Re Mu	Gg	Ar	Hi
set 4	Hi	Gg	Ar	Mu Re
set 5	Ar	Re Mu	Gg	Hi
set 6	Mu Re	Hi	Gg	Ar

If the Gg, Hi, Ar were taught in single periods there would be more solutions.

In the example shown here the pairing for Gg has been preserved.

When scheduling by computer the software keeps track of the many consistent groups, and gives you the benefits from the inherent flexibility, but when scheduling manually it can be difficult.

In each case the basic rule discussed in the example in section 4.3 must be obeyed: the width of this part of the curriculum must equal or exceed the number of periods of Re to be fitted in (with a single Re teacher).

In each case, when you have found a solution it is important to:
(a) Look for more than one solution, so that you can offer the Head of Subject more than a single choice if possible (this pays dividends in terms of diplomacy), and,
(b) Make sure that you check that the solutions actually work before you discuss them with the Head of Subject (or else you will look foolish later!).

4.8   Summary

It is valuable to draw a Schematic Diagram for all or part of the curricular structure whenever the curriculum diagram changes, or the constraints change.
It is far better to discover any problems now, when you can see the underlying reasons, and find solutions, than later when you are deep in the scheduling.

5   Staff Deployment Analysis

Once a new curriculum is decided, it ought to be analysed carefully.
In particular, it ought to be analysed to see the disposition of the most valuable of our resources, the teaching staff. One can do this simply by counting teaching periods, but there are two disadvantages — the large numbers are unwieldy and make it difficult to see how your school is changing over time, and the method will not allow you to compare your school with others.

These disadvantages are overcome by a method developed by T. I. Davies (see the bibliography) and since used by inspectors including OFSTED.

This method analyses the deployment of staff in your curriculum, expresses this deployment in terms of small, manageable numbers, allows you to see changes in your school over time, and allows you to compare your school with others, nationally.

Sometimes called 'curriculum analysis', the method is more properly called Staff Deployment Analysis.

The opposite page shows some of the symbols and formulae used in calculating the Staff Deployment Analysis. These formulae are discussed on the following pages, with some worked examples.

It is important not to get bogged down in the algebra or the arithmetic, because in practice all the calculations will be done for you, either by the spreadsheet on the CD or by your timetabler software.

The key points to understand are the principles, so that they will set the context for understanding the results and the bar-charts shown later.

5.2 The Symbols used:

N	=	**N**umber of pupils	PTR	=	overall **p**upil-**t**eacher **r**atio
c	=	**c**ontact ratio	L	=	average teaching **L**oad
T	=	number of f.t.e. **T**eachers[1]	W	=	number of periods per cycle[2]
n	=	average teaching group size	p	=	number of teacher **p**eriods
ptr	=	operational pupil-teacher ratio	$b\%$	=	relative **b**onus

Notes:

1 f.t.e. = full time equivalent. For example, if a part-time teacher is employed for only 0.4 of the cycle, then count him/her as 0.4 This figure should include the Head. OFSTED expect you to only include *qualified* teachers, in which case p refers only to the teaching periods provided by these teachers (but you may find it useful to also do the calculations counting *all* your teaching staff and all their periods).

2 The timetable cycle is typically either a week or a fortnight, so in the UK the value of W is typically 25, 30, 50 or 60 periods.

3 This method does not apply to the 'Sixth Form' (Years 12/13) – see section 5.13.

Formulae:

$$\text{Overall pupil-teacher ratio } (PTR) = \frac{\text{Number of pupils } (N)}{\text{No. of f.t.e. Teachers } (T)}$$

$$\text{Contact ratio } (c) = \frac{\text{Total No. of teacher-periods taught } (p)}{\text{Total teacher-periods possible } (W \times T)}$$

$$\text{Average teaching load } (L) = \text{Contact Ratio } (c) \times \text{No. of periods per cycle } (W)$$

$$\text{Average group size } (n) = \frac{\text{No. of pupils } (N) \times \text{No. of periods per cycle } (W)}{\text{No. of teacher-periods taught } (p)}$$

$$\text{Staff used in a year group } (t) = \frac{\text{No. of teacher-periods taught } (p)}{\text{Average teaching load } (L)}$$

$$\text{Operational PTR } (ptr) = \frac{\text{No. of pupils } (N)}{\text{No. of staff used } (t)}$$

$$\text{Actual provision } (p) = \text{No. of teacher-periods provided}$$

$$\text{Basic provision} = \frac{\text{No. of pupils } (N) \times \text{No. of periods/cycle } (W)}{27}$$

$$\text{Bonus periods} = \text{Actual provision of periods} - \text{Basic provision}$$

$$\text{Relative bonus } (b\%) = \frac{\text{Bonus periods}}{\text{Basic periods}} \times 100 \%$$

5.3   Pupil-Teacher Ratio (PTR)

This is not often a useful figure but it is the one that the local press often seize upon: *"The pupil-teacher ratio at Laura Norder High School is only 16 to 1"*. But of course this does not mean that the average or typical size of a teaching group is 16 (because teachers do not teach for every period of the week).

$$\text{Overall pupil-teacher ratio } (PTR) \; = \; \frac{\text{Number of pupils } (N)}{\text{No. of f.t.e. Teachers } (T)}$$

5.4   Contact Ratio and Average Teaching Load

The curriculum that can be offered by the school is limited by the amount of staff time that is available.
The total number of teaching periods available depends not only on the number of staff, but also on the fraction of the week that they are actually teaching. This fraction is called the **Contact Ratio**.

For example, if the average teaching load is 19 periods in a 25-period week, then the Contact Ratio = $^{19}/_{25}$ = 0.76   or 76%

How does your personal Contact Ratio compare with this ?

In practice we do not usually know the average teaching load, but we can calculate the Contact Ratio from:

$$\text{Contact Ratio } (c) \; = \; \frac{\text{Total No. of teacher-periods taught } (p)}{\text{Total teacher-periods possible } (W \times T)}$$

Example 1
In Laura Norder High School there are 800 periods timetabled.
There are 40 teachers and a 25-period week is used.
>   Total periods taught = 800
>   Total number possible = 40 x 25 = 1000 teacher-periods
>   Therefore Contact Ratio, c = $^{800}/_{1000}$ = 0.80 = 80%

The teachers, on average, spend 80% of their time in class contact
ie. they average 0.80 x 25 = 20 periods per week in class contact.

This value of 0.80 (80%) is fairly high for UK schools.
For most schools the value of c is usually around 0.70 – 0.75 (70 – 75%).
In some schools it has been as high as 85%, and (rarely) as low as 65%.
It will usually be lower in split-site schools than in single-site schools.

Remember that c relates to the *average* teaching load – for every Subject Leader, Year-Tutor, Deputy Head and Head who teaches below this ratio, other staff will have to teach above it.

The average teaching load can be calculated as in Example 1 by:

Average teaching load (L) = Contact Ratio (c) x No. of periods per cycle (W)

or by:

$$\text{Average teaching load } (L) = \frac{\text{Total No. of teacher-periods taught } (p)}{\text{No. of f.t.e. Teachers } (T)}$$

The value of the Contact Ratio also gives the *average* fraction of your staff that are teaching classes at any instant. Clearly the value of c affects the number of permanent staff available to cover for absent colleagues and for other duties. It also has implications for the degree of difficulty experienced in scheduling the timetable.

The same calculation of the Contact Ratio can be used constructively, in reverse – that is, you can decide on the required Contact Ratio and then see the effect on the curriculum or the staffing cost:

Example 2
In the same Laura Norder High School, the Head and Governors wish to expand the curriculum to 836 timetabled periods, and at the same time reduce the Contact Ratio to 76% (0.76).
What would be the cost ?

Average number of periods taught = 0.76 x 25 = 19 periods per teacher.

Number of staff required = $836/19$ = 44 staff, an increase of 4 teachers.

How much would this cost approximately (at current salary levels) ?
It may be instructive to calculate how many technicians, books, computers this sum would buy.

A quantity k, called the staff loading factor, is sometimes referred to. This is the reciprocal of c. ie. $k = 1/c$. If $c = 0.75$ then $k = 1.33$.

The only advantage in considering this factor is if you decide to provide 25 extra periods on the curriculum (in a 25-period week) – perhaps an extra registration group in Year 7 for a bigger intake. You might think that you would need the equivalent of only one extra teacher. In fact you would need the equivalent of k extra staff because each of them would be teaching only a fraction c of the week.

5.5   The Staffing Equation

Although the total number of staff is T, the effective number is only c multiplied by T. That is, cT (using c as a decimal, eg. 0.75, not a percentage).
In effect you have cT staff teaching the whole cycle (W) with no free periods. So the total number of teaching periods (p) that you have available to cover the school curriculum $= c \times T \times W$.
That is:

$$p = c \times T \times W$$

This is the Staffing Equation, sometimes called the 'First Law' of the curriculum.

This equation can be used in three different ways:

1    $p = cTW$ = the number of teaching periods that can be provided by a staff of T teachers working at a contact ratio c. It can be applied to the whole school or just to a department.

2    $T = p/cW$ = the number of teachers needed to provide p teaching periods when they are working at a contact ratio c. It can be used to to find the number of staff needed for a new school or for each part of a split-site school, or used to find the 'correct' size of a department.

3    $c = p/TW$ = the contact ratio that must be accepted if p teaching periods are to be provided by T staff.

5.6   Average Teaching-Group Size in each Year of the school

For an individual Year, the average size of a teaching group can be found by:

$$\text{Average class size } (n) = \frac{\text{No. of pupils } (N) \ \times \ \text{No. of periods per cycle } (W)}{\text{No. of teacher-periods taught } (p)}$$

To find the number of teacher-periods for this calculation, see the final column of the Curriculum Audit Form shown in Chapter 6.

The number of f.t.e. staff used for teaching any single Year can be found by:

$$\text{Staff used in a year group } (t) = \frac{\text{No. of teacher-periods taught } (p)}{\text{Average teaching load } (L)}$$

It is occasionally useful to calculate the 'operational' pupil-teacher ratio for each Year of pupils separately, via:

$$\text{Operational PTR } (ptr) = \frac{\text{No. of pupils } (N)}{\text{No. of staff used } (t)}$$

These items are discussed further in Section 5.8.

5.7　Teaching periods : Basic provision and Bonus periods

The original intention of T. I. Davies was to allow us to compare different Years within a school, to see which students are getting the 'best deal' in terms of the *quantity* of teaching time.

His key concept was the idea of a 'Basic provision' of teaching periods for any population of pupils.

For historical reasons he decided on a Basic provision of teaching periods that would give an *average* teaching-group size of 27. There is nothing absolute about this value: Davies chose it as a convenient datum-line and we have kept to it ever since. In fact it wouldn't matter what number we use as long as we all agree on the same value, just as geographers have agreed to measure the heights of mountains from mean sea level rather than the centre of the Earth. Our 'mean sea level' is a group size of 27.

The Basic provision can be calculated by:

$$\text{Basic provision of teaching periods (for an average group size of 27)} = \frac{\text{No. of pupils } (N) \ \times \ \text{No. of periods/cycle } (W)}{27}$$

In practice, in most schools, the **actual** provision is greater than this (giving an average group size of *less* than 27, as you'd expect).

The difference between the **actual** provision and the **Basic** provision is called the BONUS:

$$\textbf{Bonus } \text{periods} \ = \ \textbf{Actual } \text{provision of periods} \ - \ \textbf{Basic } \text{provision}$$

The Bonus is our 'height above mean sea level'.

As we shall see on the next page it is a key concept in showing you where you are allocating the most precious of your resources, teaching time.

If your school has rising or falling rolls, so that the number of students in each Year varies, then it is best to calculate the **Relative** Bonus, $b\%$, by:

$$\text{Relative bonus } (b\%) \ = \ \frac{\text{Bonus periods}}{\text{Basic periods}} \ \times \ 100\,\%$$

These concepts are illustrated with a real example on the next page.

Section 5.13 explains why this method cannot be used with a 'Sixth Form'.

5.8   Worked Example : Calculating the Bonuses

The diagram below shows the screen of a spreadsheet that is included on the CD provided with this book.

To use it you simply type your school's details into the yellow boxes. The software then uses the formulae from this chapter to immediately calculate all the values in the blue boxes:

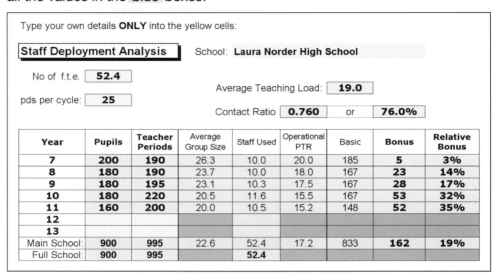

Type your own details **ONLY** into the yellow cells:

Staff Deployment Analysis   School: **Laura Norder High School**

No of f.t.e.   **52.4**

pds per cycle: **25**

Average Teaching Load: **19.0**

Contact Ratio   **0.760**   or   **76.0%**

Year	Pupils	Teacher Periods	Average Group Size	Staff Used	Operational PTR	Basic	Bonus	Relative Bonus
7	200	190	26.3	10.0	20.0	185	5	3%
8	180	190	23.7	10.0	18.0	167	23	14%
9	180	195	23.1	10.3	17.5	167	28	17%
10	180	220	20.5	11.6	15.5	167	53	32%
11	160	200	20.0	10.5	15.2	148	52	35%
12								
13								
Main School:	900	995	22.6	52.4	17.2	833	162	19%
Full School:	900	995		52.4				

The spreadsheet also draws 4 bar-charts of this data for you.

Looking at the data above you can see that this 11-16 school has 52.4 f.t.e. qualified teachers, and runs a 25-period timetable cycle.

Column 2
Looking down column 2 you can see that in this school the number of students per Year varies. We'll see later how this is compensated for.

Column 3
This column shows that the number of teaching-periods provided by the school also varies — but we cannot easily see at this stage whether the school has provided enough staffing for the large Year 7 or not.

Column 4
This shows the average size of teaching-groups in each Year. As you'd expect, Years 10 & 11 have smaller groups due the range of subjects in the options.

If you wish you can manually calculate the values for Years 12–13 (section 5.13) and enter them in the grey cells so that they can be included on the graphs.

Column 5
This shows the equivalent number of f.t.e. staff used for each Year Group. Because of the varying pupil numbers it is hard to see any real pattern here.

Column 6

This column shows the operational pupil-teacher ratio for each YearGroup, which decreases for older students, as you'd expect. As for column 4, you can manually calculate the values for your Years 12 & 13 and enter them here.

Column 7

This shows the Basic provision for this number of pupils ie. the number of teacher-periods needed to give a mean group size of 27, our 'mean sea level'.

Column 8

This shows the Bonus. Now, for the first time, a clearer picture emerges of the way the staff are being deployed in this school, with the Bonuses being much more generous for Years 10 & 11 than for Year 7.

Column 9

In schools with rising or falling rolls, when the number of students per year varies markedly (as in this example), then it is better to use the values for the Relative Bonus (as shown in column 9). Notice that the Relative Bonus shows that the provision for Year 11 is more generous than for Year 10, whereas the Bonus column showed the reverse (because of uneven student numbers).

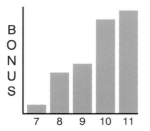

This is the bar-chart for the data in the spreadsheet opposite.
It shows how the 162 bonus periods were distributed.
You could decide to distribute the 162 periods differently.

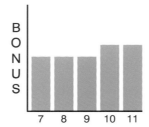

Is this pattern more, or less, fair to the students?
It distributes the same 162 bonuses in a different way.
It's your judgement.

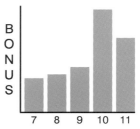

A potentially bad scenario, because the bonuses for Year 10 will normally have to continue into Year 11 as well, either by stealing from lower years or by raising the contact ratio.

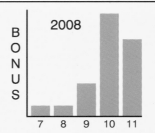

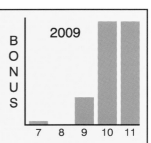

Laura Norder School in 3 successive years. The effect of a changing curriculum or a changing intake had not been allowed for. This shows the value of calculating your bonuses regularly.

5.9   Relative bonus b%

Section 5.7 explained how to calculate the Relative Bonus (b%), while the bar-charts showed how useful it is in tracking how your school changes.
The Relative Bonus also allows you to compare your school with others.

In the worked example in section 5.7 the Relative Bonus (b%) was 19%. This is quite a generous value, allowing a good degree of curricular flexibility.

The experiences of OFSTED and HM Inspectorate suggest that relative bonuses below 10% will restrict the school's curriculum considerably, while values above 20% are generous and rare.

The lower limit of b% = 10% implies a lower limit to the contact ratio c. This lower limit is c = 0.0407 multiplied by the pupil-teacher ratio (see Appendix 4 for the proof). For example, if your funding allows a pupil-teacher ratio (PTR) of 17:1 (for the main school, not including the 'Sixth Form', see section 5.13) then the lower limit for c = 0.0407 X 17 = 0.69. If your value of c falls below this figure, then b% will fall below 10%, and you will lose the curricular flexibility that you need in order to provide a reasonable range of options.

5.10   Worked Example : Relative bonus

You are newly appointed to the Headship of Laura Norder High School.
This is a 6-form-entry 11–16 school with 900 pupils (N). The funding allows you to appoint 52.9 f.t.e. staff, giving a value of 17 : 1 for the pupil-teacher ratio.

You devise your ideal curriculum and find it requires 1160 teacher-periods (in a 25-period cycle). What can you deduce?

Using the staffing equation (see section 5.5):

$$c = \frac{p}{TW} = \frac{1160}{52.9 \times 25} = 0.88 \quad (88\%)$$

This is equivalent to an average load of 0.88 x 25 = 22 periods in a 25-period week and must be considered to be too high. What would be possible?

If you decided on c = 0.72 (= 18 periods *average* in a 25-period week, giving a reasonable allowance of time to some staff for pastoral care etc.), then:

$p = cTW$ = 0.72 x 52.9 x 25 = 952 teaching periods

This is the total number of teaching-periods available to cover the curriculum.

Since the school has 900 pupils (N), in a 25-period week (W):

the **basic** provision $= \frac{N \times W}{27} = \frac{900 \times 25}{27} = 833$ periods

Thus the **bonus** for the whole school is 952 – 833 = **+119** periods.
You can then decide how to distribute these +119 bonus periods between the

five year-groups. Would you give +50 bonuses to Year 10 and + 50 to Year 11 in order to give a wide range of options, leaving only +19 for Years 7, 8 and 9?

Or would you decide on a strong injection of resources into Year 7 in an attempt to develop good work habits in your intake, hopefully to pay dividends later?

To compare this school with others we can calculate b%, by:

$$b\% = \frac{\text{total bonus}}{\text{total basic}} \times 100\% = \frac{119}{833} \times 100\% = 14.3\%$$

This is a reasonable value. It could be increased by increasing c (for example, if c is increased to 0.77, $b\%$ increases to 22%). The variation of $b\%$ as c varies can be checked most quickly by using a nomogram.

5.11   The nomogram

It can be shown (see Appendix 4) that there is a relation between the pupil-teacher ratio (N/T), the contact ratio (c) and the relative bonus ($b\%$).
This relationship can be plotted on a form of graph known as a nomogram (see the next page).
For the present refer only to the three labels at the tops of the axes and ignore the labels at the bottom (these will be used in chapter 9).

The quantity plotted on the left-hand axis, N/T, is the pupil-teacher ratio. Typically it is in the region of 16 or 17. It is determined by your funding and typically the school has no direct control over it. Mark the value of your staffing ratio on the N/T axis.
The quantity plotted on the central axis is c, the contact ratio. This typically varies over the range 0.70 – 0.80. As c varies, so does the relative bonus $b\%$ which is marked on the right-hand axis. The three quantities are always connected by a straight line (use a ruler or stretch a length of black cotton).

For example, suppose your pupil-teacher ratio is 17: 1 and you wish to see the effect of having a contact ratio of 0.77. Draw a straight line from 17 on the left axis through 0.77 on the central axis. This line cuts the $b\%$ axis at 22%, a high value. (These are the same values used in the last part of section 5.10).

Reducing the contact ratio to 0.69 (with this PTR of 17:1) gives a value for $b\%$ of less than 10% (unsatisfactory). If you wanted a $b\%$ value of 20% then you would have to accept a contact ratio of 0.76.

By pivoting your ruler or length of cotton about the school's value of N/T, acceptable values of c and $b\%$ may be found.

Once $b\%$ is determined, the number of bonuses that are available can be calculated from:

$$\text{bonus periods} = \frac{b\% \times N \times W}{2700}$$

The school must then decide how to distribute these bonuses equitably.

Using the nomogram

Staffing (chapter 5)

1 Calculate the pupil-teacher ratio $\dfrac{N}{T} = \dfrac{\text{number of pupils } (N)}{\text{f.t.e. number of staff } (T)}$

   (For the main school only - if you have a 'Sixth Form', see section 5.13).

2 Reading the label at the top of each axis and using a ruler, the nomogram will show what contact ratio (c) must be accepted to achieve a relative bonus ($b\%$) or vice versa. (See also section 5.9)

3 The national average for c is often around 0.75 in the UK but it varies from school to school, typically over the range 0.7 - 0.8
   The value of $b\%$ should be greater than 10% if the school is to have a reasonable curricular flexibility.

4 Once c is agreed, the number of teaching-periods (p) that can be provided to cover your curriculum can be calculated from the staffing equation:
   $p = cTW$ where W = number of periods in your cycle.
   More conveniently, the number of bonuses to be distributed throughout the school can be calculated from:

$$\text{bonus periods} = \frac{b\% \times N \times W}{2700}$$

Rooming (chapter 9)

5 Calculate $\dfrac{N}{R} = \dfrac{\text{number of pupils } (N)}{\text{number of teaching spaces } (R)}$ (for main school only)

6 Referring to the label at the bottom of each axis, the nomogram will then show what rooming fraction (r) must be accepted for a given curriculum bonus ($b\%$) or vice versa.

7 If $r = 0.85$ then, on average, each room will be used for 85% of the week, and, on average, 85% of the teaching spaces will be in use at any time.

8 As r rises above 0.85 there are likely to be increasingly severe restrictions on the timetable.
   If $b\%$ falls below 10%, the school is unlikely to have sufficient curricular flexibility.
   Taken together, these values imply a critical value of $N/n = 21$ (see chapter 9).

9 If required, r could be used to calculate the number of teaching periods (p) to be provided, using the rooming equation: $p = rRW$
   This equation can be applied to the whole main school or to specialist rooms within a department.
   The larger the value of r for the whole school, the more uniform the values of r must be for the individual departments.

10 Steps 2 and 6 should be iterated as necessary to obtain reasonable values of c, b, r.

The nomogram

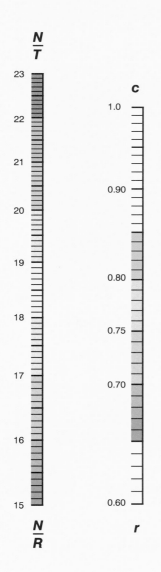

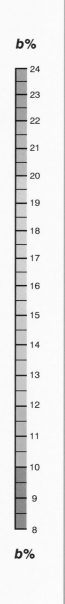

5.12   Using software to calculate the bonuses

As well as the spreadsheet shown in section 5.8 (which is on the CD), your timetabling software will often do the calculation on the data that you enter.

For example here is one of the screens in the **TimeTabler** program:

The software can do the calculations quicker for you, and it will also do more for you, including drawing the bar-charts and using some of the more

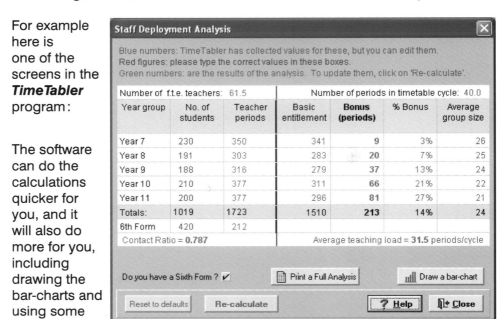

Staff Deployment Analysis

Blue numbers: TimeTabler has collected values for these, but you can edit them.
Red figures: please type the correct values in these boxes.
Green numbers: are the results of the analysis. To update them, click on 'Re-calculate'.

Number of f.t.e. teachers: 61.5   Number of periods in timetable cycle: 40.0

Year group	No. of students	Teacher periods	Basic entitlement	Bonus (periods)	% Bonus	Average group size
Year 7	230	350	341	9	3%	26
Year 8	191	303	283	20	7%	25
Year 9	188	316	279	37	13%	24
Year 10	210	377	311	66	21%	22
Year 11	200	377	296	81	27%	21
Totals:	1019	1723	1510	213	14%	24
6th Form	420	212				

Contact Ratio = **0.787**   Average teaching load = **31.5** periods/cycle

Do you have a Sixth Form ? ✔   Print a Full Analysis   Draw a bar-chart

Reset to defaults   Re-calculate   ? Help   Close

complex formulae shown in Appendix 4 to give you extra information.

5.13   The Sixth Form, Years 12 & 13

Some aspects of this method of staff deployment analysis cannot be applied to the Sixth Form (Years 12/13). This is because the students are normally allowed a variable amount of time for private study and this time is not staffed.
Also, an average class size of 27 (our 'mean sea level' for zero bonus) is scarcely relevant to most Sixth Form groups.

If the students in your 'Pre-A-level' or 'Pre-IB' are allowed little or no free time, then perhaps you can use the same method as for the Main School. The size of the bonuses may surprise you.

Local authorities and councils often apply a staffing ratio of about 1:11 when considering 'Sixth Forms'. Even at this level of staffing, it seems that in most schools the Sixth Form is subsidized by the main school.

If you wish to use Staff Deployment Analysis in a school with a Sixth Form then it is best to use one of the computer methods described in sections 5.8 and 5.12.

If you are working manually then the usual method is to separate the Sixth Form provision from the main school as follows:

(a) Calculate the contact ratio as explained in section 5.4.
(b) Add up the total number of teacher-periods in the Sixth Form curriculum.
(c) Multiply the contact ratio by the number of periods in the timetable cycle to find the average teaching load.
(d) Divide the number in (b) by the number in (c) to find the number of full-time-equivalent teachers for the Sixth Form.
(e) Subtract this number from the total full-time-equivalent staffing for your school and use the result as T for the main school (in the staffing equation, section 5.5, etc.)

If you take the number found in (d) and divide it into the number of Sixth-Formers, the result is your pupil-teacher ratio for your Sixth Form. Comparing this with the value used in your funding (often about 11:1) allows you to decide whether your Sixth Form is being subsidized by the main school.

A value of 9 : 1 means that the Sixth Form is taking more than its 'fair' share of teachers. This is commonly the case with Sixth Forms of less than 100 students.

5.14 Summary

The procedures described in this chapter need not be performed frequently – perhaps every second or third year if your situation is static. If the curricular structure changes or if your intake numbers change, then these methods will highlight the effects.

It is a particularly interesting exercise when newly joining a school.

The calculations themselves require and make no judgements. Once the principles are understood, use a computer program to make the calculations automatically, so that you can concentrate on the implications.

Now that he had all the basic data, Jim felt ready to begin...

So that's NO split groups, NO Friday afternoons,
NO room changes, NO Year 9, NO Monday mornings
and NO double periods this year, OK?

6 Collecting the data

We have now reached a half-way stage in the overall timetabling process.
We have sorted the Options and finalised the Curriculum Diagram that we intend to provide, but have yet to begin the process of scheduling it.
In order to proceed to the scheduling stage we must first assemble all the necessary data and then check this data for impossibilities.

The 3 main steps in the assembling and preliminary checking of the data are:

1   Doing a Curriculum Audit, looking at the necessary Teaching Loads, and balancing these loads to match your staffing to your curriculum.

2   Providing Subject Leaders or Heads of Departments with Data Collection Forms on which they can put their requests.

3   Checking these Data Collection Forms.

These 3 steps are covered in this chapter.

By the end of this stage (the end of this chapter) we wish to have teachers' initials shown next to each Teaching Group on the Curriculum, like this (using the diagram from section 2.7 as an example):

9A	En *AJo*	Ma *JHa*	Sc *KJo*	Fr *LMu*	Hi *JCl*	Gg *IKe*	Ar *EBi*	Mu *DWi*	Re *PUn*	Se *JCl*	Te *IHa* Te *AFr*	Pe *ASe*	
9B	En *BJa*	Ma *FHi*	Sc *BPa*	Fr *EBr*	Hi *JCl*	Gg *IKe*	Ar *EBi*	Mu *BAl*	Re *PUn*	Se *EBr*	Te *JHi*	Pe *SOr*	
9C	En *DSi*	Ma *VHa*	Sc *JSi*	Fr *EBr*	Hi *RRe*	Gg *IKe*	Ar *TTi*	Mu *BAl*	Re *AFr*	Se *TTi*	Te *IHa* Te *JHi*	Pe *ASe*	
9D	En *JRo*	Ma *JVi*	Sc *KJo*	Fr *GSi*	Hi *JCl*	Gg *IKe*	Ar *TTi*	Mu *DWi*	Re *AFr*	Se *IKe*	Te *AFr*	Pe *SOr*	
periods:	4	4	4	4	2	2	2	1	1	2	2	2	=30
	SSSS	SSSS	DSS	SSSS	SS	SS	D	S	S	SS	D	D	

6.2   Matching the departments to the curriculum

One of the first things we must check is that each department can cover the required number of periods of that subject.

This is not merely a matter of ensuring that there are enough History teachers to cover the total number of periods of History: several things must be investigated.

The questions to be considered include:

- Are members of the department also Year-Tutors (or Heads of Subject, Deputy Heads, etc) requiring extra 'free' (non-teaching) time?

- For part-time staff, do you know the amount of teaching that they will be engaged to do on the new timetable? Are there any who wish to change the number of teaching periods?

- Have resignations or appointments of staff during the year changed the structure of the department?

- Are there enough suitably qualified staff to take all the classes at all levels?

- What is the position of staff who are shared between this department and another department? If the balance of periods between the departments is to change, how will this affect each department and the member of staff involved?

- How many periods, if any, are surplus to the department? Can they be used to cover PSHE, Games, RE, Tutorial-periods, General Studies etc.?

- How many periods, if any, are a deficit in the department? Can they be borrowed from any other department?

You may have done much of this checking while drawing up the option pools (chapter 3) but it should always be done again at this stage.

Methods of checking the departments vary from school to school. One method, in three steps, is shown in the box on the next page:

This should be done in conjunction with the Curriculum Audit Form shown in section 6.3.

While this is being done for all departments, a look at the alternatives should lead to a way of balancing all the departments and covering the necessary periods of PSHE, Games, RE, General Studies etc.

This process may well involve a certain amount of negotiation (sometimes delicate negotiation) between the Director of Studies, Heads of Subjects and individual members of departments, as these 'musical chairs' moves are used to balance the staff against the curriculum.

This is discussed in more detail during this chapter.

3 steps in balancing the staffing of a department

Step 1: Find the number of periods needed to cover the subject this year.

For example: History Department

Year:	7	8	9	10	11	12/13	
Periods needed:	12	12	12	15	15	30	= **96**

(+3 compared with last year)

Step 2: Make suggestions about the teaching load of each member of the department, in order to find the total number of periods that are likely to be available. It is best to use the same unique code for each teacher that you will use in scheduling the timetable.

For example (in a 30-period cycle):

$$\text{If:} \quad \begin{array}{lll} \text{AFr} & = & 21 \quad \text{(Head of Department)} \\ \text{JCr} & = & 21 \quad \text{(Year-Tutor)} \\ \text{RRe} & = & 24 \\ \text{TBr} & = & \underline{24} \\ & & 90 \quad \text{Therefore a Deficit of } \textbf{6} \text{ periods.} \end{array}$$

The proposed teaching load should be based on the load usually given to Subject Leaders, Year-Tutors or House-Tutors, Deputy Heads etc. The numbers should be mathematically feasible. For example in the list shown above, if JCr teaches History only in the Lower School where all the History is taught in bundles of 2 periods, then JCr = 21 implies that he will teach 20 periods of History with 10 groups and then:

> either: 1 period of History sharing a group with someone else,
>
> or: 1 period of another subject, perhaps Games or RE

It is sometimes worth noting (and later providing to Subject Leaders as a guide) how the teaching load for a member of the department could break down into groups. For example (from the list above, for RRe), assuming that History is provided for 2 periods per group in Lower School and 3 periods per group in Upper School, then:

> RRe = 24   (= 9 groups x 2 periods + 2 groups x 3 periods)
>
> (or 6 groups x 2 periods + 4 groups x 3 periods)
>
> (or 3 groups x 2 periods + 6 groups x 3 periods)

Step 3: If the totals from Step 1 and Step 2 do not agree exactly, then make suggestions about possible solutions.

For example: To solve the History deficit = **6** periods

i)   If AHa in the English Department teaches 6 periods of History (she has some experience, is willing, English Department has some 'slack') then the totals balance (though there might still be split teaching for JCr, as above).

ii) If AHa in the English Department teaches 7 periods of History (= 2 groups x 2 periods + 1 group x 3 periods) then JCr could do 1 period of Games (he would like this).

iii) JCr, although a Year-Tutor, could be asked to teach 22 periods this year, with AHa = 7 periods of History and **JCr = 2 periods** of Games. Etc. etc.

6.3 The Curriculum Audit Form

To help you with the steps of section 6.2, there is a spreadsheet on the CD called the Curriculum Audit Form.

Subjects →	Ma	En	Hi	Gg	Re	Fr	Sp	Sc	Ph	Ch	Bi	Te	Ar	Mu	IT	Ga			TOTALS
CURRICULUM AUDIT FORM																			
Year 7	18	18	12																48
Year 8	18	18	12																48
TOTAL DEMAND:	129	135	96																360
Supply Available:	130	123	90																343
SURPLUS:	1	-12	-6																-17

You enter your values *only* into the yellow cells; the software calculates the answers for you and puts the results into the blue cells.

You enter the names/abbreviations for all your Subjects along the top.

Then you use your Curriculum Diagram (see chapters 2, 3, 4, 5) to enter (in each column) the number of periods needed for each Subject in each year.

The spreadsheet calculates the total number of periods for each Subject ('Total Demand') and enters the result in the first blue row.

The bottom two blue rows are provided by the linked spreadsheet, see below.

6.4 The Staff Loading Chart

This is part of the same spreadsheet workbook (on the CD), and is linked to the Curriculum Audit Form shown above.

Staff initials	Ma	En	Hi	Gg	Re	Fr	Sp	Sc	Ph	Ch	Bi	Te	Ar	Mu	IT	Ga			TOTALS	TARGET	FT or PT
STAFF LOADING CHART																					
JWi	18																		18	18	
AHa	19																		19	19	
FHi	19																		19	19	
JMa	20																		20	20	
VHa	20																		20	20	
GNe	20																		20	20	
GWa	14	6																	20	20	
TOTAL SUPPLY:	130	123	90																343	343	
DEMAND	129	135	96																360		
SURPLUS	1	-12	-6																-17		

Again, you enter your data *only* in the yellow cells; the software calculates for you and puts the results into the blue cells (on this sheet *and* on the other sheet).

Of course it is essential to have the Subjects in the same order here as in the Curriculum Audit Form, and the linkage ensures this.

Down the left-hand column, enter the initials/names of all the Teachers that you expect to have for the new timetable. It may help to colour-code departments.

- If a Teacher has resigned and a new person has been appointed, then enter their name/initials.
- If a post has been advertised but **not** yet appointed, then enter a place-holder (eg. X-Ma for an unknown Maths teacher).

Down each Subject column enter the number of periods that you expect each Teacher to teach, as discussed in section 6.2.

The blue cells show the results. They show:

- At the right-hand side, the Total Teaching Load for each person. This should match the Target that you have set, as in section 6.2.
- At the bottom, the Total Periods Available ('Total Supply') from these Teachers. (This value is also fed back to the penultimate blue row on the Curriculum Audit Form.)
- The penultimate blue row shows the periods needed for the curriculum ('Demand'), this figure being provided from the 'Total Demand' row of the Curriculum Audit Form (section 6.3).
- The bottom blue rows show the *difference* between these two figures, the '**Surplus**' (which of course can be negative).

Your task is to adjust the figures in the main (yellow) area of the spreadsheet until the 'Surplus' row contains only zeros, so that all is balanced.
You can work on either sheet, but the usual one is the Staff Loading Chart.

These spreadsheets have space for 20 Subjects and 60 Teachers, but you can easily add more. See also the appendix on 'How to use the CD'.

When you have balanced the loads then it is a good idea to take it to the Senior Leadership Group (SLG) as a proposal for discussion.
After talking it through and making any adjustments, this becomes a key document for the way ahead.

It is also a good idea to get members of the SLG to share the task of explaining any changes (especially any controversial changes) to the relevant Head of Subject. For example if a member of the SLG teaches in the Maths department, they would be the natural person to explain to the Head of Maths.

It is valuable to describe to the SLG explicitly which subjects are 'tight' and which are 'slack'. Too often, if an Art teacher hands in her notice near the deadline, the Head reacts by immediately advertising for another Art teacher, when what the school really needs is a new Science teacher. This Staff Loading Chart shows where the staffing of the school should be taking a new direction.

6.5 The Data Collection Form

The next stage is to provide each Subject Leader (SL) or Head of Department (HoD) with three things:

1. A Curriculum Booklet. This is a booklet showing the Curriculum Diagram for each year (like the diagrams shown in chapter 2). In this booklet, each SL/HoD can see all the classes for which he or she will be responsible.

The Curriculum Booklet may also draw attention (perhaps on the cover) to any changes in the structure of the curriculum.

It may also include requests such as 'Subject Leaders are asked to produce a balanced distribution of experienced staff between Upper School and Lower School' or 'Heads of Departments are urged to teach at least one first-year class personally'.

You may prefer to give copies of the Curriculum Booklet only to SLs/HoDs at this stage or you may think it better to give one to every member of staff so that everyone is aware of what is proposed.

2. Some information on the expected teaching load of each member of the department. ie. a list of the proposed number of periods for each member of the department as suggested in section 6.2.

3. A Staffing Form on which the Head of Department will provide you with the data that you need. The layout of the Data Collection Form varies from school to school. One such layout is shown here:

Data Collection		Data for the 2009/2010 timetable										History Dept.		
Staff ► / Class	AFr		JCr		RRe		TBr		AHa		No. of Groups	No. of Periods	Distribution
Y 13	Block B	5**			Block A	5**	Block C	5**			3	5	DDS
Y 12	Block A	5*			Block C	5	Block D	5			3	5	DDS
Y 11	Block C	3**	Block B,E	3,3**	Block D	3**	Block A	3**			5	3	SSS
Y 10	Blks D,E	3,3	Block C	3	Block B	3	Block A	3*			5	3	SSS
Y 9			9A, 9C	2+2	9B, 9D	2+2	9E, 9F	2+2			6	2	SS
Y 8			8A, 8B	2+2	8F	2*	8C	2	8D, 8E	2+2	6	2	SS
Y 7	7A	2	7B, 7D	2+2	7C	2	7F	2	7E	2	6	2	SS
Totals:		21		21		24		24		6			
Targets:		21		21		24		24		6			

This is available as a spreadsheet on the CD but it is probably best just printed out (from the CD) as a paper pro-forma to complete by hand.

On this form, you (as Timetabler) enter the values shown in **blue** above.
You will be giving this form to the SL or HoD and of course they are working in the current year while you are thinking of *next* year, when the curriculum may be different ...so you need to enter the details to focus them on next year.

You get the Targets (the bottom row) from the Staff Loading Chart (section 6.4).

The Subject Leader (or HoD) is asked to complete the cells shown in yellow.

To save your time later, during scheduling, it is useful to ask them to use a system of double/single asterisks on the form:

** It is crucial that this teacher teaches this group (eg. Y10 moving into Y11).

* It is important to keep this teacher but if absolutely necessary I could exchange this teacher with another (but keeping the same teaching load).

- No asterisk means that the Timetabler can exchange teachers. eg. swap over the named teacher for 7A Art with the named teacher for 7B Art.

ie. as Timetabler you are saying *"Tell me what is important, but give me some room for manoeuvre."*

The reverse side of the Staffing Form may show some notes containing some or all of the following requests to SLs/HoDs:

- to use asterisks as above,
- to use non-overlapping teacher teams for Maths and English etc., as much as possible (see the Principle of Compatibility in chapter 7),
- to apply the Combing Chart check (chapter 7) if you have previously explained this test as part of a CPD in-service training programme,
- to keep part-time teachers out of option blocks or teams of teachers, where possible (see also section 10.4),
- to check that the department has staffed all the groups for which it is responsible,
- to note briefly any specific complaints about the current timetable,
- to note in detail any timetabling limitations that will affect the department for the coming year:
  eg. – days and times for part-time teachers,
  – essential days and times for particular lessons (eg. swimming etc.),
  – requests for particular classes to be timetabled in parallel or grouped in a particular way for team-teaching,
  – any special resources for certain groups (eg. specific rooms),
- to return this Data Collection Form by a specified date.

The SL or HoD then has to use the information in (1) and (2) opposite to complete the cells shown in yellow, entering a number of periods for each teacher in the relevant cells. If they can't make the Totals match the Target value, then they must come and speak to you (see also section 6.2).

Ideally, before providing you with this information, the Head of Department will have applied the Combing Chart check (see chapter 7) to the department, so that she/he is aware of any problems arising and has done his/her best to solve them before filling in this Data Collection Form.

6.6   Checking the Data Collection Forms

When the forms are returned, it is wise to check everything. For example:

- Are the totals correct? Do they match the targets? Are the right number of groups entered for each Year?
- Are you quite sure which teachers are part-time? It can help to put a ring round their initials.
  If they are 'fixed' part-timers, are you quite sure which fixed days and times they are available?
  If they are 'floating' part-timers are you sure how many (half-) days they are prepared to be in school?
- Are you quite sure about the times requested for swimming, work-experience, 14-19 Diploma courses in the local consortium, links with the local Further Education college, local businesses, etc.?
- Is there anything in the complaints about the current timetable that may affect your approach to the new timetable?

Once the checking is completed, you can add the initials of the members of staff to your 'master' copy of the Curriculum Booklet.
This is the Master Booklet which will contain all the information that has to be timetabled. The Master Booklet will be at the timetabler's side throughout the next few weeks of work.

The staff initials should be added in pencil (nothing is finally decided yet) into the rectangles on each sheet of the Master Curriculum Booklet, next to the appropriate subject. See the diagram on the opening page of this chapter.

It helps to ring the initials of part-timers in red. The days and times of availability of part-timers can be collected on to one blank page of the booklet for easy reference.
Requests for particular times for swimming, live web-links with foreign schools, etc., should be marked against the relevant classes.

Later when you enter your data into your timetabling software, it is essential to check that your entries match the spreadsheet of section 6.4.

For example in *TimeTabler*:

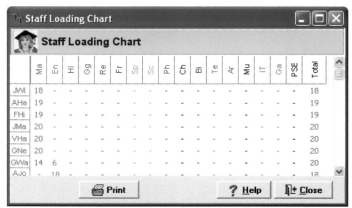

6.7 An alternative Staff Loading Chart

An alternative Staff Loading Chart is shown below.
It shows for all members of staff their teaching load, the classes they are due to teach, the Form-Tutors of each class and in the case of a split-site school, the weighting of staff by periods between the buildings.

	Name	Total	LS – US	base	7A	7B	7C	7D	8A	8B	8C	8D	9A
M A T H S	Alcock	30	6 – 24	U			Ma_6						
	Bull	32	26 – 6	L	Ma_6				Ma_6		Ma_6		
	Carr	32	20 – 12	L	En_6							Ma_6	
	Driver	12	12 – 0	(L)				Ma_4					
	XMa	26	20 – 6	U	Ma_6			Ma_2		Ma_6			

The first columns, at the left, show the name of the department and the member of staff, followed by his or her total teaching load.

The next two columns are relevant only to a split-site school. The first of these two columns shows the split (in periods) between the Lower School site and the Upper School site. This will be important information at the scheduling stage when we are determining priorities. The next column simply shows in which building (Lower/Upper) the teacher will be based for registration and pastoral purposes.

The remaining columns of the chart show, for each class and for each teacher, the subject and the number of periods.
For example, in the Maths Department of the split-site school shown in the diagram above, Alcock is teaching for a total of 30 periods; 6 periods in the Lower School, 24 in Upper School, so he is based in Upper School. The 6 periods he is to teach in Lower School will be spent teaching Maths (Ma) to class 7C.

Bull is teaching 32 periods; based in Lower School; some of his Lower School classes are shown; in each case he is teaching Maths. The circle, added at a later date, shows that Bull is to be the Form-Tutor of 8C.

Carr is to teach 32 periods, split 20–12 between the buildings (this is a more difficult split and so he will have a higher priority at the scheduling stage than Alcock and Bull). Carr is based in Lower School and is evidently a member of the Maths Department but also teaches English for 6 periods to 7A.

Driver is a part-timer (the name is ringed) teaching only 12 periods.

XMa (X-Maths) is an unknown person, yet to be appointed, probably a probationer with only 26 teaching periods. Unfortunately (or deliberately?) Driver and XMa are splitting the teaching of a class (7D) between them.

The chart should balance arithmetically both horizontally and vertically. Horizontally, for each teacher, the totals of the classes should agree with the 'total' column; vertically, for each class, the totals of the subjects for a class should agree with the total number of periods in the timetable cycle.

One of the valuable features of this layout is that it shows the intended distribution of each teacher throughout the classes of the school. The Head may wish to make changes here.

The Chart is useful when deciding Form-Tutors, if you wish to ensure that each Form-Tutor also teaches his form. (The final result of choosing Form-Tutors must be one ring in each class column).

In a split-site school the Chart is useful when deciding on an order of priorities for the scheduling of staff that commute between buildings.

6.8 Summary

In most schools it is the Subject Leader or Head of Department who specifies who will teach each group. Collecting and then checking this data is an essential step.

The Timetabler now has a Curriculum Diagram, with a Teacher attached to each group, something like this:

	En	Ma	Sc	Fr	Hi	Gg	Ar	Mu	Re	Se	Te	Pe
9A	En AJo	Ma JHa	Sc KJo	Fr LMu	Hi JCl	Gg IKe	Ar EBi	Mu DWi	Re PUn	Se JCl	Te IHa / Te AFr	Pe ASe
9B	En BJa	Ma FHi	Sc BPa	Fr EBr	Hi JCl	Gg IKe	Ar EBi	Mu BAl	Re PUn	Se EBr	Te JHi	Pe SOr
9C	En DSi	Ma VHa	Sc JSi	Fr EBr	Hi RRe	Gg IKe	Ar TTi	Mu BAl	Re AFr	Se TTi	Te IHa / Te JHi	Pe ASe
9D	En JRo	Ma JVi	Sc KJo	Fr GSi	Hi JCl	Gg IKe	Ar TTi	Mu DWi	Re AFr	Se IKe	Te AFr	Pe SOr
periods:	4	4	4	4	2	2	2	1	1	2	2	2	=30
	SSSS	SSSS	DSS	SSSS	SS	SS	D	S	S	SS	D	D

Having obtained the data and checked the arithmetic, the timetabler naturally feels an urge to move immediately to the scheduling stage. This is a mistake. Almost certainly there are mathematical impossibilities in the data.

There are some simple tests that have been devised to identify some of these impossibilities so that they can be removed by modifying the data before the difficult task of scheduling begins.

These tests are explained in the next four chapters.

7 Timetable test 1
The Combing Chart

The **First Law** of Timetabling states that: *the sets of data received on the Data Collection Forms are almost certainly incompatible!*   Because of the wide range of options that we offer in our schools and because we usually allow departments some freedom in choosing the staff to teach the groups, the sets of data we receive almost certainly contain some mathematical impossibilities.

The **Second Law** states: *Any impossibilities in the data will force the Timetabler to make compromises during the actual scheduling stage of the timetable, and any compromises then are likely to damage the quality of the timetable!*

All scheduling is likely to involve some compromise, although obviously we wish the compromising to be as inconsequential as possible. Compromises made in a logical way at this present stage are likely to have less consequence and be more acceptable to the staff than compromises forced on the timetabler during the scheduling stage.

The compromises that have come to be accepted by the teaching staff vary somewhat from school to school. Timetablers naturally vary in the amount of patience and ingenuity they can maintain in order to obtain a better solution. Some of the compromises that may be forced during scheduling are listed in the box on the next page.

There is no known method of determining whether a given set of data can be timetabled without compromise (other than by completing a full timetable).

However, there are tests which will detect some of the **im**possibilities and pinpoint the **reasons** for them. This chapter covers the first of these tests.

Some of the **compromises** that may occur during scheduling:

1   Alteration to the requested period spread. This happens most frequently to English, Maths and Modern Languages.
    eg. French scheduled for 5 periods on 4 days instead of 1 period per day.

2   Alteration to the requested period breakdown.
    eg. Art or Science scheduled as single periods in Year 7 although doubles were requested.

3   Specialist subjects taught in ordinary classrooms.
    eg. all four periods of Science taught in a classroom.

4   The requested teacher replaced by an alternative in the same department.
    eg. a young new teacher replaces the Head of Department for a tough Year 10 class.

5   The requested teacher replaced by an alternative in the same department for some periods during the week.
    eg. class 9A has two teachers for Maths (called 'split teaching').

6   The requested teacher replaced by a member of another department.
    eg. some time ago, a Deputy was heard to say (at the scheduling stage):
    'Those two Technology teachers will have to teach Maths.'

7   Setting scheduled for only some of the periods.
    eg. Year 9 Maths setted for only 3 out of the 4 periods.

8   Multiple periods spanning a break or a lunchtime.
    eg. a double period of Science across a break.

9   Alteration to the expected number of periods.
    eg. Yr 12 Chemistry allocated only 4 periods instead of the usual 5 periods.

10 Inability to allocate any teacher.
    eg. a Deputy was heard to say (at the scheduling stage):
    'This Year 10 subject will have to be cancelled.'

In considering the feasibility tests in this chapter (and the next three chapters) it is important to remember that it is **teachers** that clash, **not subjects**.
ie. conflicts are not introduced directly by the curriculum on which we have decided, but only indirectly by way of the staff who are chosen to teach the groups.

For some groups the Subject Leader's choice of a teacher will be made for sound educational reasons; for other groups the choice may be arbitrary.
Once the feasibility tests have pinpointed an area of difficulty, one can look for simple and acceptable modifications to the data on the Data Collection Forms.

These modifications may be crucial but simple. Perhaps, by happenstance, a certain teacher is due to teach 7A, according to the Data Collection Form.
For timetabling, the feasibility tests show that it would be far better if he taught 7B instead. The Head of Department does not mind, the teacher does not mind, but for the timetabler the difference could be crucial.

7.2   Teacher teams

Teams of teachers are obviously more difficult to schedule than single teachers. The number and size of the teacher teams in our schools tend to increase as Subject Leaders request them for a variety of reasons:

- to allow team teaching or 'setting' (by attainment or ability level), eg. in Mathematics, English, Languages,
- to allow a choice of subjects, eg. in the option pools,
- to allow separation by sex, eg. for PE,
- to reduce class size, eg. if two classes are scheduled together and allocated three teachers,
- to allow a cycle of rotation during the year, eg. in Technology.

The way in which these teams are chosen can have a huge effect on the scheduling difficulty and final quality of the timetable.

In choosing the teams for these activities, we want the teams to be compatible so they can be timetabled within the number of periods in the timetable cycle.

Worked Example 1

Consider a small department consisting of three teachers, AA, BB, and CC. Each is due to teach for 20 periods, in a 25-period week.
On the Data Collection Form, the Subject Leader requests that:

> teachers AA and BB teach together for 10 periods
> and teachers BB and CC teach together for 10 periods
> and teachers AA and CC teach together for 10 periods

Question: is this possible?

To see if this is a reasonable request, we can draw a **time-chart** (see below). The vertical axis (see below) shows the three teachers.
The horizontal axis shows a length of time in periods.
By drawing a horizontal bar for each teacher in a teacher-team, we can see the total number of periods needed for this small department:

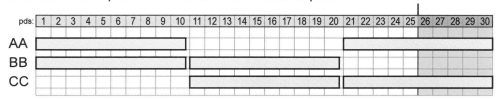

We can see that this arrangement requires 30 periods (even though each teacher teaches only 20 periods). It could not possibly fit into the 25-period week, just because the staff are in teams.

The red area shows the periods needed beyond the 25-period week – the staff would have to teach at the weekend!
The chosen teams were not compatible with the available timeframe.

Worked Example 2

A small Mathematics department consists of 6 teachers, numbered 1 to 6. Each teacher is to teach for 20 periods. They are in an 11–16 school (Years 7–11) where each of the five year-groups is divided into 2 half-year 'bands' (called A and B). Each band requires a team of 3 teachers, for 4 periods.

The Head of Maths might request the teams shown here:

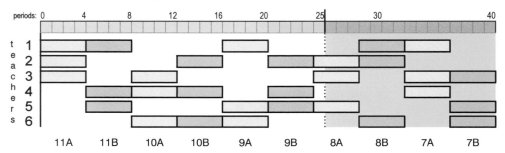

The chart shows that the team for Year 11 band A is made of teachers 1, 2, 3. For band 11B, the teachers are 1, 4, 5. These two teams cannot teach at the same time because they have teacher 1 in common (and teacher 1 cannot teach two classes at the same time).

For 10A the teachers are 3, 4, 6. This team cannot teach at the same time as the 11A team (because of teacher 3), nor can this team teach at the same time as the 11B team (because of teacher 4). The three teams considered so far would need 3 x 4 = 12 periods of the week.

Inspecting the other teams one by one shows that *none* of them can teach at the same time as any other team. Each team overlaps every other team.

Each teacher teaches five classes, each of 4 periods, and so teaches 20 periods per week. However, since no team can exist at the same time as any other team, the total length of time needed for the teams to teach all 10 bands is 10 x 4 = 40 periods. In a 25-period week this is clearly impossible.

That example was an extreme case where all the teams clash.

Now consider an ideal situation, unlikely to be obtained in practice but something to aim for. The diagram below shows the *same* Maths department with the *same* 6 teachers teaching the *same* number of groups:

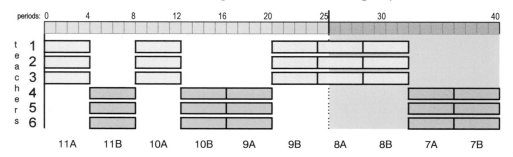

In the diagram the team for 11A does not overlap the team for 11B. The teams are said to be non-overlapping or **disjoint** or compatible. This means that 11A and 11B can be timetabled at the same time. Similarly with 10A, 10B etc.

Comparing the two diagrams above for this Maths department, we can see the difference between them: the second diagram can be squeezed up by sliding the 4, 5, 6 teams to the left, under the 1, 2, 3 teams.

The whole diagram will then fit into a time of only 20 periods, as shown below:

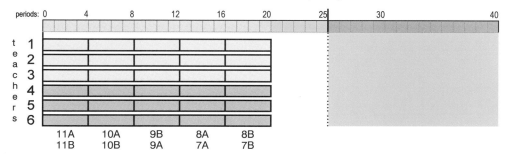

It is clear that these non-overlapping ('disjoint'), compatible teams give much greater flexibility at the scheduling stage.

In fact there are two advantages with non-overlapping teams:
- Non-overlapping teams will fit into a smaller number of periods (overlapping teams may not fit into the school week).
- There is a greater number of different ways of fitting non-overlapping teams. In the last diagram, the labels show 11A paired with 11B, but 11A could well be paired with 10B while 11B could be paired with 8A etc. This interchangeability gives you much greater flexibility at the scheduling stage.

These diagrams are called '**Combing Charts**'. The horizontal bars for the teams can be thought of as the teeth of combs which allow or prevent other teams moving or 'combing' to the left.

7.3 The Principle of Compatibility

In the light of the previous section let us see how a department might choose **ideal** teacher teams. Consider a large department – English, Maths or perhaps Science – consisting of 12 teachers, numbered 1–12.

Suppose that for one of the year-groups we need a team of 6 teachers.
Clearly there are many ways of choosing 6 teachers, but suppose we choose the teachers numbered from 1 to 6. This team is marked as 6-team-**A** in the diagram on the next page.

Suppose now that we need a team of 6 teachers for another year-group.
There are only two possibilities if we want non-overlapping teams – either we choose the team of the *same* 6 teachers (6-team-A) **or** we choose the team of the *other* 6 teachers (6-team-**B**).

The teams are subsets of the department. Because team A and team B are non-overlapping teams they are called **disjoint subsets**.

In choosing other teams in this department, we should follow the same principle.

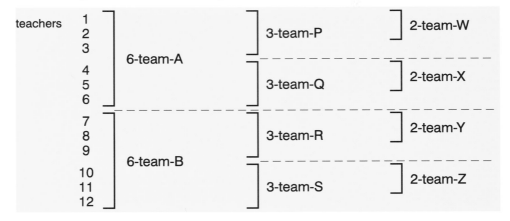

Suppose, for other parts of the school, we need teams of 3 teachers. Ideally each 3-team should be chosen from **within** one of the 6-teams. For example, in the diagram, 3-team-P (teachers 1, 2, 3) is entirely within 6-team-A. This means that 3-team-P can teach at the same time as 6-team-B, if we wish to schedule them that way. Choosing a 3-team such as teachers 1, 2, 7 would be less satisfactory because it would clash with *both* team A *and* team B.

Once 3-team-P is chosen to be teachers 1, 2, 3 (as in the diagram), the only other disjoint subset of team A is 3-team-Q (teachers 4, 5, 6). Similarly teams R and S are disjoint subsets of team B.

When it comes to choosing 2-teams, these should be chosen from **within** the 3-teams, as shown. At each level, each team should be chosen from **within** a larger team. In the diagram the horizontal dashed lines show the boundaries which should not be crossed.

This principle is called the **Principle of Compatibility**. It can be applied to sets of resources other than teachers, as we shall see in later sections of this chapter. The principle states that, *to fit sets of resources into the minimum number of periods, with the maximum flexibility, disjoint subsets should be chosen.*

In applying the principle to the staffing of your school, two points to note:

1. The rigid application of the principle is an ideal: there are likely to be sound educational reasons preventing your teacher teams from being entirely non-overlapping. However, it is important for Subject Leaders to realise that each departure from the principle implies a loss of flexibility, with a consequent possibility of compromises in the final timetable.
   If such compromising forces a change of teacher, then the change will always be towards a greater obedience to the principle.
2. In applying the principle, it is the choice of the largest team that is the most critical. In the example, the initial choice of 6-team-A limited the possibilities for all the other teams.

7.4   Choosing teacher teams — worked example

Imagine you are the Head of the English Department at the Laura Norder High School. The department is composed of 10 teachers, numbered 1–10.
The timetabling of your department has been difficult and unsatisfactory in recent years and you resolve to improve the situation.

(a)   Teachers 1, 3, 5, 7, 9 are due to continue with their classes into the new Year 11 (as a team of 5). You need to choose a team of 5 for the new Year 10. What are the alternatives? Which is the better alternative?

(b)   You remember that you have promised teachers 9 and 10 that they can teach the new Year 10. What do you do? What reason do you give?

(c)   For Year 9, you need to choose a team of 4.
Teachers 1 and 2 also teach History and they have full timetables.
Teacher 3 is the Year Leader for Year 9.
Which team of 4 would you choose?

(d)   A colleague proposes to the School's Curriculum Study Group that English in Year 8 is taught by a team of 6 teachers. What is your response?

If we assume that we need consider only the educational factors that have been mentioned in the questions, then we suggest the solutions should be:

(a)   Since Year 11 has a 5-team of all the odd-numbered teachers, then the choice is either all the odd teachers or all the even teachers.
If the odd team is chosen again, then the even team will not teach any of the Upper School classes. In some schools this may be preferred. However, if all members of the department are to be given the chance of teaching students in Years 10-11, then the even team must be chosen.

(b)   If you decide on the even team then teacher 9 (odd) must be told of your decision, with reasons. Ideally all members of the department should be made aware of the Principle of Compatibility and the ways in which it affects the timetable. As Head of Department you might also resolve not to make any promises in future until your position is clear!

(c)   Since teacher 3 (odd) is the Year 9 Tutor, the 4-team should be chosen from within the odd 5-team (so that it will be disjoint with the even 5-team). As teacher 1 is involved elsewhere, the 4-team should be teachers 3, 5, 7, 9.

(d)   A team of 6 could be chosen for Year 8 but it could not be disjoint with the 5-teams for Years 10 and 11. If despite this a 6-team was chosen, then the best choice would be the 6 members of the department who were not in the 4-team for Year 9. Then at least Year 9 and Year 8 could be scheduled at the same time. However, for greater flexibility the Year 8 team should be a disjoint subset of the other teams. It might be worthwhile suggesting to the School's Curriculum Study Group that there would be benefits to your department and to the whole school if Year 8 was scheduled as two half-year groups, each requiring disjoint 3-teams.

If, in practice, not all the teams are disjoint subsets then we need a feasibility test to apply to the department. For this we use a Combing Chart.

7.5 Drawing a Combing Chart

If, in practice, not all the teams are disjoint subsets then we need a feasibility test to apply to the department. For this we use a Combing Chart, as shown in the next section.

Here are 4 Rules for drawing a Combing Chart:

Rule 1
Start with the biggest team (strictly speaking, start with the team which has the most conflicts with the other teams, but this usually approximates to the biggest team).

Rule 2
When adding another team to the chart, if that team is for the *same* population of students as an existing team, then obviously it must fit to the side, taking up more of the available periods.

Rule 3
When adding another team to the chart, if that team is for a *different* population of students from an existing team then ideally it should fit into the same periods, with no clashes. ie. it should be a disjoint team, if possible. If it is not disjoint (ie. with clashes) then again it must fit to the side.

Rule 4
If the maximum teaching load of any individual teacher on the chart is *n* periods, then ideally the chart should 'comb' down into *n* periods. This is the green area on the charts shown in this chapter.

If the teams take up more periods than there are periods in the timetable cycle then they will be impossible to schedule. This is the red area on the charts in this chapter.

The area between green and red is shown in orange on these charts.
The more of the orange area that is used, the more difficult it will be to schedule, and the more likely that you will have to make compromises.

7.6 The Combing Chart — worked example

In practice we do not get ideal teacher teams. Even where Heads of Departments understand the principle of compatibility, there will usually be some reason why the teams are not perfectly disjoint.

We need a feasibility test to apply to a department to see if the teacher teams will fit into the school week. This test ('timetable check number 1') consists of drawing a Combing Chart like the diagrams in section 7.2.

For example, consider a Mathematics department of 6 teachers staffed as shown on the next page (for a 30-period cycle):

We usually begin with the biggest teacher team. In this example all the teams are equal in size so we begin with the 'least-alterable' – Year 11.

For 11A we draw horizontal lines, each 5 periods long, opposite each of the teachers involved (see below).

At this point we are not considering the period breakdown; that is, we are not considering whether the 5 periods will be taught as 5 singles or 2 Doubles and a single, etc. There is little point in looking at the finer detail until the main structure appears feasible.

Year and Band (5 periods each)	Teachers
11A	1, 3, 4
11B	3, 5, 6
10A	1, 2, 3
10B	4, 5, 6
9A	1, 2, 3
9B	2, 4, 5
8A	1, 5, 6
8B	1, 2, 6
7A	4, 5, 6
7B	2, 3, 4

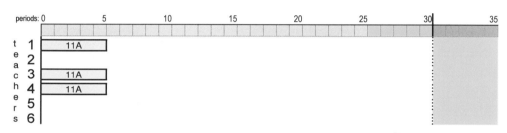

The next team to be added, 11B, has teacher 3 in common with the team for 11A and so it must go into a new block of time.
Similarly, 10A has teachers 1, 3 in common with 11A and teacher 3 in common with 11B, so that 10A team must use a further block of time.
Similarly the 10B team clashes with the teams for 11A and 11B; however it does not clash with the 10A team and so it can fit into the same block of time as 10A.

If you care to continue this process yourself with the other teams, you should get a final picture as shown below.

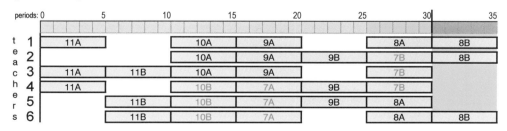

The columns, each 5 periods wide, could have occurred in a different order if you had considered the teams in a different order but the chart would be essentially the same. Clearly the object is to 'comb' the teams to the left as much as possible, into a shorter period of time.

In this example 35 periods are needed — a mathematical impossibility in this 30 period week. The Subject Leader can see **why** his teams must be changed (without feeling suspicious about a timetabler saying 'It can't be done'). Further, the Subject Leader can see which teachers to interchange to improve the situation.

The Subject Leader may wish to adjust *one* team in order to bring the total time-span down to 30 periods. For the timetabler this will not be enough. True, it allows a solution for *this* department, but this department has to dovetail into other departments. Leaving this department with a period-spread of 30 periods will not allow a total solution unless this department is given the highest priority in scheduling (and then other departments will suffer compromises as a result).

In practice the golden rule is: *if the maximum teaching load of a member of the department is* **n** *periods, then the Combing Chart for that department should aim to fit into* **n** *periods.*

In our example, the maximum teaching load for anyone is 25 periods, so the chart should comb down to 25 periods. This could be achieved by interchanging teacher 4 in the 9B team with teacher 6 in the 8B team. Then the 9B team will fit against the 11A team and the 8B team will fit against the 11B team, the whole fitting into 25 periods.

Even this is not ideal as it gives an almost unique pairing of classes – the only alternatives to the pairings shown would be 10A-with-7A and 9A-with-10B. We want the chart not only to comb as much as possible to the left, but also to comb to the left *with as many permutations as possible*.

Unless there are strong educational reasons against it, interchanging teachers 1 and 4 between the teams for 8A and 7B would improve the situation by making these teams compatible with the teams for 10A, 10B, 9A, 7A.

Note: When making changes on the Combing Chart, it is useful to remember that if there is an unavoidable conflict between two teams, it is worthwhile positively compounding the conflict: two clashes are no worse than one. When taken to the limit this approach leads naturally to non-overlapping teams.

The Combing Chart is the first main timetabling check.

The Training Pack
It is valuable for all members of staff to have some knowledge of the principle: it can form the basis of a useful in-service training meeting, particularly for Subject Leaders.

On the CD is an INSET/CPD **Training Pack** that you can use to teach your Subject Leaders about the Principle of Compatibility and the Combing Chart.

The Pack consists of two Tutor-Briefing Sheets (for you); two Fact-Sheets for you to explain to them; and two Activity-Sheets for them to work through. Typically it takes about 50 minutes in a meeting of Subject Leaders.

Thereafter, your Subject Leaders should be expected to check their data before submitting the Data Collection Form to you.

Using a computer

Often it is easier to use a computer to draw a Combing Chart, particularly if it is a Combing Chart for more than one department, see section 7.7.

For example, here is the Combing Chart Screen in *TimeTabler*:

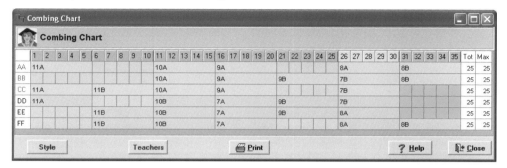

It shows the same situation as in the previous diagram, and the green/amber/red traffic-light system has the same meaning as explained in section 7.5.

7.7   The Combing Chart for more than one department

Staff who are able to teach more than one subject are valuable when you are trying to cover the curriculum and balance teaching loads (as explained in sections 6.2—6.4).

However when it comes to scheduling they can cause difficulies because they link two or more subjects together, making the Combing Chart more difficult.

Consider a case where a teacher 'HG' offers both History and Geography.

Conflicts are less likely to occur in scheduling if the following rules are observed:

a)   Teacher HG should not be a member of a team in either the History department or the Geography department – that is, he should teach pure class activities only.

b)   If teacher HG must be a member of a team, try to limit this to only one team in each department.

c)   Whether teacher HG teaches in a team or not, try to arrange for him to teach the **same** class for **both** subjects. This does not eliminate the teacher conflict, but it does link it to a conflict which already exists (the conflict between a class and itself) and so it reduces the total number of conflicts.

For example, if HG teaches 9A for History and 9B for Geography, then 9A History cannot occur simultaneously with 9B Geography. However, if HG teaches 9A for *both* History *and* Geography then, because of HG, 9A History cannot occur simultaneously with 9A Geography – but it never could do that because 9A cannot have two subjects simultaneously.

In cases where a teacher is shared by two departments, a Combing Chart drawn by each Head of Department will not show the full picture. To see that, the timetabler should draw a Combing Chart *for both departments combined*. In this case it is definitely much quicker to use computer software (see the previous page).

Interchangeable teachers

The timetabler may also wish to draw a large Combing Chart to investigate the mixed teams in the option pools. This is particularly useful when there are interchangeable teachers.

For example, in Year 10 band A there may be two French groups, one in pool 2 and one in pool 4. The Head of Department has requested teachers AB and CD for these groups but does not care which teacher takes which group. For you, the timetabler, one arrangement might be very much better than the other. A Combing Chart of the teacher teams in the option blocks will help you to decide which is the better arrangement for scheduling.

Consider an example. The Year 11 and Year 10 teacher teams shown below are to be timetabled across a full year-group in each case.

		teachers	
Year-11 team-1 (4 periods)	1, 4, 8, 10	
Year-11 team-2 (4 periods)	2, 5, 9, 11	12 periods
Year-11 team-3 (4 periods)	3, 6, 7, 12	
Year-10 team-1 (4 periods)	2, 5, 7, 10	
Year-10 team-2 (4 periods)	2, 3, 7 with 8 *or* 9	12 periods
Year-10 team-3 (4 periods)	1, 4, 6 with 9 *or* 8	

These teams could be the teams for option pools or the teams for Maths or English sets. In Year-10 team-2 and team-3 there are alternatives: the Head of Department has specified that teacher 8 should teach one group and teacher 9 the other group, but it does not matter which. We can draw a Combing Chart to find the better arrangement.

Usually it is best to begin with the largest teacher team. Here they are equal in size so we begin with the Year 11 teams.

A word of warning here: the Year 11 teams do not have any teachers in common and so it might be thought that they could be combed to the left of the chart and all fitted into the same 4-period block. This is **not** possible. The Year 11 teams are all due to teach the **same** students and cannot do so simultaneously! (See the diagram on the next page.)

The Year 11 teams will fit into 12 periods. The Year 10 teams would also fit into 12 periods. Ideally all the teams should fit into the same 12 periods. This would be the best case. The worst case would be if the teams were entirely incompatible, in which case 24 periods would be needed for these teams.

To find the number of periods actually needed, we can continue by trying to fit in Year-10 team-1. This clashes with each of the Year 11 teams and so cannot be combed to the left but needs an extra 4-period space as shown here:

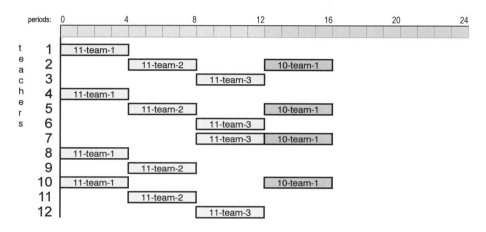

Now consider Year-10 team-2 and team-3.
Let us begin by looking at the *first* alternatives for the teachers (i.e. teacher 8 in team-2 and teachers 9 in team-3). In this case both teams clash with everything fitted so far. 24 periods would be needed to fit the teams and the solution space is considerably reduced.

Now consider the *other* alternative (ie. teacher 9 in team-2 and teacher 8 in team-3).
In this case Year-10 team-2 will fit against Year-11 team-1 and Year-10 team-3 will fit against Year-11 team-2 (it is left to the reader to draw in the bars on the diagram).

This time a total of 16 periods is needed. Although this is less than the first alternative, it is still not a very good solution. The diagram shows a unique fit; there is no flexibility; none of the teams can pair up in any way other than those shown. Ideally the teams ought to be able to pair up in many different ways (as discussed in section 7.2).

Of course in this example we have looked only at some of the teacher teams. When all the other teams for Year-11 and Year-10 are fitted, it may be that the same combinations of teachers may appear, so allowing alternative pairings of teams. The more the principle of compatibility is followed, the more these alternative pairings will occur, giving more flexibility in scheduling.

The effect of the period-breakdown

In looking at these Combing Charts we have so far ignored the effect of different period-breakdown – that is, we have assumed that each group is taught in one large block of time (4 periods for each group in the current example).

In practice this is not the case. If all the groups are taught in single periods or *all* the groups are taught in double periods then there is no problem.

In practice some of the groups may be taught in single periods, some in double periods and perhaps some in triple or quadruple periods. This means that even if your Combing Chart fits into the length of the timetable cycle, it still may not be possible to schedule it into the timetable cycle.

Consider the effect of varying period-breakdown in the current example. Suppose Year-11 team-1 is Technology, to be taught in one quadruple period while Year-10 team-2 is Science, to be taught in two double periods. Now all the periods for Year-10 team-2 will *not* fit against Year-11 team-1. Only one double will fit against Year-11 team-1 and the other double must go at the end, now making a total of 18 periods, see below:

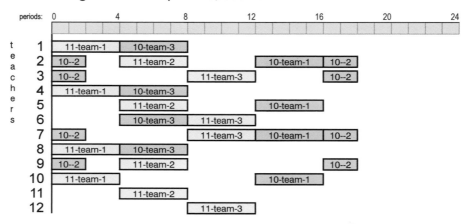

And if the lessons for some of the teams had to be in single periods, this would further increase the time-span needed.

In general there is little point in looking at the finer detail of period-breakdown until the main structure appears feasible.

Some timetablers like to draw a Combing Chart showing all the teacher-teams in the school (ignoring period-breakdown, at least initially). Although this can be done manually (!), it is far easier to use computer software (see section 7.6).

(An alternative way of investigating the teacher-teams for the option pools is given in chapter 8, the Conflict Matrix).

When looking at the whole school, as well as using a Combing Chart (plotting teachers against time), you can also use a similar diagram but plotting classes against time. This of course is the Schematic Diagram of chapter 4.

7.8 The Principle of Compatibility and Time

Your timetable cycle is divided into subsets of periods by days, breaks and lunches. These subsets are clearly disjoint and non-overlapping. The ways in which departments specify the period-breakdowns for their subjects must be compatible with the way in which the timetable cycle is divided.

For example, in a school operating a 35-period week with a 2–2–3 day, a Technology department might request 3 triple periods and 13 double periods for a particular room. This might appear to be possible (if difficult) because $(3 \times 3) + (13 \times 2) = 35$ periods. However a diagram shows it is impossible:

periods:	1	2	3	4	5	6	7
Mon	D1		D2		T1		
Tues	D3		D4		T2		
Wed	D5		D6		T3		
Thurs	D7		D8		D9		
Fri	D10		D11		D12		

D13 is incompatible within the time-frame

In a similar way, a Head of Department might request 5 double periods for a part-timer who is available only for four afternoons per week.

If we consider now a 40-period week, similar considerations show that a 3–2–3 day is not a good one for scheduling unless there is a large number of triple periods (or a lot of singles to go with doubles). For a timetable requiring many double periods, it is poor. A Head of Department may specify a particular science laboratory or technology room for 16 double periods in a 5-day week: with either a 2–2–3 day or a 3–2–3 day that is impossible.

If a teacher or a room is to be used only for double periods, each can be used for a maximum of 30 periods per week in a 2–2–3 or 3–2–3 arrangement.

For schools with a 40-period cycle, a 2–2–4 day or a 2–2–2–2 day is easiest to schedule, but this consideration may be over-ridden by other factors (e.g. the public transport services or other factors demanding a short afternoon).

Similarly in a 25-period cycle, a Subject Leader may specify 12 Double-periods (=24 periods) and expect this to be achieved — but in fact a 2–2–1 day allows only 10 doubles in a week. 12 doubles are not possible.
Similar considerations apply to a 50-period fortnight.

A 30-period or 60-period cycle with a 2-2-2 day does not have these problems.

The fitting of a department's requests into the time periods of a school week could be checked when the Combing Chart is drawn (section 7.6). Instead

---

of leaving the horizontal axis as simply 0–25 periods, it could be divided by vertical lines into 2–2–1 or 2–1–2 days etc. Then the horizontal bars should be drawn in such a way that they do not cross any of these vertical lines.
As mentioned earlier, it is best if Heads of Departments do this — then they will appreciate the necessity for change it their specification will not fit.
A pro-forma ruled sheet (sometimes called a Visual Planner) can be provided to the Heads of Departments with the Data Collection Form.

There is a further consideration regarding time: this is concerned with the time span of each option block and the compulsory core subjects. There will be a more compatible arrangement, easier to schedule, if all the option blocks and the blocks of compulsory core subjects are equal in time or are simple multiples or sub-multiples of each other. They will fit together more easily.

Some schools have staggered lunch breaks (see section 11.18), or early starts and late finishes on some days for some year-groups.
These tactics can give greater flexibility to the timetable and allow more efficient use of the limited resources of a school.
A 'non-rectangular' week allows greater utilisation of your resources:

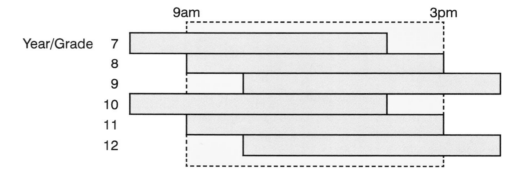

7.9   The Principle of Compatibility and Class-combinations

Whenever classes are combined together for setting, team-teaching, options etc., the principle of compatibility can be applied to the ways in which they are combined. The class-combinations should be disjoint, non-overlapping.

For example, consider the proposal in this diagram for the grouping of English and Mathematics in Year 10:

classes		English		Maths	
10A	En		Ma		
10B	En			Ma	
10C		En		Ma	
10D		En	Ma		

This will be difficult to schedule because the class-combinations for English and Maths are overlapping: each of the Maths combinations clashes with **both** of the English combinations. Clearly a consistent combination of classes would be easier to timetable.

As a more common example, consider this curriculum diagram:

9A	En	Ma	Fr		Pe
9B	En	Ma	Fr	etc	Pe
9C	En	Ma	Fr		Pe
9D	En	Ma	Fr		Pe
9E	En	Ma	Fr		Pe
9F	En	Ma	Fr		Pe

If the classes are grouped as triplets for most of the week, changing to pairs for PE can lead to difficulties.

This is a common feature in schools (either because of limited PE facilities or because of the need to have a Boys group and a Girls group), but is likely to cause you scheduling difficulties. As you can see, PE for 9CD clashes with both half-year-groups!

For compatibility the class-combinations for PE should be a subset **within** the other class-combinations.

See also the examples described in sections 2.15 and 2.16.

In some cases, class-combinations within year-groups may be non-overlapping but still cause clashes with other year-groups because of the way they are staffed.

For example, for English the classes might be staffed as shown here:

teachers		11ABC	11DEF	10AB	10CD	10EF
	1	En		En		
	2	En		En		
	3	En			En	
	4		En		En	
	5		En			En
	6		En			En

In this case the class-combinations within Year 11 are non-overlapping, as required by the Principle of Compatibility. The Year 10 class-combination are also disjoint within Year 10. However, because of the way they are staffed, 10CD clashes with *both* the Year 11 teams.

7.10   The Principle of Compatibility and Room-combinations

We have seen that the Principle of Compatibility has implications for the grouping of teachers, units of time and classes. It also has implications for the grouping of rooms.

If a school were to teach classes entirely in specialist rooms then the principle would apply as severely to room-combinations as it does to teacher-combinations and class-combinations. Ideally the possible room-combinations should be disjoint. It helps the timetabler if there is a suite of Maths rooms and the number of rooms corresponds to the number of staff in the teacher teams, but this is by no means essential. In practice, schools use alternative classrooms for many subjects.

Subjects such as Science, Technology, PE and Music will always be subject to rooming constraints, but the major constraint is usually one of total usage in the school week. This is discussed in chapter 9.

7.11   Summary

The Principle of Compatibility applies to teacher-teams, period-combinations in the school day, class-combinations and room-combinations. Strict adherence to the principle is usually impossible in practice but the greater the departure from the principle, the greater the loss in flexibility with a consequent loss in quality in the timetable.

The first of the timetable feasibility tests is the Combing Chart (section 7.5). Normally this test should be completed by each Head of Department so that each can see the implications of staffing decisions and can see why changes may be necessary.

It is possible for the timetabler to use the Combing Chart to check several interlocking departments and even the entire upper school option scheme. However such a chart can be very complicated and sometimes a better method is to use the second timetable feasibility test — the Conflict Matrix.

By cancelling Maths we could save... nearly got it...
...two... ...no, three hours... ...Hang on...!

8   Timetable test 2
The Conflict Matrix

In most schools the new Year 10 is different from the old Year 10 (because of the new option blocks reflecting the students' choices), but the old Year 10 still exists (as the new Year 11). Conflicts between these two years can be severe, partly because these are usually large teacher-teams, and partly because the option blocks usually contain *mixed* teams from several different subject areas.

For these reasons, Years 10 and 11 tend to dominate the timetable, and are given a high priority in scheduling. It is therefore particularly important to know whether the proposed staffing of these teacher-teams is feasible.

The Principle of Compatibility and the Combing Chart are invaluable aids in choosing and testing the teacher teams within a department. However the Combing Chart can become complicated when used to check teams from the several departments in the option blocks. Another method of investigating the teacher-teams is to draw up a Clash Table or **Conflict Matrix**.
(The grander title is usually used, to distinguish it from the Clash Table used earlier to investigate the students' choices, see chapter 3.)

A Conflict Matrix is also useful to help you draw a Schematic Diagram (see chapter 4), and it can be useful if you are using 'block timetabling' of columns as has been common in Scotland (see chapter 13).

Initially the Conflict Matrix considers only the staffing of the teacher-teams.
If this proves feasible then other factors – period-breakdown, rooms, even teaching equipment – can be included.

As well as identifying particular areas of conflict at an early stage, so saving time at the scheduling stage, the Conflict Matrix also helps the timetabler to decide which parts of the option scheme have the highest priority and should be scheduled first.

8.2 The Conflict Matrix — worked example

To simplify the example, consider a school in which the staffing for each of Years 10 and 11 consists of **only** five teacher-teams. Each of these teacher-teams teaches across the full year group. The teams are as follows:

			teachers
Year 11	Maths	Team 1	1, 2, 3, 4, 5
	English	Team 2	6, 7, 8, 9, 10
	Option A	Team 3	11, 12, 13, 14, 15
	Option B	Team 4	16, 17, 18, 19, 20
	Option C	Team 5	21, 22, 23, 24, 25
Year 10	Maths	Team 1	1, 3, 11, 15, 31
	English	Team 2	12, 24, 30, 32, 35
	Option A	Team 3	13, 14, 18, 20, 38
	Option B	Team 4	2, 14, 15, 20, 22
	Option C	Team 5	4, 11, 12, 13, 18

In this example some of the teams are Maths and English teams across the whole year; some of the teams are for option blocks across the year, but these labels are not important, because it is the **teachers** that cause conflicts.

The first question to be considered is: does this represent a feasible or an infeasible situation? To answer this we produce a Conflict Matrix by first drawing a grid of squares and then labelling each column with a Year 11 team and each row with a Year 10 team, as shown here:

Then consider each cell of the matrix in turn.

If that Year 10 team and that Year 11 team have a teacher in common, then that cell should be marked as a conflict to show that they cannot co-exist.

It can be marked with a cross to show the conflict. More usefully it can be marked with the names of the teachers who are causing the clash.

This has already been done for the first row of the matrix on the previous page; you may like to complete the other cells yourself before looking at the result shown below.

When all the clashes have been marked in, it is time to consider what the pattern means.

Year 11

		1	2	3	4	5
	1	1, 3		11, 15		
	2			12		24
Year 10	**3**			13, 14	18, 20	
	4	2		14, 15	20	22
	5	4		11, 12, 13	18	

For the school in this example, this pattern is bad news: if the Year 10 curriculum consists only of the teams shown, **none** of the Year 10 teams can fit against Year-11-team-3 (11-3). Something must be done about this impossibility.

In practice this would involve inspection of the teacher teams and discussion with Heads of Department to see which members of team 11-3 need not be members of the Year 10 teams.

In the absence of other information, it would seem simplest to do something about teacher 12. (Of all the clashes between 11-3 and the Year 10 teams, the clash with 10-2 involves only one teacher: teacher 12.)

There are two ways of removing the conflict caused by teacher 12:

1   **Deletion.** Allow teacher 12 to remain in team 11-3 but remove him from team 10-2. Or vice versa.

2   **Interchange.** Perhaps teacher 12 and teacher 38 are both due to teach Biology in the Year 10 option pools. If it does not matter who takes which group, then interchanging them removes the clash between 11-3 and 10-2. It adds a clash between 11-3 and 10-3 but three clashes are no worse than two. As with the Combing Chart, it is always worthwhile positively compounding conflicts to give flexibility elsewhere.

If we suppose that in one of these ways the conflict is removed between 11-3 and 10-2, then these two teams can be scheduled to occur simultaneously providing they have the same period-breakdown. See ① in the diagram below. The - - - dashed lines show how other cells are used up.

Looking further at the diagram, we can see that 11-2 seems to have a lot of flexibility because there are no clashes in that column. In fact, that flexibility is illusory: when we look at 10-4 we see that it has only one blank cell. So 10-4 must occur simultaneously with 11-2, providing that they have the same period-breakdown. See ②, which uses up all the empty column of 11-2.

This illustrates the steps used in the initial analysis of the matrix:

1. Ensure that each team has at least one empty cell.

2. If a team has only one empty cell then it must occur simultaneously with another team, providing the teams have the same period-breakdown. The empty cell lies at the 'crossroads' where the teams meet.

Continuing with the analysis of this matrix, we find that other teams now have only one empty cell. Now that 11-2 has been paired off, 10-5 has only one empty cell: it must be paired with 11-5. See ③.
Similarly 10-3 must then be paired with 11-1. See ④.
Finally, 10-1 can then only go with 11-4. See ⑤.
This is summarised in the diagram below with the coloured numbers and dashed lines showing how the cells are used up at each step:

Year 11

In this example this analysis leads to a *unique* solution — not a good situation as the effects of period-breakdown, part-time teachers, rooms and other resources have yet to be considered. In practice, at this stage you should expect to find *several* ways in which the teams could be paired.

The Conflict Matrix can include any team of teachers. If any English or Mathematics Teachers also teach in the option pools (eg. Drama, IT) then the teams for the English and Maths sets must be included.

8.3 Including the effect of period-breakdown – worked example

If a Conflict Matrix proves to be feasible when the teacher-teams have been considered, you may wish to see the effect of including the period-breakdown for each team. This is done by writing the period-breakdowns on the other two sides of the matrix, using a simple code: S for single periods, D for double periods, T for triple and Q for quadruple periods.

For example, consider the simplified Conflict Matrix shown here:

This matrix is a deliberately simplified diagram showing the effects of five teams in each year.
It assumes there are **only** the five teams in each year!

The names of the teachers in the teams have been omitted: the clashes that they cause are shown by the grey shading:

The period-breakdown is as shown: the Year 11 periods are shown underneath, the Year 10 periods to the right.

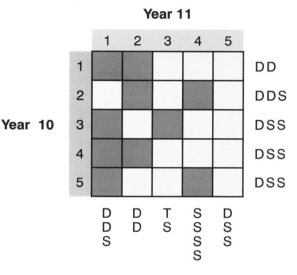

For example, Year 11 team-1 (which will be written in this section as 11-1) teaches for 5 periods, as 2 doubles and one single period (DDS).

To investigate the feasibility of this matrix, consider first the team with the least flexibility. This is the team 11-1 as it has only one empty cell. This means that 11-1 *must* be scheduled to occur simultaneously with 10-2.
Fortunately they have the same period-breakdown and so this is possible. That is, each D of 11-1 will fit against a D of 10-2 and the S of 11-1 will fit against the S of 10-2.
This can be shown in the matrix by marking 'DDS' in the empty cell and crossing out the DDS below 11-1 and the DDS to the right of 10-2.

It is useful to sketch a **Schematic Diagram** at the same time (see chapter 4). The Schematic Diagram will begin by showing 10-2 under 11-1 (for 5 periods, as DDS), as shown:

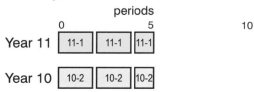

Chapter 8 - The Conflict Matrix

The next team to consider is **11-2**. It has just two empty cells, against 10-3 and 10-5, so it is the next tightest team. This team needs DD. There are 4 ways in which the DD of 11-2 can be paired with parts of 10-3 and 10-5.

The 4 ways are:

(a) One D of 11-2 with the D of 10-3; then the other D of 11-2 with the D of 10-5.

(b) One D of 11-2 with the D of 10-3; then the other D of 11-2 with one S from 10-3 and one S from 10-5.

(c) One D of 11-2 with the D of 10-5; then the other D of 11-2 with one S from 10-3 and one S from 10-5.

(d) One D of 11-2 with one S of 10-3 and one S of 10-5; then the other D of 11-2 with the other S of 10-3 and the other S from 10-5.

Since there is little to choose between them, let us choose (a) (it looks the simplest). Whenever you make an arbitrary decision like this, you should carefully record it and the alternatives, so that if you reach an impossible situation later (a cul-de-sac on the diagram) you can retrace your steps and take another alternative.

Choosing (a) we can mark a D in the empty cell shared by 11-2 and 10-3 and a second D in the empty cell shared by 11-2 and 10-5. We also cross out the DD below 11-2 and one D from the DSS of 10-3 and one D from the DSS of 10-5. The Schematic Diagram will show the same pairing of teams.

It is usually best to proceed by alternate vertical and horizontal movements. Having moved vertically down the 11-2 column, let us now move horizontally along the 10-5 row. 10-5 needs two more singles to complete it: one S with 11-3 and one S with 11-5.

The next step is to move up the 11-3 column. The triple of 11-3 can be matched with a double of 10-1 plus a single of 10-4. At this stage the matrix looks like this:

Year 11

		1	2	3	4	5	
	1			D			~~D~~D
	2	DDS					~~DDS~~
Year 10	3		D				~~D~~SS
	4			S			DS~~S~~
	5		D	S		S	~~DSS~~

1	2	3	4	5
~~D~~	~~D~~	~~T~~	S	D
~~D~~	~~D~~	~~S~~	S	S
~~S~~		S	S	~~S~~
			S	

It is left to the reader to complete the diagram — the next step would seem to be to move along the 10-1 row or the 10-4 row. (There is more than one way of completing the last two columns of the matrix.)

The Schematic Diagram below shows one of the possible solutions:

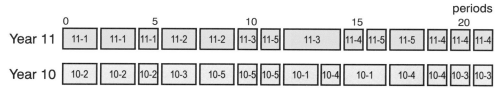

The fact that more than one Schematic Diagram can be obtained indicates that there will be some flexibility at the scheduling stage. In effect, the final timetable will consist of vertical slices of one of these Schematic Diagrams, rearranged to take into account the period-spread throughout the week, the effect of part-time staff, etc.

If any part of the Conflict Matrix gives only one possible pairing – like 11-1 and 10-2 in the example – then those two teams should be treated at the scheduling stage as a single item (see chapter 11).

For those who wish to follow this method in more detail, into 'Schematic Matrices', there are references in the bibliography.

8.4   Including the effect of other resources – rooms, equipment, part-time teachers, external courses

If, after including the teacher teams and the period-breakdowns (as in section 8.3), the Conflict Matrix still proves to be feasible, then you may wish to see the effect of including other resources.

For example, you may have two Drama teachers but only one Drama Studio, two teachers of Music but only one Music Room. These conflicts can be shown on the matrix in the same way that teacher clashes are shown.

Normally, however, they should not be treated as absolute conflicts — for example, the Music teachers could take turns in using the Music Room, while 'theory' lessons take place in another room.

Normally the effects of part-time teachers cannot be shown on the Conflict Matrix. However, if you have two part-timers in the options scheme (most unfortunate) and if the times that they are available do not overlap, then this is an absolute conflict that can be marked in the matrix.

If Year 10 and Year 11 both go out to a local college for courses or work experience then if (typically) the college will not accept both year-groups at the same time, then you should mark as a conflict the intersection of the relevant row/column, because they cannot co-exist.

8.5 Conflict Matrices for more than two year-groups

If your Year 10 or your Year 11 is divided into two or more bands then more than one Conflict Matrix will have to be drawn. If your school has a 'Sixth Form' (Years 12 and 13) then you will wish to see how the Sixth Form teams fit against the Year 10 and against the Year 11. Taking n groups two at a time, the number of Conflict Matrices required is $\frac{1}{2}n(n-1)$.

One way of drawing these matrices manually is shown here:

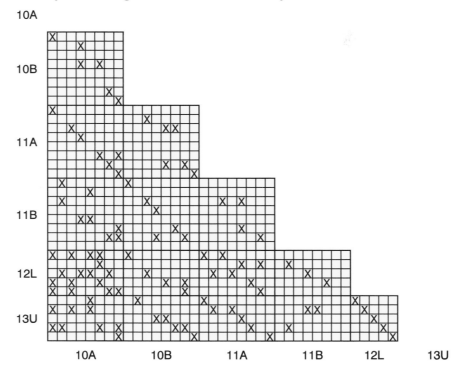

In this example the clashes are shown simply by crosses. This layout gives the conflicts for each pair of classes with the minimum amount of paperwork.

As well as the options teams, the English and Mathematics teams should be included. You might wish to include lower school teacher-teams also.

It is clear that such a diagram is much more difficult to analyse clearly – cruder analysis will have to suffice.

Two things can be seen clearly:

1. The total number of clashes, when compared with the same diagram for previous years, gives a crude measure of relative difficulty. It is useful to know from the beginning whether this year's timetable is likely to be 'slightly easier' or 'much more difficult' than last year's. The total number of clashes will naturally be greater if you have heterogeneous option blocks and if you change the blocks from year to year, as most schools do.

2. The pattern of the clashes gives the timetabler some idea of the priority that should be given to different areas when it comes to the scheduling stage. For example, in the diagram, the number of clashes in the 12L–10A block is greater than in any other block. This means that, to schedule the teams, a higher priority must be given to fitting the 10A teams against the 12L teams. Yet this is a *scheduling* priority and you may feel that a higher *educational* priority should be given to Year 11 and the 13U teams because their classes have already embarked on two-year courses. This may lead you to try to reduce the conflicts in the 12L–10A block at this stage, rather than allow them to distort the timetable at the scheduling stage.

Whether staff changes are made at this stage or not, if you are scheduling manually you will find it useful to have the Conflict Matrices to hand when you begin the scheduling stage.

Of course if you are using timetabler software it can take account of all this for you.

The large matrix above shows directly which two teams cannot fit together on the timetable, but it can also be used to see the clashes between three or more teams. For example, suppose you have scheduled 12L-team-3 and 13U-team-4 to occur simultaneously and the matrices show that:

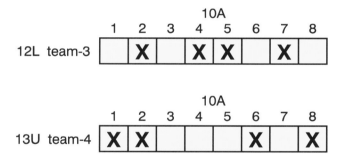

Then adding the matrices together, we get:

This shows that if 12L-team-3 and 13U-team-4 are scheduled together, then of the 10A teams, only team 3 can occur at the same time (and only if the period-breakdown is the same).

8.6　The Conflict Matrix — a worked example

Imagine you are the timetabler for Laura Norder High School, and the teacher-teams for Year 10 and Year 11 are as shown on the diagram:

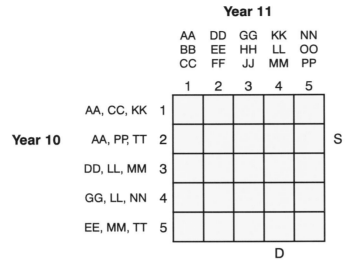

Year 11

	AA BB CC	DD EE FF	GG HH JJ	KK LL MM	NN OO PP
	1	2	3	4	5
AA, CC, KK　1					
Year 10　AA, PP, TT　2					S
DD, LL, MM　3					
GG, LL, NN　4					
EE, MM, TT　5					

D

Please complete the diagram.
Assume that the diagram shows all the teams in these two year-groups.

Q1. Which team will be hardest to timetable?

　　　If that team were scheduled to Monday period 1, which other team would have to be scheduled to Monday period 1?

Q2. Suppose now that Y11-team-4 requires a double period and Y10-team-2 must have single periods. What is the situation now?

Q3. Discussions between the Timetabler and the Head of Faculty now reveal that teacher LL in Y10-team-4 and teacher TT in Y10-team-5 can be interchanged with no disadvantage to the pupils. How does this improve the situation?
　　　Which team would you now timetable at the same time as Y11-team-4?

Q4. Now suppose also that teachers MM and TT both always need the Drama Studio (or some other unique resource, eg. music room, minibus).
　　　What is the situation now?
　　　Which teacher would you consider first of all, with a view to negotiating his/her removal or exchange ?

A1. Team 11-4, because there is only one gap. Team 10-2 has to be scheduled at the same time.

A2. It is impossible to schedule now, because now you cannot put 11-4 at the same time as 10-2.

A3. This now gives a gap at the intersection of 11-4 and 10-4, so these two teams can be scheduled at the same time (if their period-breakdown matches).

A4. This makes it impossible again, because there is now an extra clash, between 11-4 and 10-4.
　　　The cell at the intersection of 11-4 and 10-1 has only one teacher (KK) so this probably the first place to look for a solution, if KK can be removed from one of these two teams.

8.7   The Training Pack

You may wish your Subject Leaders to be familiar with the Conflict Matrix. Though it is not as useful to them as the Combing Chart (see section 7.6), it can still help them to understand why not everything they ask for is possible, and so help you in your negotiations with them.

On the CD is an INSET/CPD **Training Pack** that you can use to teach your Subject Leaders about the Conflict Matrix.

The Pack consists of two Tutor-Briefing Sheets (for you); a Fact-Sheet (2 pages) for you to explain to them; and an Activity-Sheet for them to work through. Typically it takes about 30 minutes in a meeting of Subject Leaders.

8.8   Using a computer

As with most other aspects of timetabling, a computer can do the donkey work for you, leaving you to weigh up the consequences and judge the best way forward.

For example, here is the Conflict Matrix Screen in **TimeTabler:**

Resting your mouse over any cell gives you more details.

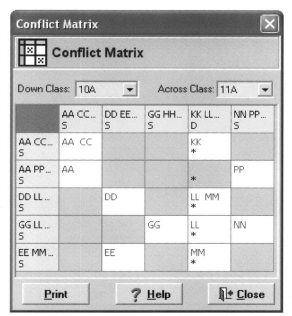

8.9   Summary

Although a Combing Chart (chapter 7) is useful for checking teams within a department, when many departments come together in the options scheme a Conflict Matrix is more useful.

A Conflict Matrix is particularly useful when the option blocks apply across a full year-group. The matrix allows the timetabler to check the feasibility of the staffing of the blocks. Period-breakdown, rooms and other resources can also be included.

A Conflict Matrix is a useful preliminary to drawing a Schematic Diagram (see also section 4.4).

9 Timetable test 3 Accommodation

In chapter 5 we saw how the curricular provision of a school depends on the number of teachers. The curricular provision also depends upon other resources; in particular it depends upon the accommodation that is available.

By definition, each group that is taught needs a teacher. In the same way each group also needs a learning-space (teaching-space) whether this is a classroom, laboratory, workshop, gymnasium, swimming pool, playing field or cross-country course. This learning-space could be in school, in a local college or a local business, or in another school in a consortium.
In this chapter the word 'room' is used whatever the type of learning-space.

Staff do not teach for every period in the week; on average they teach for a fraction c of the school week (see section 5.4).
In the same way, rooms are not occupied for every period in the week; on average they are used for a fraction r of the school week. This fraction r is called the **rooming fraction**.
Its value is crucial in determining success or failure at the scheduling stage.

I know you're not happy now, but you'll soon get used to teaching Science in the swimming pool...

9.2 The rooming fraction

The rooming fraction r can be defined by:

$$r = \frac{\text{average usage of rooms (in periods)}}{\text{number of periods in the timetable cycle}}$$

For example, if the average usage of the rooms in your school is 21 periods in a 25-period week, then $r = {}^{21}/_{25} = 0.84$. This is a typical value.

Remember that r refers to the *average* usage of accommodation — for every textiles room, library or drama studio that is used below this fraction of the week, other rooms will have to be used above it.

To calculate the value of r for your school, calculate the total number of periods provided in the curriculum and divide this by the total number of periods for which the rooms could be used if they were never empty. That is:

$$\text{rooming fraction } (r) = \frac{\text{number of periods taught in the curriculum}}{\text{number of learning-spaces } \times \text{ number of periods in the cycle}}$$

Remember to include all the 'rooms' that are used for teaching. For example, if the playing fields, on average, are occupied by two classes, then count the playing fields as two rooms. However, omit off-site lessons (eg. at college) (in the top line of the formula), and omit their off-site rooms (in the bottom line).

The value of r also gives the average fraction of rooms that are occupied at any time. For example, if $r = 0.85$, then (on average) 85% of the rooms are occupied at any time.

Clearly the value of r has implications for the timetable. If the value of r rises too high then the timetabler will have to make some compromises at the scheduling stage. As r increases, more and more specialist subjects have to be taught in non-specialist rooms (or vice-versa).

Observation and analysis by a group of HM Inspectors led them to suggest that r could rise to 0.85 without compromising educational objectives. However, as r rises above 0.85 there are likely to be increasingly severe restrictions on the curriculum and the timetable.

As r rises above 0.85 there will be restrictions on your curriculum (as distinct from restrictions on your scheduling). These restrictions can arise from a mismatch between your ideas about the curriculum and the architect's ideas. This can be explained best by referring to the diagram on the next page. This shows values of r for two different schools.

In school A, due to falling rolls, r is very low. The overall value of r for all types of accommodation is only 0.60. That is, on average, only 60% of the rooms are occupied. Because the overall value is low, values of r for individual types of room can vary widely.

For example, if the school's curriculum requires it, the science laboratories can be timetabled at over 90% usage – the timetabler would give them a high priority at the scheduling stage, knowing that there would be ample flexibility later because the classrooms would have only 40% usage. Such a school can decide its own curriculum, to a large degree independently of the architect's designs.

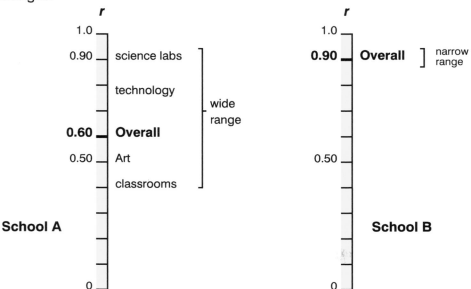

However **in school B** the overall value of r is 0.90. Because the overall value is so high, all types of room must be used at about 90% usage.

Specialist rooms could not be timetabled at much over 90% because the timetabler would not have much flexibility with ordinary classrooms – they also have to be timetabled at about 90% usage.

All types of room are forced into a narrow range of values of r. The ICT rooms will have to be used for 90% of the week, whether the school likes it or not; all the Technology rooms will have to be used for 90% of the week, whether the school likes it or not. The curriculum must conform more closely to the architect's design. This is one area where schools gain if rolls fall.

In most schools the science laboratories are used at a high value of r. This is because laboratories cost about twice as much to build as general classrooms. HM Inspectorate suggested that science laboratories may be timetabled at 90% usage if support services are good; otherwise they suggested that 70% may be the upper limit.

It is worth remembering that the structure of the school day can limit the rooming fraction. As we saw in section 7.8, with a 2–3–3 or a 3–2–3 day, the maximum number of double periods is 15. That is, a maximum of 30 periods out of 40. This gives a maximum rooming fraction of 0.75 if the accommodation is used only for double periods.

9.3   Priorities — worked example

One of the difficulties at the scheduling stage is deciding an order of priority for fitting different parts of the data. The rooming fraction can help to clarify this. The timetabler can calculate the overall value of r and the individual values of r for different types of accommodation, using the same equation as before:

$$r = \frac{\text{number of periods to be timetabled}}{\text{number of teaching spaces x number of periods in a week}}$$

Then the values of r for different types of accommodation can be arranged into a list showing the order of priority for scheduling (assuming for the moment that all other factors are equal).

Consider an example. Imagine you are the new Head of the English Department of the Laura Norder High School.
All 12 members of the English Department are teaching 30 periods (in a 40-period week). The departmental suite consists of 10 rooms.
The Head of Science tells you that his department teaches 300 periods in 8 laboratories.
The Head of Art complains that, although he has 4 Art rooms, only 96 periods of Art are shown on the Curriculum Diagram.
What can you deduce?

For the **English** department:

$$r = \frac{\text{number of periods timetabled}}{\text{number of rooms x 40}}$$

$$= \frac{12 \times 30}{10 \times 40} \qquad = \frac{360}{400} \qquad = \mathbf{0.90} \qquad (90\%)$$

This 90% room usage is high but the consequences for the department have to be judged in comparison with other departments.

For the **Science** department:

$$r = \frac{300}{8 \times 40} \qquad = \mathbf{0.94} \qquad (94\%)$$

This is very high. Clearly, for priority in scheduling, Science will take precedence over English (particularly as Science lessons require a laboratory more than English lessons require an English room).

For the **Art** department:

$$r = \frac{96}{4 \times 40} \qquad = \mathbf{0.60} \qquad (60\%)$$

Clearly the order of priority for these three departments is:
1.   Science
2.   English
3.   Art

Whether the English department will be given a high priority after science depends on the value of r for other departments.
If the overall value of r is high, English classes may have a low priority on this basis (although other factors such as teacher-teams may increase the priority). If the overall value of r is reasonable (0.85 or less) then several departments will have a low r (to balance the Science and English). This might suggest that there is a mismatch between the curriculum and the allocation of rooms.
Perhaps another department should donate a room to the English department.

If all the rooms are treated as specialist rooms, as implied in this example, then the principle of compatibility applies to them (see section 7.10).

9.4   Rooming Equation

In section 5.5 we saw that the number of teaching-periods (p) that can be provided depends on the number of teachers (T) and their contact ratio (c). This led us to the staffing equation: $p = c\,T\,W$

There is a corresponding equation for rooms. The number of teaching-periods (p) that can be accommodated depends on the number of learning-spaces (R) and their rooming fraction (r).
Although the total number of rooms is R, the effective number is only R multiplied by r. That is, rR. In effect we have rR rooms being used all the time, for all W periods in the timetable cycle.
So the number of periods (p) is:

$$p = r \times R \times W$$

This is the Rooming Equation, sometimes called the 'Second Law' of the curriculum. See also Appendix 4.

As it stands, the equation will tell you the number of teaching-periods that can be accommodated in R rooms at a rooming fraction r. This can be applied to the whole main school or to specialist rooms within a department.
As in section 9.2, R must include all the learning-spaces that you use.

Alternatively the subject of the equation can be changed to r:

$$r = \frac{p}{R \times W}$$

If p was determined from the curriculum (chapter 2) or from the staffing equation (section 5.5) then r can be calculated from this equation.

Remember that since p applies only to the main school, so also does R. If you have a 'Sixth Form' (Years 12/13), then a corresponding number of rooms will have to be subtracted from the total accommodation. This can be done by looking at the current timetable and finding the average number of rooms occupied by the Sixth Form classes.

By comparing the Staffing Equation ($p = cTW$) with the Rooming Equation ($p = rRW$), we can see that: $cT = rR$

So: $T = \dfrac{rR}{c} =$ the number of staff, working at a contact ratio c, that can be accommodated in R rooms at a rooming fraction r

This can be used to find the 'correct' size of a specialist department. For example, if 7 laboratories are to be used at 90% usage when the contact ratio is 0.75, then

$$T = {0.90 \times 7}/{0.75} = 8.4 \text{ staff}$$

If there are 9 full-time Science teachers then 0.6 of a teacher (= 18 periods in a 30-period cycle) will be timetabled out of a laboratory.

Some other curriculum equations are shown in Appendix 4. For example: $p < 0.85\,RW$. That is, to keep r less than 0.85, the number of teaching-periods provided by the school or by a department must be less than the number of rooms multiplied by 0.85 x the number of periods (W) in the timetable cycle.

9.5   The nomogram

In section 5.11 we saw how a nomogram connects the staffing ratio (N/T), the contact ratio (c) and the relative bonus (b%). The same nomogram (section 5.11) can also be applied to rooms.

This time the labels at the *bottom* of the axes are used.

The quantity plotted on the left hand axis is N/R, the number of pupils divided by the number of teaching spaces (in each case for the main school only). This value is usually in the range 16–22. It is determined by external factors such as funding: the school has little direct control over it.

The quantity on the right hand axis is still b%. This quantity was found when the nomogram was used in section 5.11. Joining the quantities on the left and right axes by a straight line gives the intercept on the central axis, which is r, the rooming fraction.

For example, suppose that your school has N/R = 20.5 and it is proposed to have b% =18½%. Draw a straight line from 20.5 on the left axis to 18½ on the right axis. This cuts the central axis at r = 0.90.

This is rather high but the only ways of reducing it are to obtain more accommodation or to reduce b% by reducing the contact ratio.

To summarize the use of the nomogram:

1. Calculate N/T and N/R.

2. Using the top labels and knowing N/T, decide c and b%.

3. Using the bottom labels and knowing N/R and b%, decide r.

4. Iterate as necessary to achieve reasonable values of c, b%, r.

9.6   Johnson's Rule

Still looking at the nomogram (section 5.11) and considering the labels at the bottom of the axes, we can see that two of them (r and b%) have critical values.

The b% axis should have a *minimum* value of 10% if the school is to retain sufficient curricular flexibility for its option scheme (see section 5.9).

The r axis should have a *maximum* value of 0.85 if the school is to retain sufficient scheduling flexibility to keep rooming compromises within acceptable limits.

When taken together these two limits give a *maximum* value to the quantity N/R.

Joining b% = 10% and r = 0.85 on the nomogram, the line cuts the N/R axis at just under 21. That is:

$$\frac{N}{R} < 21 \qquad \text{or} \qquad N < 21\,R$$

This is Johnson's Rule: *If the number of pupils (N) divided by the number of teaching spaces (R) is greater than 21, then the school has lost curricular flexibility or scheduling flexibility or both.*

If N/R is greater than 21, the school cannot have b% greater than 10% unless r rises above 0.85 (loss of scheduling flexibility); the school cannot keep r below 0.85 except by allowing b% to fall below 10% (loss of curricular flexibility).

Clearly a school which has N/R greater than 21 has a powerful argument for requesting more funding to provide more accommodation (or else reduce the school's intake).

9.7   Worked example

Imagine you are the Head of the Laura Norder High School, an 11–16 school with 1440 pupils (N), and 80 full-time-equivalent teaching staff (T).
The number of teaching spaces (including all sports facilities) is 65 (R).
The curriculum you wish to provide for the next school year requires 1760 teaching-periods (p) in a 30-period timetable cycle.

Questions:

1. What is the 'basic provision' of teaching-periods for this number of pupils?

2. What would be the bonus?
   What would be the relative bonus? Comment on the value.

3. Use the nomogram (of section 5.11) to determine the necessary contact ratio (c). Comment on the value.

4. Use the nomogram to determine the rooming fraction (r). Comment.

5. An inspector suggests that your staff should have more class contact time. Suggest a reply.

The answers are on the next page.

Answers

1. See section 5.7

    The basic provision $= \dfrac{\text{no. of pupils x no. of periods in cycle}}{27}$

    $= \dfrac{1440 \times 30}{27} = \mathbf{1600}$ periods

2. The bonus $=$ actual provision $-$ basic provision

    $= 1760 - 1600 \qquad\qquad = \mathbf{160}$ periods

    Relative bonus $b\% = \dfrac{\text{bonus periods}}{\text{basic periods}} \times 100\% = \dfrac{160}{1600} \times 100\% = \mathbf{10\%}$

    This is the lower limit, for curricular flexibility.

3. The staffing ratio $N/T = 1440/80 = 18.0$. This is not generous.

    Using the nomogram (top labels), with $N/T = 18.0$ and $b\% = 10\%$, gives $c = \mathbf{0.73}$. (Alternatively, one can use $p = cTW$)

    In a 30-period week this is an average of 22 periods per week.

    In earlier years this would have been considered rather low. Whether it is reasonable today depends on how much pastoral care and support for discipline is needed from Deputy Heads and Year Tutors or House Tutors.

4. $N/R = 1440/65 = 22.2$

    This is greater than 21 so the school must suffer a lack of flexibility.

    Using the nomogram (bottom labels), with $N/R = 22.2$ and $b\% = 10\%$, gives $r = \mathbf{0.90}$. (Alternatively, one can use $p = rRW$)

    This value is high, so all types of accommodation must be used at about 90%. The curriculum is being forced to conform to the building.

5. If the school is an inner-city comprehensive, perhaps a split-site, then the value of c is not low. Under more favourable conditions, even if it is agreed that c ought to rise, it cannot do so without raising r. This will force the curriculum to conform even more closely to the accommodation and it will force even more compromises during scheduling.

    The school clearly needs more accommodation in order to:

    (i) reduce N/R to less than 21

    (ii) reduce r to 0.85 or less, to allow better scheduling

    (iii) raise $b\%$ above 10% to allow better curricular provision

    As a bare minimum, to get $N/R = 21$, the school needs $R = N/21 = 1440/21 = 69$ rooms. That is, at least 4 more rooms.

    The types of room that are needed could be decided by looking at r for each type of accommodation.

9.8 Summary

The curricular provision in a school depends on the number of teaching spaces (rooms) (R) and the rooming fraction (r).

r = fraction of rooms* occupied for teaching (on average)

$$= \frac{\text{average number of rooms* in use } (cT)}{\text{total number of rooms* } (R)}$$

$$= \frac{\text{average usage of rooms* (in periods)}}{\text{number of periods in the timetable cycle}}$$

$$= \frac{\text{number of periods provided on the timetable } (p)}{\text{number of rooms* } (R) \ \times \ \text{number of periods in the timetable cycle } (W)}$$

*rooms = all learning-spaces (teaching-spaces)

Number of teaching-periods $(p) = r R W$

As r rises above 0.85, there are likely to be increasingly severe restrictions on the curriculum and the timetable.

If $N/R > 21$ then the school has lost curriculum flexibility or scheduling flexibility or both.

Values of r for different types of accommodation help to give an order of priority for scheduling.

Further formulae can be found in Appendix 4.

The particular problems of split-site schools are discussed in chapter 10.

*Do you think Watkin meant to timetable **all** of Year 5 in the History Room this lesson?*

10 Other timetable checks

In the last three chapters we have seen how the data can be checked for impossibilities in:
- the staffing of departments (using the Combing Chart),
- the option blocks and other big teacher-teams (using the Conflict Matrix),
- the use of accommodation (using the rooming fraction).

With these impossibilities removed, a complete solution to the timetable may be possible without any further compromise.

However this could be decided only by attempting to schedule the data. For the complicated timetables that are attempted in most large schools today, it is worthwhile looking further for ways of providing still more flexibility.

In this chapter we look at ways of providing this extra flexibility.
If you have a 'Sixth Form' there are extra checks discussed in chapter 12.

A later part of the chapter is concerned with the problem of deciding priorities. This is an essential last step before going on to consider the scheduling stage in the next chapter.

I suppose it's too late to mention that I don't work on Mondays

10.2 Zarraga's Rule

One of the limitations on your timetable is the way in which the Teacher-teams of the Upper School interact with the 'pure class' activities of the Lower School. Zarraga's Rule can help you to reduce the interaction and find more flexibility for your scheduling. (The formal statement of Zarraga 's Rule is given later.)

Consider this example. Here is a teacher-team in Year 10, consisting of 6 teachers called AA, BB, CC, DD, EE and FF:

Monday...   Tuesday...   Wednesday...

Dr	**AA**
IT	**BB**
Sc	**CC**
Sp	**DD**
Hi	**EE**
Pe	**FF**

These 6 teachers are due to teach Year 10 all at the **same** time, in *parallel*. It might be an Option Block as shown here, or it could or a column of Maths 'sets'. Let's suppose that you have scheduled this block to Monday-period-1.

Now it may happen, by chance, that your Heads of Department request the **same** 6 teachers to all teach the **same** Lower School class, say 7A.

Monday...   Tuesday...   Wednesday...

	En	Ma	Sc	Fr	Hi	Gg
Class 7A	**AA**	**BB**	**CC**	**DD**	**EE**	**FF**

In this case these same 6 teachers are due to teach 7A, at **different** times, in *series*. This situation can lead to serious difficulties in scheduling.

Suppose for example that long after you have scheduled Year 10, you eventually come to schedule class 7A and look for a teacher to teach them on Monday-period-1 (ie. the same period as the Year 10 team above).

In this example you would find that teacher AA is not free, because he is teaching in the Year 10 team (above).
If you then try to schedule teacher BB with 7A, you find he is also not free -- he is also teaching in the Year 10 team. Similarly with teachers CC, DD, EE and FF.

If all the other teachers needed for 7A are not free, because they have been scheduled with other classes or with unavailable part-timers, then you are in difficulty.
The class is available, the room is available, the time-slot is available, but **none** of the teachers is free !

At the scheduling stage it is extremely difficult to see the reason for this. But applying this test at an early stage shows up the problem, and the solution is easy; see below.

And if you have reduced the number of staff teaching in Year 7 (eg. to try to emulate a primary school ethos, so that you have perhaps only 5 teachers for each class instead of the more traditional dozen) ...then the situation will be even more difficult !

The solution is easy:
Clearly this situation is less likely to arise if the 6 teachers who are in parallel in Year 10 are *not* put in series for the same Lower School class.
Unless there is a good educational reason against it, the 6 teachers should be allocated to *different* Year 7 classes. For example:

	Monday...		Tuesday...		Wednesday...	
class 7A	**AA**					
class 7B		**BB**				
class 7C			**CC**			
class 7D				**DD**		
class 7E					**EE**	
class 7F						**FF**

Naturally you should discuss these changes with the Subject Leader, but because there is normally no issue of continuity of teaching, there is usually no problem.

I do not know who originated this idea but since it was first put to me by M.N. Zarraga of STAG, I think of it as **Zarraga's Rule**: *As far as possible, teachers who are members of the same teacher-team in one part of the school should be allocated to different classes for pure class activity in another part of the school.*

Applying this rule to Lower School classes, consulting with Heads of Departments as necessary, can lead to a surprising increase in flexibility in the later stages of scheduling.
The more heterogeneous the option blocks, the more important it is to apply this rule.

You may think that this example is slightly far-fetched. But in practice you will have not just a Year 10 block but also a Year 11 block of teachers at the same time (and maybe Years 12 and 13 as well), and perhaps a block of Maths sets in Year 9, all of them causing conflicts for 7A. So the more flexibility and freedom you can find, the better.

How to use Zarraga's Rule:

While Zarraga's Rule is very useful, it is harder to use in practice than the other tests like the Combing Chart. The first step is to find what conflicts there are, either manually or using a computer.

Manually, you can do it by analysing and comparing all your teacher-teams, one by one ...but it is much easier to get a computer program to do it.

In *TimeTabler*, you just click on the button labelled Zarraga's Rule, to see:

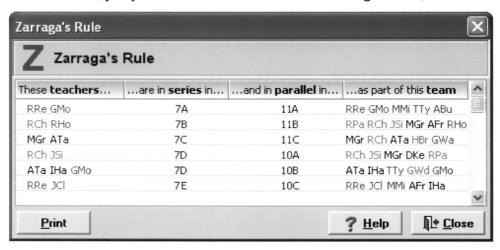

These **teachers**...	...are in **series** in...	...and in **parallel** in...	...as part of this **team**
RRe GMo	7A	11A	RRe GMo MMi TTy ABu
RCh RHo	7B	11B	RPa RCh JSi MGr AFr RHo
MGr ATa	7C	11C	MGr RCh ATa HBr GWa
RCh JSi	7D	10A	RCh JSi MGr DKe RPa
ATa IHa GMo	7D	10B	ATa IHa TTy GWd GMo
RRe JCl	7E	10C	RRe JCl MMi AFr IHa

The second step is to look at the (lower school) classes to see what beneficial changes you can make. For example, from the first line of screen above you would aim to change the staffing of 7A so that RRe and GMo are not both teaching 7A.

A crude way to use Zarraga's Rule is to look at the screen above and say simply: *'The most common subject colour in the first column is blue* [which in this school is Humanities], *so maybe I need to take particular care with the staffing of the Humanities lessons'.*

Subjects v. Teachers

Note that although we have shown the Subject labels in the diagrams on the previous spread, they are really irrelevant, because it is **Teachers** that cause clashes. However these subject labels illustrate how the teacher-teams in upper school do create a large degree of interaction between the various subject departments.

For example, you may think that your En and Ma departments are separate because they have no teachers in common. But in the Year 10 team shown in the diagrams on the previous spread, an English teacher (AA) teaching Drama is inescapably linked to a Maths teacher (BB) teaching IT in the same block. (And in a different way Pe and Gg are linked via teacher FF.)

Hence the value in doing the Combing Chart for *pairs* of departments (or even triplets), see chapter 7.

10.3 Balancing the teaching power for lower school classes

While you are looking at possible teacher changes for lower school classes in the light of the previous section, it is also worthwhile looking at the quality of teaching to be provided to those classes. It is important (not only for justice, but also to control disruption) that the strengths and weaknesses of the teaching staff should be distributed equitably.

This can be considered most easily by looking in the 'master' booklet (section 6.6). The master booklet shows the Curriculum Diagrams with the relevant staff initials entered next to each group of pupils.

Looking along each row (that is, for each class or population of students) the group of teachers allocated to each class can be seen easily.

In judging the relative strengths and weaknesses of these groups of teachers it may be helpful to allot a simple (and confidential) numerical value to each teacher.

For example:

1 = non-qualified, probationary or weak teacher
2 = strong classroom control but routine teaching style
3 = adequate classroom control with good, lively teaching style
4 = excellent teacher

In this way a total value can be found for each class and any imbalance corrected by interchanging teachers (and consulting with Heads of Departments as necessary). Obviously such judgements must be made carefully, in the light of all that you have observed of these teachers and these classes.

Two other criteria may be considered at the same time:

1   It may be preferable for the ratios of old/young teachers to be uniform.
2   It may be preferable for the ratios of male/female teachers to be uniform.

As a further refinement you may wish to ensure that no class is allocated a group of teachers with weak health or a strong involvement with examination boards for which they might require several days' absence during the year.

10.4 Deciding priorities

When you eventually arrive at the scheduling stage and look at the virgin timetable, if you are scheduling manually it is important to have an order of priority for fitting the various items on to the timetable.

Initially it is easier to look at priorities and constraints under seven separate headings before combining them into one overall order of priority.

The 7 headings are:

1. Fixed Points
2. Part-time teachers
3. Split-site schools
4. Teacher-teams
5. Rooms
6. Lesson-spread (pattern) and length
7. Other constraints and priorities

These are discussed on the next six pages.

1   Fixed points

These must be given the highest priority. For the timetabler it is essential to know the exact days and times well before scheduling begins. Examples include:

(a)   Fixed times for swimming
For example, if the local swimming pool is available only on a Tuesday morning then swimming lessons for Year 7 must be scheduled for Tuesday mornings.

(b)   Shared playing fields
If your playing fields are shared with another school (or if the transport to sports facilities is available only at certain times) then Games will have a high priority. Some schools like to restrict games for a whole year-group to the last part of an afternoon. The timetabler needs to know whether it should be at the end of a particular afternoon for each Year, or whether any afternoon will do.

(c)   Linked courses at other schools in a 14-19 Consortium or at an FE College.
Many schools arrange courses for students aged 14-19 to attend courses at other schools in the consortium or at the local FE College, or for work experience. These are often vocational courses in media studies, building construction, IT, etc. One advantage of these courses is that their staffing may not count directly against the school's establishment.

There can be disadvantages: for example, some pupils tend to get 'lost' on their way to the college unless there is adequate staff supervision, and good registration arrangements. The restriction on the school timetable can be severe because of specific times dictated by the college, affecting large teacher-teams in Year 10 and Year 11. There may also be a difficulty if the dates of the terms for school and college do not coincide.

(d)   Sixth Form consortia
Urban 11–18 schools with small Sixth Forms often group together into consortia to maintain provision of less-popular or specialist subjects. One member of a consortium will provide Latin, another Psychology, etc.

As before it is essential to agree on days and times at an early stage. Difficulties arise if the schools are some distance apart or if the period-breakdowns of the school days are dissimilar. For example, if one school operates a 2–2–2–2 day while another school prefers a 2–2–2 day, it may be preferable to timetable shared subjects on mornings only. See also section 2.18.

(e)   Management meetings
Some schools restrict these to certain times, often unnecessarily.

(f)   Year-Tutors or House-Tutors
Some schools may place a high priority on pastoral staff being free at particular times to meet with the Educational Welfare Officer.
Other schools may require particular staff to be free after assembly on certain days or to be free last period for bus duty, etc.

2   Part-time teachers

Part-time teachers are often a serious constraint on the timetable and often must be given a high priority. For the timetabler, part-time teachers are usually a curse.

There are 2 kinds of part-time teachers:

- 'Fixed' part-timers. For example, Mrs Smith insists on being out of school all day Friday and Monday to have her long weekend. If you are using computer software then you will tell the program this information at the start, and it will ensure that you do not use Mrs Smith on Friday or Monday.
  If you are working manually you will need to keep checking on this, because it is dangerously easy to 'solve' a problem by accidentally using Mrs Smith on a Friday and not realise this until the new timetable starts operation!

- 'Floating' part-timers. For example, Mrs Jones has a contract to teach 4 half-days and does not mind which 4 half-days.
  Clearly this gives you more flexibility, particularly if you are using timetabler software which can take full advantage of this flexibility.

With any part-timer it will be important to reduce or eliminate any 'trapped time'. For example, Mr Brown will not be pleased if he is scheduled to teach (and be paid for) only periods 1 and 5 and is left free (but unpaid) for periods 2, 3, 4!

Wherever possible part-time teachers should **only** be allowed to teach pure class activities. If a part-timer is allowed to become a member of a team then his or her 'part-time-ness' is transferred to the other members of that team.

For example, if a part-timer is available only on Monday and Tuesday and is a member of the teams for some Year 10 and Year 11 options, then these teams must teach on Monday and Tuesday and so all the other classes taken by all the members of the teams will tend to be squeezed into Wednesday, Thursday and Friday. This effect tends to 'ricochet' round the timetable and can produce a serious skew to the timetables of some departments and some classes seemingly unconnected to the part-timer.
This is especially serious if it clashes with fixed 'consortium days' when students are moving to other schools in the consortium.

Obviously, if *two* part-timers are in the same teacher-team then the team can teach only at times that are common to both part-timers! This, by itself, may make your timetable impossible!

The availability of part-time teachers should allow for (and be consistent with) the required period-spread of the subject. For example, a part-time teacher of French who is available for only three afternoons will not allow the 5-single-periods-on-5-days that support good French teaching.
The availability of part-timers should be ascertained as early and as clearly as possible. The timetabler can hope that there will be some flexibility in the agreed time although, as the law stands, it seems that part-time teachers can insist that they teach for exactly the same days and periods as they taught on the last timetable unless their contract specifies differently.

3   Split-site schools

Split-site schools or 'federal' schools or members of a consortium of schools are usually more difficult to timetable than single-site schools.

One reason is that if the split-site school has three laboratories on each of two sites, there is a total of six but only three are available at any time to each population.

It may be useful to calculate the rooming fraction for the room-types on each site, see chapter 9. For example, if the Science labs on Site 1 have a rooming fraction of 95% while the Science labs on Site 2 have a rooming fraction of 70%, then it looks likely that some pupils will have to commute from Site 1 to Site 2 for their Science.

A more serious difficulty is that a teacher cannot really be expected to teach a class in the upper school for period 1 and then teach a lower school class for period 2, without any break between. Some schools apparently do expect this 'instant commuting' but one cannot think how they can justify it on educational or practical grounds.

The severity of the problem depends on the distance to be travelled. Even some single-site schools with a spread-out layout have this problem.

Other schools solve this problem (and create another) by limiting commuting to only one or two teachers, thus emphasizing the split nature of the school.

With half or more of the staff commuting, the situation can be relieved by operating a 2-2-2 day or a 2-2-2-2 day (with morning and afternoon breaks long enough to allow commuting between buildings).

Care should be taken to ensure that each teacher is based clearly in one of the buildings. For example, in a 25-period cycle a member of staff teaching 10 periods in each building will have obvious difficulties.

For the timetabler, a colleague who teaches 20 periods (in a 25-period cycle) and is split 18–2 between buildings will cause no difficulty; a split of 15–5 will cause more difficulty to the timetabler as he tries to block the teacher into one building for a whole session. It is probably wise to direct Subject Leaders to limit the split to 12–8, but the effect of this on the timetable will vary from department to department.

For example, if Technology is always taught in big blocks of time then 12–8 or even 10–10 is easier to schedule. However for French, which should be scheduled with a lot of single periods, even 15–5 may cause severe difficulties for the timetabler and for the teacher (who may have to commute frequently).

If you work in a split-site school then the split for each teacher can be shown on the Staff Loading Chart, as explained in section 6.7. By inspecting this chart a list can be drawn up showing the order of priority for scheduling the members of staff who commute.

See also the box opposite on split-site schools.

Movement in Split-site Schools

In secondary schools, most of the teaching is done by subject specialists. This means that for a class to get their total curriculum they need to be taught by perhaps a dozen different teachers. In order to do this either the teachers can stay in one room and the pupils move around to the staff, or the classes can remain static and the teachers move around the school to find their classes. The third option is to do some of each, depending on the subject.

In single site schools the staff are usually static and the pupils move. Many staff have their own room, often a specialist room. This has significant advantages for the staff and some advantages for the pupils.

In a split-site school, where the distance between sites is significant, it is usually thought that moving the teachers between sites is more desirable than moving the pupils. This means that the staff teach in more rooms.

An obvious general rule is: '*Any attempt to reduce pupil movement between sites will usually increase teacher movement, and vice-versa*'.

Looking at ways to reduce movement:

- Specialist rooms
  One aim is to have the necessary specialist accommodation on both sites. For example, is it possible to have sufficient Art rooms, Science labs, etc on each site? See chapter 9 on how to check if the rooming fractions balance.

- Dual bases
  Can you allocate a room on each site to act as 'home', for each commuting teacher? Of course each of these rooms will be shared with someone else, but the aim would be to have most rooms shared by no more than two teachers, and for all their lessons to be scheduled into these rooms.

- Improve on the last timetable
  Analyse the current timetable to see where (why) most of the movement occurs. For example, in one school the pupils were trekking back to their 'own' building just for registration, when an 'assistant form tutor' could have done this with no movement by the pupils.

- Allocate the staffing differently
  If all (or more of) the staff could be persuaded to teach either Key Stage 3 or Key Stage 4/5, then not only could the pupils stay on their home site most of the time, but staff would not have to move either.
  For example, the scenario might be that the lower school would be an 11-13 school which sends it pupils on certain mornings/afternoons to the upper school for Technology, while the upper school is a 14-18 school which perhaps employs some teachers from the lower school to do some examination work.

4   Teacher teams

By inspecting the Conflict Matrices (chapter 8) and the Curriculum Diagram (chapter 2) one can draw up an order of priority for the scheduling of the teacher teams, whether these are teams for Mathematics, English and French sets, or teams for the option blocks.

A simple rule to apply is that the more teachers involved and the more periods for which they are due to be scheduled, the greater the difficulty. That is, the product of teachers multiplied by periods can be used to decide the order of priority (this corresponds roughly to the area of the item to be fitted to the 'card' timetable model, see chapter 11).

Clearly the order of priority should be modified after considering other constraints that are mentioned in this chapter.

Remember to include the teacher teams needed for any management meetings or for any essential departmental meetings that are to be timetabled.

5   Rooms

Using the ideas developed in sections 9.2 and 9.3, the timetabler should calculate the rooming fraction for each type of teaching space. Clearly a Chemistry laboratory with $r = 94\%$ will have a higher priority than an Art room with $r = 60\%$. A list can be drawn showing the order of priority for different types of room.

6   Lesson length and pattern-spread

The timetabler should be aware of the lesson length requested by each Subject Leader and the preferred pattern of the periods throughout the week. For example: five singles of French on five days; a single period of PE and a double period of Games on different days; no more than three days (including the weekend) to elapse between Spanish lessons, etc.

7   Other constraints and priorities

A variety of other factors may be considered. For example:

- The priority given to the Upper Sixth will depend upon the flexibility shown in the Clash Table (section 12.9).
- It may be decided to give some priority to scheduling Numeracy and Literacy or other academic lessons in the mornings for difficult classes in some years.
- Food Technology for Year 10 may be preferred in the morning to allow the pupils to eat the results of their practical sessions.
- If you have a staggered lunch-break (eg. Years 7, 8, 9 eat during period 4 and go to lessons during period 5, while the reverse applies to Years 10 and 11) then you will need to ensure that each teacher has a lunch-break. In this example a teacher must not teach Year 10 during period 4 and then teach Year 7 during period 5.
- It may be decided that a department which has suffered in previous years should have a higher priority this time.

- It may be decided to give some priority to reducing the movement of younger pupils round the building between single periods by careful consideration of the sequence of lessons.
- Other particular constraints may apply to your school, eg. 'The local primary schools use our Sports Hall on Wednesdays', or 'A group of Subject Leaders is involved in a liaison project and cannot teach last period on a Tuesday'. A common one is 'Every class in the school has PSHE during period 1 on Thursday'.

If you are new to the school then it is essential – but sometimes quite difficult – to discover all these particular constraints, before you start the timetable.

When all these 7 factors have been considered and an order of priority decided under each of the 7 headings, then the timetabler can consider an overall order of priority.

Fixed points normally take precedence over everything else. Next in order of priority might be a part-time teacher who is a member of a large teacher team, commutes between the two sites of a split-site school and is teaching Physics (for which the rooming fraction is 92%).

Considering other composite constraints like this, the timetabler can draw up lists of priority to help at the scheduling stage. It will usually be sufficient to draw up four lists under headings such as: 'extreme priority,' 'high priority', 'important', 'lower priority but still needing consideration' etc.

Clearly a timetabler program can prioritise using many more factors and with more in-depth 'look-ahead' analysis.

10.5   Solving problems : Diplomacy

If you need to change the data either now or later during scheduling, then it's often a question of negotiation and diplomacy.

Indeed, when timetabling, diplomacy is as important as problem-solving skills.

Before approaching a colleague (eg. the relevant Subject Leader):

- Try to find at least *two* ways to resolve the problem, so that you can offer them a choice, so that they feel less pressured.
- Make sure that all of your solutions will actually work, or you will look foolish later!
- Decide on *who* to approach and *how*.
- Don't expect an instant response. You may feel it's urgent but they may need a short while to consider the options or to speak to someone in their team.
- Allow them the option to suggest a solution of their own.

10.6 Looking for more flexibility

If at this stage you feel the need to look for more flexibility, there have been many suggestions in the previous chapters but some of them are collected here to remind you. You may also find this list useful if you get stuck later during scheduling.

- If you feel the problem is to do with the structure of the curriculum, then you may need to draw a Schematic Diagram for a part of the curriculum. See chapter 4. As a result you may wish to consider including more subjects within a tight consistently-setted block, see section 2.10.

- Draw a Combing Chart for pairs of linked departments, if you haven't already done this. You may find this pinpoints a problem teacher, who you may need to swap. See chapter 7.

- Look at the Conflict Matrices (chapter 8). Where a conflict is unavoidable, try to increase the conflict there, so you may gain freedom elsewhere.

- If a team of teachers meet frequently in the option blocks, do not give them the same class in lower school for pure-class teaching. See section 10.2.

- Where teachers are in more than one option block, try to confine their teaching to one Year/Band. For example, someone teaching:

  French in Year 10 Option-Block-1 *and* in Year 10 Option-Block-3

  is better than:

  French in Year 10 Option-Block-1 *and* in Year 11 Option-Block-3

  because you cannot ever schedule the first two together (because they are the same students), but the second two activities could be at the same time if there were no clashes. See also section 7.7.

- Look at how dual-subject teachers have been used, see section 7.7.

- Look at how part-time teachers have been used, see section 10.4.

- Where teachers meet classes for only 1 lesson per week (eg. Re, Music, etc) it can cause difficulties if their teaching is restricted mainly to Years 7/8. Can this be relaxed?

10.7 Summary

This chapter has considered methods of introducing additional flexibility, particularly in the staffing of the lower school pure-class activities.
The chapter has also been concerned with deciding the priority to be attached to the various items that have to be fitted, now that the scheduling stage has been reached.

11 Scheduling

At last we reach the stage most people think of when we say 'timetabling'.
At this stage we allocate particular activities to particular times of the week, and so produce a device which controls the movement of a large number of people, bell by bell, for many weeks.
The final timetable is a very powerful device and its construction places a heavy responsibility on the timetabler and on his ability to remember all the requests, preferences, whims and habits of his colleagues, and to judge fairly their relative merits for staff, pupils and the school as a whole.

Clearly we wish to obtain a timetable of the highest quality, a timetable which is *enabling* rather than restrictive. We do not wish to include any of the compromises that were listed in section 7.1, particularly as compromises made early in the scheduling stage may tend to avalanche further compromises at a later stage.

Obviously the construction needs to be done in a logical manner. The number of permutations is too great for any other method. Indeed, for an average school, if just one year-group were to be scheduled in a random manner, the number of ways of doing this would greatly exceed the number of atoms in the observable universe!

Logic, however, means different things in different schools. In one school in Derbyshire, 'logic' consisted of the Head of Mathematics being allowed to schedule his Sixth Form Maths on the timetable board, followed by the Head of English who scheduled his Sixth Form groups and so on, down a pecking order of departments until the Sixth Form timetable was finished. Then the Head of Maths had first chance at the Year 11 timetable, followed by other departments in order, until that year-group was completed. It is not clear at what stage in this process violence or nervous breakdowns occurred.

Other teachers report 'do-it-yourself' methods, bartering in the staffroom: *'8A haven't had any science this week, I'll swap one period of 10D for two periods of 8A this afternoon'*.

In a special school in Lancashire the Head was doing the timetable, and promised it by the first day of term but failed. During the first few days of term an increasingly frantic Head ordered staff: *'Every time the bell rings, just send your class to the next room down the corridor'*.

Some people think of scheduling as a process of completing a jigsaw puzzle, but it is not as simple as that – when you buy a jigsaw at least you know that it has a solution! With a timetable there may not be a solution – or, more likely, there will be many solutions, depending on the compromises that you make. Our job is to get the best of those solutions.

If you don't care about compromises then scheduling is easy. Any old Deputy Head could do the timetable on the back of an envelope during an evening at the pub ...but Year 9 might get all their Maths on a Monday!

Even when the timetable is viewed as a jigsaw puzzle, it must be thought of as a kind of 5-dimensional jigsaw, because there are five main variables to be considered. These are (in order of decreasing importance):

- the **Class** (population) of pupils to be scheduled,
- the **Time** at which the lesson takes place,
- the **Teacher** who takes the class,
- the **Room** in which the lesson takes place,
- the **Subject** label, saying what they will be taught, eventually.

In order to keep control over these variables, we must build up the timetable on some kind of 'model'.

This model can be a mechanical model (as was usual in the 20th century) or a computer model (as is usual today).

In order to demonstrate and understand the ***principles*** of scheduling, and to see clearly what the processes are, in this chapter we will use a mechanical model for most sections. (See chapter 15 for scheduling with computers.)

11.2 Five timetable models

Your timetable model should include all of the five main variables. A good model will also show clearly other variables such as the grouping of classes and the length of lessons. When using the model, two important factors are security and flexibility in use. These factors, as well as portability, are discussed below.

All the manual timetable models have two physical dimensions – the length and width of the sheet of paper or plastic board or whatever is used. Two of the five main variables are shown on these two axes. The two variables that are usually shown are the first and second in the list given earlier – the **classes** of pupils and the **times** of the school week.

The classes should run from the oldest Year-group at the top down to Year 7 at the bottom. The periods should run from Monday-period-1 at the left to the last period in the timetable cycle at the right.

Here is part of such a timetable model for a school operating a 5-period day:

classes	Monday 1	2	3	4	5	Tuesday 1	2	...
Year 11								...
Year 10								...
9-band X								...
9-band-Y								...
8A								...
8B								...
etc								...

The different timetable models that are available each use the same basic grid but have different ways of representing the information.

The table compares five common timetable models:

	Timetable model	Flexible?	Secure?	Portable?
1	Pencil & paper grid	★	★★★	★★★
2	Pegs in a pegboard grid	★	★★	★
3	Coloured cards on a card grid	★★	★	(★★★)
4	Magnetic plastic on a steel grid	★★	★★	★★★
5	Grid in a computer's memory	★★★	★★★	★★★

One, two or three stars are given under each of three headings.

The more stars the better, but note that the categories have varying importance. By far the most important is the first one – we must have a model which is **flexible** in use if we are to obtain a high quality timetable.

Each of these models is discussed in turn.

---

1   Pencil and a paper grid

If you teach in a school with a very simple curricular structure then this may be the model for you. You will need a large rubber eraser and tough paper. It is useful to develop a strong wrist for your non-writing hand so that you can use the rubber without changing hands each time. This model is secure (the information will not fall off the model), portable (for carrying home or to departmental meetings etc.) and cheap. The final version can be photocopied to provide staffroom copies etc.

Unfortunately, this model is not sufficiently flexible for use in large schools where there are large teacher-teams. Each time an activity is moved to another period, the information has to be erased and copied again – with large teacher teams this becomes unbearable. Complicated 'musical chairs' moves cannot be attempted easily and if such a move fails then it is very tedious restoring the original position. Clearly a better model would allow the physical movement of information without the need to erase it. All the other models allow this.

2   Pegs in a pegboard

A proprietary 'Prograph' pegboard consists of a large plastic board honey-combed with thousands of small pigeon-holes (each about 7 mm x 7 mm). Into these pigeon-holes fit small plastic pegs. For each class and for each period there are normally three pegs to be fitted: a peg labelled with the Subject; a peg labelled with the Teacher's Number; a peg with the Room number.

It is by far the most expensive of the models listed, costing several hundred pounds for most schools (a school of 1000 pupils needs over 6000 pegs and about 30 sq. ft of board). It is not easily portable, being large and heavy and usually screwed to a wall.

It ought to be secure — a perspex sheet is provided to fit over the front to prevent pegs coming out. In practice some unhappy events have occurred.

One headmaster took home a Prograph board on the back seat of his car to complete his timetable over the weekend. Duly completed he brought it back to school on Monday morning. Unfortunately he had forgotten to fit the front plastic sheet, there were some road-works on his route, the car jumped and in the school car park he was seen scrabbling on the floor of his car, desperately picking up dozens of pegs.

In another school, a deputy head had completed about three-quarters of his timetable when he went home one night, leaving off the front perspex sheet. A cleaner came into his room to sweep up, nudged the board with the broom handle and knocked some of the Prograph pegs on to the floor. Being a kind and considerate cleaner, she picked up the pegs and fitted them into some empty spaces on the board — presumably where they looked the prettiest! It would have been ironic if this produced a better timetable than the one intended!

The greatest disadvantage of the Prograph method is that the information to be stored remains in a large number of small pieces. Moving one class for a single period means moving only two or three pegs but moving large teacher teams for double or triple periods can mean moving a very huge number of pegs, always with the possibility of dropping some, especially if the move does not work and you have to restore the original position.

In a typical scheduling situation you may need to make 'musical chairs' moves involving six large teacher-teams — with the Prograph model this requires the movement of perhaps 100 pegs! Also, when moving large numbers of pegs there is always the possibility of moving some members of a team but forgetting the others — a fatal mistake!

3 Coloured cards on a card grid

This is a home-made model. A large piece of cardboard is marked out in a grid laid flat on a desk. Coloured cards are then moved in position on the grid.

The big advantage of the card model is that the cards can be as large as you like and can integrate as much information as you like – you are not restricted to the situation in the previous model of '3 pegs for each class and each period'.

This means that if a teacher team is to teach 4 classes in parallel, the card for this team is cut so that it is 4 classes in depth. In this way moving one card moves the whole team and there is no possibility of moving only part of the team by mistake (unless you use a pair of scissors to cut the card).

Also, if the subject is intended to be taught for a single period the card will be cut so that it is only one period horizontally; if it is intended to be a double period it will be cut larger to be two periods horizontally. In this way multiple periods cannot be broken up into smaller periods (unless you use scissors).

Of course, colour should be used to give quick visual clues: the base colour for each card should indicate the subject area. Abbreviations for the subject, the teacher and the room-number are written on the card. Further details of the layout and labelling of the cards are given later in this section.

Before completion it is not portable – the timetabler must work entirely at school or entirely at home. Once completed, the timetable is made secure by glueing down the coloured cards to the base card. It is then portable and easily carried to departmental meetings etc.

4 Magnetic plastic and tinplate base

This is the best manual model — it combines flexibility and portability with reasonable security and cost. It is made from sheets of coloured magnetic plastic which can be cut to size using scissors. The plastic is available in several colours from office suppliers and extra stripes of colour can be added if necessary, using self-adhesive coloured plastic tape, available from the same suppliers. The plastic can be labelled using pencil, ball-point or felt-tip pens. The magnetic attraction is strong — turning the timetable model upside down and hitting the back of the board will not easily displace the 'cards'.

This is in contrast to a huge magnetic timetable model mounted on a large wall in the RAF camp at Cosford, which worked well until some officers played indoor rugger in the room on the other side of the wall, and a heavy tackle caused the wall to shudder so most of the magnets slid down!

The coloured 'cards'

The design of the coloured 'cards' is a common feature of the last two manual models and is discussed here in more detail.

1. The shape of the cards will vary depending on the banding or setting, and on the period-breakdown of the subject. Here are three examples:

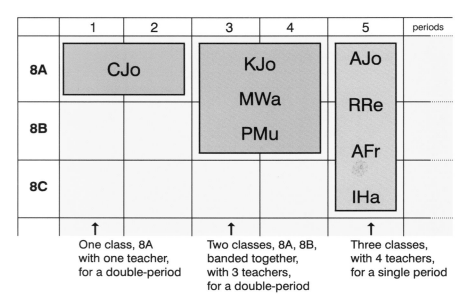

On the whole, the greater the area of the card, the greater the number of teacher-periods involved and so the higher the priority for fitting that card. That is, one of the rules of scheduling is: *large cards first*.

2. Colours help you to identify the subjects quickly. Some people use the following colour scheme:

green — English (language and literature)
red — Mathematics
brown — Languages (different languages can be shown by different colours of ink for the labels, or different shades)
yellow — Science (different sciences distinguished by different inks for the labels: eg. green – Biology, red – Chemistry, blue – Physics)
blue — History, Geography etc. (again inks can be used to distinguish)
orange — Technology subjects, including Art,
pink — Music (green labels); PE (red labels)

Curiously, other timetablers, who have devised colour schemes independently, have often chosen the same colours — is there a basic greenness about English?

3. Cutting a card for a homogeneous option pool is straightforward because only one colour is needed. For a heterogeneous option pool, more than one colour is needed if we wish to provide strong visual clues to help the timetabler. For example, if a heterogeneous pool consists of History, Science and French then three colours — blue, yellow and brown — are needed if the subjects are to be identified quickly during scheduling. This can be achieved by adding strips of colour to a card.

4. The staff initials can be marked on the card in the teacher's 2-letter or 3-letter code.

5. In addition, the name of the subject can be written on the card — for example to distinguish between the different science courses. This helps others to read the timetable model during the year it will be in use.

6. Part-time teachers or others with particular restrictions can be marked with a large asterisk or else their initials should be ringed clearly.

7. It is worthwhile marking the name of the class in one corner of the card, to ensure that it is placed on the correct class row. It also helps in case the card becomes displaced by accident.

The important thing is that all the information should be immediately available on the cards and there should be strong visual clues to help the timetabler as he moves the cards along the rows of the model.
The diagram below illustrates how all this information is integrated on to the card or piece of magnetic plastic.

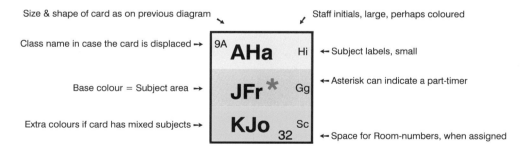

Of the five variables listed earlier — class, time, teacher, room, subject — four of them are thus shown explicitly on the model.
The exception is the room which is usually dealt with at a later stage. However, if your school has only one specialist room of a particular type and this room is to be used by more than one teacher, then the room number should be shown on the relevant cards to prevent double-assignment clashes.

The basic rules of the 'card' model

It should be clear that since each card belongs to one class or one band of classes, the first major rule of the scheduling game is that **the cards may only move 'horizontally'** and never 'vertically'.

That is, each card may move 'horizontally' along the school week to different times, but the teachers on a card are scheduled for a specific class and so the card must not move up or down.

The second major rule of the timetabling game is that **there must not be a clash 'vertically'**. This is, two cards having a teacher's initials in common cannot both be scheduled for the same time of the week — they cannot be allowed in the same 'vertical' column of the model.

This means that as you bring across a card from the feeder board, your eyes are constantly scanning, to see which times of the week are free for this particular card, with no clashes. This is where the visual clues provided by the colours are so important. If you are bringing across a yellow card (science) then your eyes are rapidly scanning the columns, ignoring all other colours, looking only for yellow cards — and each time one is found, checking to see if the cards have a teacher in common (or in the case of certain specialist rooms marked on the cards, to see if they have a room in common).

You can cut out and label *all* the cards for the whole timetable before beginning any scheduling. Or you can do them in Batches, one year at a time, as you progress.

The cards should be arranged directly next to the class to which they belong, on a 'feeder' board. As the cards move across from the feeder board on to the main board (larger cards first), a bar-chart develops on the feeder board, indicating which classes have fewest degrees of freedom and are nearest completion.

As we shall see later, this is very useful during the later stages of scheduling.

Here's a simplified picture of the timetable model:

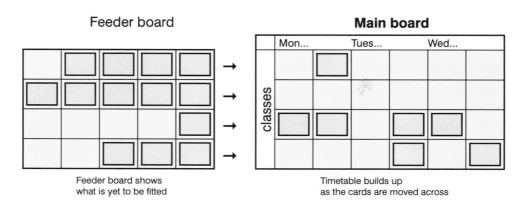

11.3 Ten rules for scheduling

In an attempt to give some guidance for new timetablers, here are ten rules for scheduling:

1. Have all the information immediately available

It is vital to have all the information to hand and preferably built into the timetable model itself (as with the coloured card model). It's a good idea to have close at hand a fully-annotated copy of the final version of the Curriculum Diagrams.

If you suddenly get an incredibly brilliant idea which is going to solve all your scheduling problems, but then find that you have to shuffle through piles of paper to check one item of information, you are likely to lose your way in a rising tide of frustration.

2. Link each teacher with a room where possible

Of the five main variables — class, subject, teacher, room, time — shown on the timetable model, the least explicit is the room. For this reason it helps if you can link a teacher to a room as much as possible. The staff will also prefer this – people like to work from a fixed base with known equipment and storage. Of course it is unlikely that you will be able to do this completely – most schools have more teachers than rooms.

As mentioned earlier, if you have only one specialist room of a certain type and two or more staff are due to use it, then you should show that room explicitly on the relevant cards.

3. Start with the worst constraint

The question of deciding priorities was discussed in section 10.4.

After considering your priorities in the ways suggested in that section, you should be able to draw up lists of priorities under headings such as 'extreme priority', 'high priority', 'important', 'lower priority but still needing consideration'. These lists can then be kept at hand to guide you.

In general the larger the **area** of the card (implying more teachers for more periods) and the more special markings on it (specifying part-time teachers, special restrictions or special subjects) then the greater the priority for it to be fitted early. It may help if the high priority cards are arranged at the right of the rows on the feeder board.

Fixed Points: there will usually be some cards that are absolutely predetermined (eg. swimming baths, links with a college, diploma-days, a shared Sixth Form) and these must be placed first and fixed in place.

Thereafter, fitting the first large teacher-team on to the almost virgin timetable can be a dramatic moment.

It can be a worrying time because, with too much freedom in placing the cards, the human timetabler cannot judge whether the placements are ideal or whether they somehow contain the seeds of later disaster.

4. Look ahead to possible problems

Although we have a limited ability to look ahead it obviously makes sense, as you place each card, to consider how that card will affect other cards that are yet to be fitted. Scanning the feeder board or the lists of priorities will tell you which are the cards due to be placed soon. The timetabler soon develops the knack of looking at the card in his hand and always considering:

- the positions (times) that are possible because of what has been fitted already, *and*
- which of these positions looks best for other cards that are about to be fitted.

5. Consider carefully before saturating any period with a particular subject

One may have mixed feelings about this rule because instinct sometimes runs counter to the application of the principle of compatibility.

As an example, imagine you are scheduling a school with six laboratories. Suppose that for Monday period 1 you have already placed cards that will need to use five of these six laboratories. Suppose further that you now need to bring on a card that requires just one laboratory. Clearly you could place that card on Monday period 1 because one laboratory is available. Indeed, it follows from the principle of compatibility that you should do this in order to minimize the number of free resources in that period.

However, instinct says that, given alternatives, it would be better to place the card elsewhere and delay 'saturating' this particular period with this particular subject. Later, in dealing with the simpler pure-class activities of the lower school, you might find that a science class is forced into this period and then you would need a laboratory for it. At the half-timetable stage, trying to keep one of the labs free for each period seems a useful thing to do, if you know you will need single laboratories at a later stage.

Applying the principle of compatibility more rigidly and saturating the period would have a stronger appeal when larger teacher teams were involved.

6   Bias numeracy and literacy lessons towards the morning?

Many timetablers would disagree with this suggestion but it is certainly worthwhile considering the best time of day for certain subjects particularly where a difficult class or a weak teacher is involved.

On the whole it would seem best that subjects where the pupils are usually able to move around the room (e.g. Art, Technology, Games) should be timetabled towards the end of the day. The same argument would suggest that subjects like Mathematics and Science should take place earlier in the day. (We do not know of any research to support this.) Another school of thought suggests that the first period after lunch may be a good time in inner-city schools because many children will then have broken their fast by eating for the first time since the previous evening.   Another view is that they may feel sleepy after eating. On the whole it is probable that the room and the direction of the wind have a greater effect on the pupils' behaviour!

7 Do not fill up a day with Technology, Games etc. — leave room in each day for Maths, English etc.

Unless you are conscious of this point you may find that you have given one class Art and Games on Tuesday morning followed by Technology all Tuesday afternoon. By squeezing Mathematics, Science, History etc. out of Tuesday you will necessarily squeeze them into the other four days of the week.

Your pupils may not truant on Tuesdays but perhaps they will be more likely to absent themselves on other days. Diploma-days may promote this effect.

8 Aim for an even spread along the rows (time) — with no clashes vertically (classes)

Again the colours of the cards are a great help. As s/he places or replaces each card, the timetabler should scan 'horizontally' along the rows to see the time interval between similar cards.

Of course the timetabler should already know the preferences of the different departments. Language teaching, which relies on the 'drip-feed' method, particularly in the lower school, will require an even spread throughout the cycle (preferably 5 single periods on 5 different days). Other subjects requiring regular practice, such as Mathematics, will need a similar consideration.

Sometimes the timetabler will have to judge between the requests of the staff and the requirements of the pupils. For example, some Mathematics departments are fond of double periods in the lower school. The attention span of undergraduates is said to be 20 minutes so the attention span of 12-year-olds must be rather shorter. This requires a determination by the teacher to provide a variety of experiences during the lesson — something not always in evidence in Maths lessons.

Sometimes scheduling tactics can help here — for example, scheduling a double period *across a break*. This gives the pupils the benefit of a break halfway through the lesson without having to pack their bags (and the benefit that they return to work after the ideal revision interval of 10–15 minutes).

It gives the teacher the benefit of being in one room for two periods and being able to develop a large topic if he or she wishes.

Science and Technology departments may sometimes ask for 'the last two periods in an afternoon followed by the first two periods on the next morning'. The timetabler will have to judge the advantages of these requests against the limitations imposed on the timetable.

The timetabler should check that a class does not have all the lessons in a certain subject during afternoons only (and certainly not always last period in the afternoon — such scheduling is given swift condemnation in the staffroom!).

Throughout this consideration of subject spread (along the rows), one overriding rule applies: there must be no clash vertically. That is, no two cards carrying the same initials can ever be in the same column at the same time (because a teacher cannot teach in two places at the same time).

Continuing in this way and dealing with all the activities shown on the priority lists, the timetabler will gradually bring across more and more cards from the feeder board, meeting and solving problems as he or she goes along.

S/he will probably schedule all of the Upper School and most of the Lower School in this way.

However, when all of the main priorities have been dealt with, there may come a time when it is not clear which part should be tackled next. This is where rules 9 and 10 are useful:

9 Fill in first those classes which are nearest to completion,

and

10 When filling in a class, concentrate first on the teacher whose personal timetable shows least freedom

A beginner might think that if some classes are 90% completed and others are only 50% completed, then it would be best to provide an even figure by concentrating first on the classes which are only 50% complete in order to bring them up to the 90% mark. This would be a mistake.

A class which is only 50% completed (and so 50% empty) has plenty of flexibility, many 'degrees of freedom'. Such a class can be left for a while.

A class which is 90% completed (and so only 10% empty) has less flexibility, fewer ways of being completed, fewer degrees of freedom. This class must be timetabled sooner.

Taking the extreme case, a class which has 24 of its 25 periods fitted has only one single period to be fitted and only one place to put it. This class should be tackled immediately by fitting the single period card into the empty gap or, if it causes a clash there, finding a 'musical chairs' solution that will solve the problem (see the diagrams in section 11.5).

One of the features of the card model is that the boards show you immediately what is yet to be fitted for each class and which class is the tightest and has priority to be tackled first. In action, the timetabler regularly scans the 'bar-chart' displayed by the cards on the feeder board, seeing which class has priority now and which classes will have priority soon.

That is rule 9. Rule 10 helps in those cases where, having found which class is due to be tackled next, you find that there is more than one teacher involved and you cannot decide which teacher to concentrate on.

The same principle applies: the teacher with the least flexibility, the fewest degrees of freedom, should be tackled first.

Identifying this teacher is not as straightforward as identifying the class.

It can be done by scanning the feeder board (or the main board, but by now this will be rather full) to count the number of unfitted cards for each of the teachers concerned. This allows you to calculate the degrees of freedom.

Degrees of Freedom

Knowing the number of unfitted cards, and the number of free positions for each teacher, will allow you to decide who has the least flexibility and so the highest priority. A simple guess is usually sufficient.

However, if you wish, you can calculate the degree of freedom by:

$$\text{degree of freedom, } f = \frac{\text{number of places for fitting this teacher's (or class's) cards}}{\text{number of cards yet to be fitted for this teacher (or class)}}$$

For example, if you wish to fit in 2 double periods for a particular teacher and there are 6 places in the week where a double could go, then $f = {}^6/_2 = 3$. Usually there is no need to calculate this number accurately, a 'guesstimate' is sufficient.

The value of f gives you a guide as to what to do:

(a) If f is much greater than one there is plenty of flexibility and no need for the timetabler to do anything yet.

(b) As f decreases and tends towards a value of one, the timetabler should consider it more and more as its priority increases.

(c) If $f = 1$ the card should be fitted immediately. This might be considered the ideal time. The ideal timetable might be thought of as one where every card in turn had a value of $f = 1$, so that a timetable was just possible while at the same time the Heads of Department and the timetabler had asked for the most they could get from the timetable.

(d) If it is less than one then you are in trouble and must give priority to fitting this card by moving other cards. See the 'musical-chairs' moves later in this chapter.

In these paragraphs we have been assuming a kind of repelling force as the cards on the feeder board force themselves off the feeder board and on to the main board. However, in the later stages of scheduling, when you may be fitting pure-class activities, you may find a slightly different situation.
This is when the blank spaces on the main board exert a kind of attractive force, pulling particular cards off the feeder to particular positions on the main board.

This change of emphasis arises because you may find that for a particular period in the week, the class is free and the room is free but only one of the staff is free and so must be fitted into that period. Sometimes you may find that none of the staff due to teach this class is free and then you must start 'musical chairs' moves with the cards in order to find someone who can take the class for that period.
This change of emphasis, from feeder board cards to main board blanks, comes only in the later stages of scheduling and is more difficult to see for a human timetabler (although a computer copes easily, by scanning every period regularly). If you have applied Zarraga's Rule (section 10.2) then you should have less difficulty with this problem.

For convenience, the 10 scheduling rules are listed again here:

1   Have all the information immediately available.
2   Link each teacher with a room where possible.
3   Start with the worst constraint, and/or large cards.
4   Look ahead to possible problems.
5   Consider carefully before saturating any period with a particular subject.
6   Consider the best time of day for subjects with some classes.
7   Do not fill up a day with Technology, Games etc. — leave room in each day for Mathematics, English etc.
8   Aim for an even spread along the rows (time) — with no clashes vertically.

In later stages:

9   Fill in first those classes which are nearest to completion, and
10 When filling in a class, concentrate first on the teacher whose personal timetable shows least freedom.

11.4   Worked example

To illustrate some of the rules given in the last section consider the simple and artificial scheduling problem shown here:

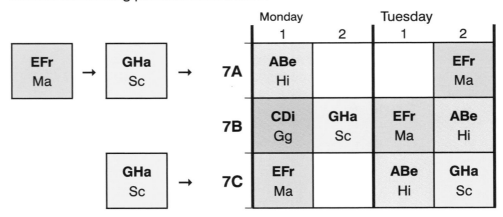

The diagram shows three Year 7 classes with their timetable partially completed and three activities yet to be placed.

The problem is to fit all the activities into the time-frame shown, in such a way that the two Maths lessons for 7A are separated as much as possible and the two Science lessons for 7C are also separated as much as possible.

You are urged to attempt this problem *before* reading the solution given below.

The first point to note is that there are only 4 teachers and 4 subjects involved in this simple problem. All the History is taught by teacher ABe, all the Science by GHa etc.

The second point is that adding even a small amount of colour to the diagram (for different subjects) makes it very much clearer to see the pattern.

Thirdly you will find the problem becomes very much easier to solve if you use **movable** coloured cards rather than pencil and fixed paper.

Rules 1 and 2 already apply. Rules 3 and 4 do not help us much in this artificial example although we might guess that Science has a higher priority than Maths. In this simple example we won't consider rules 5, 6, 7.

Rule 8 reminds us of the basic rules — the cards may only move along rows; the cards must not clash vertically.

We must decide where to start. 7B is already completed and should be disturbed as little as possible.

Rule 9 helps us to decide which class we should start with: 7C has less freedom and so is given the higher priority.

If the Science card for 7C is moved across to the empty space, it clashes with GHa taking 7B. ABe for 7C could move earlier to Monday-period-2 so that GHa for 7C could go in Tuesday-1, but this would put the two Science cards next to each other — the opposite to what was requested. A better solution is to move EFr for 7C to Monday-2 (no clash) and then place GHa for 7C in Monday-1 (so that the Science cards for 7C are separated as much as possible).

Turning now to 7A, we assume that the Science card has a higher priority than the Maths card (because of labs) and so bring it in first (rule 3). GHa for 7A cannot go in Monday-2 (clashes with GHa for 7B) but it can go in Tuesday-1 (no clashes).

Now we bring across the Maths card. EFr for 7A cannot go in Monday-2 (clashes with EFr for 7C) but if ABe for 7A is moved across to Monday-2 (no clashes) then EFr for 7A can go in Monday-1 (no clashes and the Maths cards for 7A are separated as much as possible, as requested).

This gives the best solution with the Maths and Science each separated as much as possible. Other (less good) solutions are possible. For example the whole of column 1 (i.e. Monday-1) can be interchanged with the whole of column 2 (Monday-2).

Now where did I drop Mrs Jenkins...?

11.5   Nine tactics and 'musical-chairs' moves

In the last example all the moves were very straightforward 'one-steps': a card simply moved into an empty space where it caused no clashes.
On a real timetable model the moves are often more complicated.
Some examples are given in this section.

Most of the moves are 'musical chairs' manoeuvres: the cards move round the timetable model until, hopefully, they all find a place to sit down.

In each of the following examples of tactical moves, it is supposed that the timetabler's attention is concentrated on the top left-hand corner of the diagram where teacher AB is shown to be scheduled for class 7A for period 1.

The aim of each move is to free teacher AB for period 1 *or* to free class 7A for period 1 *or* to free both class and teacher for period 1.

1.   A two-step to clear teacher AB from period 1

See diagram 1.
In this case a simple interchange, involving only class 7A, clears teacher AB from period 1 so that he may be used elsewhere for period 1.

This move depends on AB initially being free for period 4 and on teacher PQ initially being free for period 1 — otherwise they cannot move as shown.

The timetabler must scan the full length of 7A's row to find periods where these conditions apply. When the two periods concerned are not on the same day, the move may mean that one of your constraints is broken — for example it could mean that you will now have two periods of French on the same day whereas previously they were well spread.

2   A two-step to clear class 7A for period 1

See diagram 2.
This move involves two classes, not necessarily adjacent to each other.
The move relies on there being a symmetry about the positions of AB and the positions of the blanks for the two classes involved. In order to spot such a move, the timetabler need only look at cards for AB, and only those cards which lie in columns containing a blank for 7A.

As with all these moves, the result may be unsatisfactory, because it may spoil the period-spread that has been carefully built up with earlier placements.

3   A two-step to clear both teacher AB and class 7A for period 1

See diagram 3.
This useful move is quite easy to spot: the timetabler scans along the 7A row to find a suitable place for AB; if AB is teaching 7B at that time, the timetabler scans the 7B row to find a suitable place for AB to move to.

1. A 2-step move to clear teacher AB from period 1

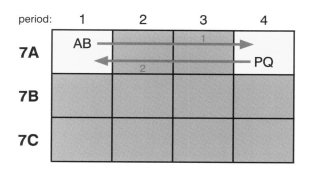

2. A 2-step move to clear class 7A for period 1

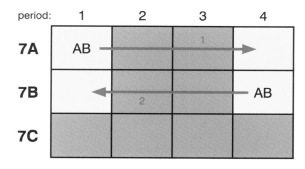

3. A 2-step to clear both teacher AB and class 7A for period 1

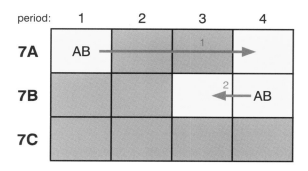

4   A three-step to clear teacher AB from period 1

See diagram 4.

The diagram is self-explanatory.   Three teachers are involved but only one class.

Of course the periods involved are not usually all on the same day (as shown in the diagram) but widely spread throughout the 25 or 30 periods of the week.

For all of these moves it is useful to mark possible positions on a manual model using coloured plastic markers (eg. Lego bricks). When making a large move these markers can also be used to mark the original positions in case the move does not work and you have to restore the original situation!

5   A three-step to clear class 7A for period 1

See diagram 5.

Three classes are involved but only one teacher.

As before, the result may upset your period-spread for the subject taken by teacher AB.

6   A three-step to clear both teacher AB and class 7A for period 1

See diagram 6.

This move involves finding a vacant place for AB in another row at another time (like move 3 but extended by a further step). Sometimes it is easier to look at this move backwards, ie. in reverse order.

Obviously these steps can be extended to give more complicated moves. Four-step moves are not too difficult and manual moves up to six-step are possible when coloured pegs are used as markers. In a computer program like *TimeTabler* it will do 16-step moves for you!

7   A combination of two two-steps to clear both AB and 7A for period 1

See diagram 7 on the next page.

Obviously combinations of two or more moves can be made.

This example is a combination of move 2 and move 1.

Alternatively it can be seen as a combination of move 3 and a simple one-step. Or a 3-step move.

It can be seen as a variation of move 6.

It involves two classes and two teachers, the result being:

AB with 7A period 4; AB with 7B period 3; PQ with 7B period 1.

4. A 3-step move to clear teacher AB from period 1

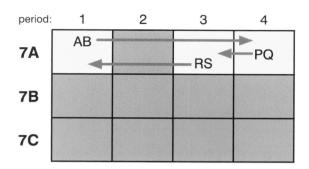

5. A 3-step move to clear class 7A for period 1

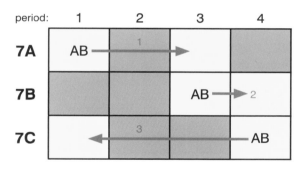

6. A 3-step to clear both teacher AB and class 7A for period 1

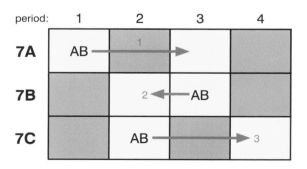

7. A combination of 2-steps to clear both AB and 7A for period 1

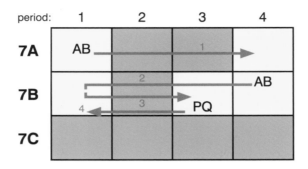

8. A multiple 2-step or 'roll-over'

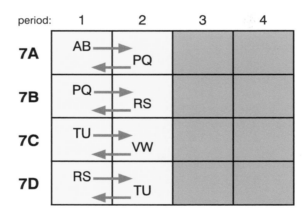

9. Interchanging teachers to clear class 7A for period 1

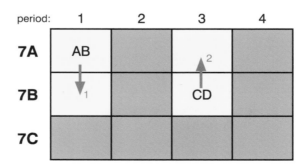

8 A multiple two-step or 'roll-over'

See diagram 8.

In this example, teachers PQ, RS, TU are teaching for both of the periods shown, while teachers AB and VW are teaching for only one period each.

By making the moves shown, AB will teach for period 2 instead of period 1.

This move is not the same as a total interchange of all of the column for period 1 with all of the column for period 2 (although, of course, this can be done). In this move only this set of interconnected teachers are interchanged, the rest of each column remaining unchanged.

This move relies on the last member of the chain reaction (in this case VW) being able to move. Because the move usually involves two adjacent periods (for example, the two halves of a double period) it is usually quite easy to see this move and to deal with large numbers of cards, for as many as a dozen classes.

A similar move can be used to clear a class. For example, if VW were missing from the diagram, the same set of moves could be used to clear class 7C for period 1.

There are two situations when a 'roll-over' move is particularly useful:

(a) At the rooming stage, when you wish to get AB into a specialist room which is available for period 2 but not for period 1.

(b) At the final polishing stage when you are trying to improve the quality of your timetable. This move may allow you to get a better sequence of events or a better traffic flow round the building (see also section 11.8). In this case the move can be used even if 'AB' and 'VW' are the same teacher, so forming a closed circuit.

9 Interchanging teachers to clear class 7A for period 1

See diagram 9.

This is a more extreme remedy. Suppose, in the example shown, that AB and CD are both Geography teachers. It may be acceptable to exchange classes, as shown, particularly if the classes are in the lower school and similar or equal in age, ability and number of periods.

If you make an exchange like this then:

(a) Remember that all the lessons of that subject for both classes must be exchanged or else you will have a split class.

(b) Remember to re-label the class names on all the cards involved.

(c) Explain to the Head of Department why it has happened.

You are more likely to need to make this move if you have not applied Zarraga's rule (section 10.2). In the example shown in the diagram, one might suppose that the move had to be made because none of 7B's teachers were available to take the class for period 1.

11.6   When something won't fit, what do I do?

As a guide to finding a solution in difficult circumstances, consider the following steps, in order:

1.   If you have a 'Sixth Form' (Years 12/13) then see also section 12.10.

2.   **Find a time in the week when the Class is free for the required number of periods.** Then:
(a)   Are the teachers (and rooms) free or able to be freed by 'musical-chairs' moves like numbers 1, 3, 4, 6, 7, 8, in the last section?
(b)   What constraints are violated by these moves — for example, does it give two periods of French on the same day, or PE and Games on the same day?

3.   **Find a time in the week when the required Teachers (and Rooms) are free for the required number of periods.** Then:
(a)   Are the classes free or able to be freed by 'musical-chairs' moves like numbers 2, 3, 5, 6, 7, 8 in the last section?
(b)   When looking to fit a double period, a good place to begin is where there is already a single blank on the main board. Then you can try to find a way of making that single blank grow into a double blank.
A variation on this method is to find a single period already fitted which can grow into a double period (displacing another card if necessary), thus leaving only a single period to be fitted.
(c)   Consider what constraints have been violated (see 2(b) above).

4.   **Find a time in the week when as many as possible of the required Classes and Teachers (and Rooms) are free.** Then:
(a)   Can the remaining classes and teachers (and rooms) be freed by 'musical-chairs' moves like those given in section 11.5?
(b)   As in 2 (b)above.

5.   If there is still no solution, can a solution be found by:
(a)   **Splitting multiples into smaller amounts of time?**
eg. a double becomes two single periods.
(b)   **Grouping periods into larger multiples?**
eg. two single periods become a double period (a good place to look is where one single is already fitted – see 3(b) above).

6.   If there is still no solution, **find a time when the Class(es) are free or can be made free.** Then:
Can suitable teachers (and rooms) be allocated by changing the specification of resources and using moves like number 9 in section 11.5?

7.   If there is still no solution you will have to consider changing the *curricular* structure — for example, breaking up a parallel setting arrangement.

11.7 Allowing for different period-breakdowns

A difficulty sometimes arises when two activities are in parallel on the curriculum, but require a different period-breakdown when they are scheduled.

Consider an example. Suppose a school decides to introduce a second foreign language, Spanish, for 4 periods per week, to two classes in Year 9, as an alternative to Design Technology (DT) and Food Technology (Fo).

Part of the Curriculum Plan might appear like this:

The problem
(on the
Curriculum Diagram)

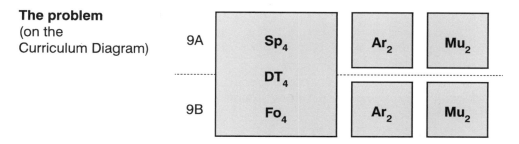

The difficulty arises because in this school Spanish requires 4 single periods while Design Technology and Food Technology prefer one quadruple period.

A possible scheduling solution is shown in this diagram:

The solution
(on the timetable model)

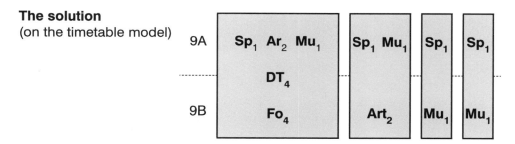

This solution requires that:

(a) about half the population of 9A and 9B takes Spanish, and

(b) the Music department agrees to single periods.

Differing period-breakdowns need to be considered carefully when they appear in any teacher-team.

For example, in Year 10 it is usually fine to put Technology subjects in an option block with Art or Science (or ICT? or Business Studies?) ...but if Technology needs a double-period then consider the consequences before putting a language in the same block.

See also the comments in section 4.5.

11.8 Improving the quality

Timetabling is essentially about the deployment of human beings.

The timetabler needs to think constantly about the effect of his actions on people — both pupils and staff.

Merely satisfying the arithmetical demands of the data to produce a workable timetable is not sufficient. We should provide a high quality, **enabling** timetable that will allow staff and pupils to give of their best.

When looking at the quality of your timetable, you may wish to consider the following aspects:

(a) There should be a good period spread, particularly in subjects like French and Mathematics. Hopefully the completed timetable will already show that the periods for each subject are distributed well, but if there are any flaws it is worthwhile spending some time in trying to improve matters. Straightforward two-step moves (like moves 1, 2, 3, in section 11.5) are the first things to look for.

(b) While making these moves it is worthwhile keeping a look-out for other situations such as 'French for period 1 followed by Spanish for period 2'. There will be less confusion if such similar subjects are separated by at least a break or a single period.

(c) The 'free' (non-teaching) periods for the staff should be well distributed. The importance attached to this will vary from school to school but it is worth considering, especially for those in weaker health or those who are frequent commuters in split-site schools. Again two-step moves provide the most likely solutions.

Some staff will want their 'frees' spread across the cycle, while others (perhaps senior staff or those with significant responsibilities) might welcome blocks of time, perhaps for visiting other institutions.

The number of staff free in any period should be as even as possible —this will be important for the person responsible for arranging 'Cover' for staff absences.

(d) The timing of lessons can have a strong effect on some classes of pupils. For example, Maths lessons which always occur late in the afternoon for a class of less able pupils can have disastrous consequences.

Scanning along the rows should show up any imbalances like this.

You may then wish to consider block exchanges — for example, exchanging the whole of one double period (across the entire timetable) for another double period.

Eight-period days with equal morning and afternoon sessions have a clear advantage here — for example, you might exchange the whole of Tuesday morning for the whole of Tuesday afternoon.

The 2-2-2-2 school day has a further advantage: in theory any quarter of a day can be exchanged for any other quarter.

In practice there may be difficulties with any exchange: fixed points for swimming, consortium activities, part-time staff, etc. will prevent an exchange of those periods.

A good sense of judgement is needed before any exchange: improving the timetable for one class almost always means *dis*improving the timetable for another class.

(e) The sequence of two single periods can be important. For example, consider these two possibilities for French and PE:

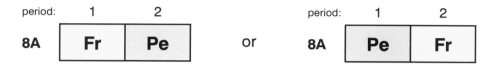

The first is clearly the better arrangement. In the second the pupils are likely to arrive at the French lesson hot, damp, late and possibly volatile.

(f) As a further example of the importance of the sequence of two lessons, consider the following simple case study.

Mr M, a Mathematics teacher, is weak; the pupils leave his lessons in some disorder, feeling very lively, perhaps frustrated at his poorly structured lessons.

Mr G, a Geography teacher, is middle-aged, has good discipline but requires standard situations, promotes a rather inflexible classroom atmosphere.

If you were to schedule Maths for period 3 followed immediately by Geography for period 4 then the pupils are likely to have a poor Maths lesson followed by a lesson where Mr G reacts against the lively mood of the pupils as they arrive boisterously at his classroom. In turn, the pupils are likely to react against his rather inflexible manner and a poor atmosphere results.

If, instead, you were to interchange the two lessons then the pupils could well have a good Geography lesson followed by a Maths lesson as good as before (or perhaps better, if some of Mr G's calmer influence carries over to period 4).

After two or three timetables, most of these considerations will come naturally to the concerned timetabler. Knowing the school well and observing it in action, he or she will instinctively feel doubtful about some combinations of teacher, class, room, time of day, day of week, traffic route and previous or following lesson.

It is for these reasons that the timetabler needs a sound knowledge of teaching and of the school — see also Appendix 3.

11.9 'Oliver Cromwell' Worked Example

The sheets for this example are in a PDF **on the CD** at the back of this book. Please use that PDF to print out the sheets, to cut out the lesson cards, and then move them around on a timetable grid (also provided in the PDF), to solve the problems posed below.

Place your movable cards in this starting position:

	Monday 1	2	3	4	Tuesday 1	2	3	4
7A					7A G.Chaucer English		7A B. Russell Maths	7A O.Cromwell History
7B	7B G. Boole Maths	7B M. Faraday Science	7B O.Cromwell History	7B A. Renoir French	7B G. Boole Maths	7B M. Faraday Science	7B A. Renoir French	7B G.Chaucer English
7C	7C O.Cromwell History		7C G.Chaucer English	7C W.Hamilton Maths				

The PDF on the CD gives you the remaining (unplaced) activities, like this:

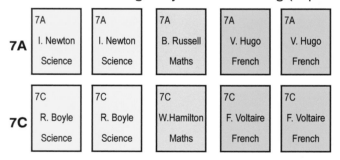

Your task is to complete the timetable according to the usual timetabling rules (see section 11.3) and the further information below. Remember that each additional task 1-10 listed below is in **addition** to previous demands.

Some solutions are given at each stage. Try not to cheat by looking first! And try not to cough or sneeze your cards out of position!

Task 1:
Complete this simplified timetable by placing all the remaining cards.
Assume that you can move **any** of the cards on the grid (in a real timetable this may not be possible because of clashes with the teachers of other classes).

Task 1 continued:

Now check your timetable for quality. For example, for each class the two Science lessons should be on different days. Similarly for French and Maths. Is any subject placed at the end of both days?

Does the pattern of each day feel right from a learner's point of view?

Comment 1: At this stage there are many possible solutions.

For example, without disturbing 7B at all, we get:

	1	2	3	4	1	2	3	4
7A	Fr	Ma	Sc	En	Sc	Fr	Ma	Hi
7B	Ma	Sc	Hi	Fr	Ma	Sc	Fr	En
7C	Sc	Fr	En	Ma	Sc	Ma	Hi	Fr

Task 2:

The Head of Maths now reminds you that you promised to ensure 'setting' in Maths across all three classes in Year 7.

Can you ensure this happens on Monday and Tuesday?

Re-check for quality as in (1) above.

Comment 2: Again there are several solutions. Here is one with Maths in period 1 each day (and still not disturbing 7B):

	1	2	3	4	1	2	3	4
7A	Ma	Fr	Sc	En	Ma	Fr	Sc	Hi
7B	Ma	Sc	Hi	Fr	Ma	Sc	Fr	En
7C	Ma	Fr	En	Sc	Ma	Sc	Hi	Fr

Task 3:

Your school is short of laboratories, and because of the requirements of other year-groups, **only one** laboratory is available in each period for Year 7.

Can you achieve this **as well**? Re-check for quality as in (1) above.

Comment 3: One solution (of several) is:

	1	2	3	4	1	2	3	4
7A	Ma	Fr	Sc	En	Ma	Fr	Sc	Hi
7B	Ma	Sc	Hi	Fr	Ma	Sc	Fr	En
7C	Ma	Fr	En	Sc	Ma	Fr	Hi	Sc

Task 4:

Similarly, all three classes for French need the **same** language lab. Can you ensure that **only one** class is taking French at any time? (**In addition** to all the earlier requirements.) Re-check for quality as in (1) above.

Comment 4: One solution is shown:

History & English are acting as the lubricants here.

	1	2	3	4	1	2	3	4
7A	Ma	Fr	Sc	En	Ma	Hi	Sc	Fr
7B	Ma	Sc	Hi	Fr	Ma	Sc	Fr	En
7C	Ma	En	Fr	Sc	Ma	Fr	Hi	Sc

Task 5:

The Head of Science points out that two extra laboratories can be freed elsewhere, and requests that Science be setted across these three classes, 7ABC. Is this possible? If not, he will settle for 7A and 7B being setted together (on both days). Can you achieve this **and** maintain the condition for French in (4) above? Re-check for quality as before.

Comment 5: It is not possible to 'set' Science across all 3 classes (while keeping all the previous requirements for Ma and Fr). However it is possible to 'set' Science across 7AB. One solution is:

	1	2	3	4	1	2	3	4
7A	Ma	Fr	Sc	En	Ma	Sc	Hi	Fr
7B	Ma	Hi	Sc	Fr	Ma	Sc	Fr	En
7C	Ma	En	Fr	Sc	Ma	Fr	Sc	Hi

Task 6 :

Your timetable still has some flexibility. What alternative solutions can you find?

Task 7:

O. Cromwell, a part-timer, says he will only be available for mornings (ie. periods 1 and 2). Can your timetable satisfy this condition **also**?

Comment 7: One solution is shown here:
This shows a complete swap between Tuesday 1-2 and Tuesday 3-4.
Note that because of Oliver Cromwell, Sc and Ma both now go at least once in the afternoon, and one of these subjects has to be in the afternoon on both days.

	1	2	3	4	1	2	3	4
7A	Ma	Fr	Sc	En	Hi	Fr	Ma	Sc
7B	Ma	Hi	Sc	Fr	Fr	En	Ma	Sc
7C	Ma	En	Fr	Sc	Sc	Hi	Ma	Fr

Task 8:

G. Chaucer, the Year-Tutor for Year 7, traditionally has his 'free' periods before and after lunch (ie. free for periods 2 and 3). Can you achieve this **as well** ?

Comment 8: If Chaucer is to avoid teaching periods 2 and 3, then we need a 'roll-over' of Monday 1-2 and also of Tuesday 1-2, to give:

	1	2	3	4	1	2	3	4
7A	Fr	Ma	Sc	En	Fr	Hi	Ma	Sc
7B	Hi	Ma	Sc	Fr	En	Fr	Ma	Sc
7C	En	Ma	Fr	Sc	Hi	Sc	Ma	Fr

Task 9:

Finally, O.Cromwell asks you to arrange for him to teach 7A immediately after 7B on Monday morning so that he can use the same materials conveniently! Can you attain this condition in addition to **all** the others ?

Comment 9: This is more tricky (while maintaining ALL the previous requirements) but can be done in 3 steps:
(i) For 7A, swap Chaucer (Mon-4) with Cromwell (Tues-2).
(ii) Swap all of Tues-2 with Tues-4 (so Chaucer is not used in periods 2–3).
(iii) Swap all of Mon-4 with Mon-2 (so 7A History follows 7B History).

	1	2	3	4	1	2	3	4
7A	Fr	Hi	Sc	Ma	Fr	Sc	Ma	En
7B	Hi	Fr	Sc	Ma	En	Sc	Ma	Fr
7C	En	Sc	Fr	Ma	Hi	Fr	Ma	Sc

The knock-on consequence of Cromwell's request is that Maths is now in the afternoon, as shown.

Task 10:

What flexibility is left in your (section of the) timetable? ie. what interchanges can still be made ?

Comment 10: There is still some flexibility (while keeping **all** the previous conditions):
a) Monday & Tuesday could be entirely interchanged.
b) Monday periods 3 & 4 can be swapped.
c) Tuesday periods 2 & 3 can be swapped, so one Maths lesson is in the morning.
d) In 7C, Hi and Sc can be interchanged on Tuesday (followed by a swap of Tuesday periods 1 & 4 to keep Cromwell free in afternoons).
e) Combinations of these.

Of course in a real timetable you would be limited by all the teams that had already been assigned for other parts of the school. But you wouldn't necessarily have to be kind to Oliver Cromwell!

11.10 Order of Scheduling : an outline

See also sections 10.4 (Priorities) and 12.10 (scheduling the Sixth Form).

1. Fixed Points and external constraints.

2. Years 11 and 10, because there are large teacher-teams.
    [Perhaps also include any large 'unique' teams in Years 12 and 13?]
    At each stage 'unique' teacher-teams take priority over teams with choices/alternatives, especially if they include part-timers.
    And 'large cards' (big teams and multiple-periods) take priority.

3. Large teacher-teams from Years 9, 8, 7.

4. Smaller teacher-teams, in descending order of size.
    [Including other Sixth Form teams.]

5. At later stages watch out for:
    * nearly complete classes,
    * nearly complete teachers,
    and complete them first (see section 11.3).

Within each of these 5 stages you will need to take account of the many other constraints such as part-timers, shortage of specialist rooms, pattern of lessons throughout the cycle, and other priorities discussed in section 10.4.

One of the advantages of using timetabler software is that it is quick and easy to experiment and try different routes, particularly at stages 2, 3, 4 above.

11.11 Rooming

With the exception of some specialist rooms, the allocation of rooms is usually left until the timetable is completed (and inspected for quality).

The ideal rooming allocation would give each teacher his preferred room and put each class into one particular room for all its periods in that subject.
Whether you can do this depends on the value of the rooming fraction (and how closely the number of pupils divided by the number of teaching spaces approaches 21, see chapter 9).
If you cannot allocate a particular class the same room for all its lessons in a particular subject, it should always be possible to fit the lessons into a maximum of two rooms. It would be quite wrong for a class to have its five French periods in five different rooms. Learning (as well as teaching) is partly a matter of habit, and pupils need the security of the same room, same desk, same walls, same teacher to support their learning habits. Perhaps the ideal timetable would also ensure the same time of day for every French lesson.

You may wish to delegate some of the rooming to the relevant Heads of Departments. For example, the Heads of the Science and Technology departments can be expected to allocate their specialist rooms. Delegating in this way will not only lighten your load, but also will give other members of staff a greater understanding of your problems and perhaps a greater appreciation of your efforts.

Of course in timetabler software you can specify each teacher's first/second/ third Room preferences (which may be different for different age-groups, eg. in a split-site school).

Clearly specialist rooms are allocated before considering general classrooms. At this stage you may need to consider the capacity of (small) rooms.

When allocating rooms it is worthwhile considering how they will affect the traffic-flow round the building. This is particularly true if your school is geographically well spread out. It is wearisome for pupils (particularly younger pupils) to trek long distances for each lesson, and wearisome for the staff as pupils arrive late for the lesson. You can often help the traffic-flow by a simple 'roll-over' on the schedule (as described in section 11.5 part 8), though you need to check whether it disadvantages other classes.

A list of the rooms left free for each period of the week will be needed during the year (eg. when organising an exam timetable).

If you are using timetabler software these free rooms are listed automatically and printed on demand or displayed on the school web-site.

Remember that there will often be room changes during the first few weeks of term (as colleagues swap), so be prepared for this and the need to update timetable printouts.

11.12 Dealing with Specialist Rooms at different stages

A summary of how to consider these Rooms at stages of the timetable. See also section 11.11 on Rooming.

- Schematic Diagram stage (see chapter 4)
  Check the number of groups against the number of rooms. eg. if only one Drama space, two Drama teachers cannot appear in the same time-slot.

- Combing Chart stage (see chapter 7)
  You can include specialist rooms in the clashes that prevent combing, especially useful if Subject Leaders draw their own chart.

- Conflict Matrix stage (see chapter 8)
  Include specialist rooms as clashes on the grid.

- Rooming fraction (see chapter 9)
  This can give you a priority order of rooms.

- Scheduling stage
  On a manual model show specialist rooms on the cards before you start.
  Of course in timetabler software you can specify a specialist room for any activity, so the software can ensure that no clashes occur.

11.13 Checking the timetable

When you have finally completed the scheduling and apparently fitted all the information correctly on to the model, it is wise not to heave too large a sigh of relief until you have checked it.

On a manual model the first check is to look up and down each column very carefully, to ensure that you have not used (a) any teacher and (b) any (specialist) room twice in the same time-slot.

If you are using timetabler software then of course all this checking is done for you automatically. The program will ensure that clashes are impossible, so that the timetable is guaranteed to work when term starts.

The second check is to scan along the rows to check the rhythm and pattern of the lessons for each subject (to see that they suit the pedagogy of each particular subject), and to look for the timing of particular lessons.

For example you may feel instinctively that the combination of Mrs Murray teaching Maths to class 10Z for the last lesson on a Friday afternoon is not a good combination. Even if you are using timetabler software you will need to do this check, because only the 'computer between your ears' can make these human judgements.

Using timetabler software will guarantee no conflicts, so that you can be sure that the timetable will work when term starts. But if you are working manually you will be nervous until the end of the first timetable cycle. Remember Sod's Law: *'If something can go wrong, it will, and at the worst possible time'*.

The method of checking this aspect of the timetable at one school was remarkable. Late in the summer term, all the staff and pupils were given copies of the new timetable and then the school bells were rung every five minutes. Each five minutes represented a full period on the new timetable, which the pupils and staff tried to follow, bell after bell, so that a full school week was simulated in about three hours! This was followed by a staff meeting to discuss the new timetable!

Uh-oh? What do you mean 'uh-oh'?

11.14 Printing and Publishing the timetable

This can be a chore (if you are using a manual model then it is a huge chore). The box shows some of the printouts you may need:

'Master' timetables

1. A master **Class** timetable showing all the classes in the school, year by year, with their teacher / subject / room for each period.
2. A master **Staff** timetable showing all teachers, either alphabetically or more usually by departments, with their class / subject / room for each period.
3. A master **Room** timetable showing all rooms, in the most logical order, with the teacher / class / subject occupying them in each period.

4. A **Departmental** (subject) timetable showing all the teachers in that department (with their class / subject / room in each period).
5. A **Year** (or 'House' or vertical-group) timetable, showing all the classes in that Year with their teachers / subjects / room for each period.

Individual timetables

6. Individual **Class** timetables, showing the teacher / subject / room for each period.
7. Individual **Teacher** timetable, showing his/her class / subject / room.
8. Individual **Room** timetable showing its class / teacher / subject.
9. Individual **Student** timetable, showing his/her subject / teacher / room for each period, including their specific choices in the option blocks to ensure a smooth start to the new term for the students.

'Free' timetables

10. 'Free Staff' timetables, showing which teachers are 'free' in each period.
11. 'Free Room' timetables, showing which rooms are 'free' in each period.

Each of these timetables can be produced by timetabler software and:

- Printed on paper, as a Booklet (eg. 1 – 3 above).
  This is probably the most efficient way to keep all your colleagues informed and also to allow them to locate colleagues or classes during the year.

- Printed on paper, as individual sheets (eg. 4 – 11 above).
  This is the most common way to give out individual student timetables (or whole class timetables to lower school classes).
  See also the specific printouts listed on the opposite page.

- Printed as an HTML web-page, to be:
  – sent as an email attachment to colleagues,
  – posted as a web-page on the school intranet or web-site, for access by staff, students and by parents (who have legal rights to this information).

11.15 Printouts of the timetable

As well as a general timetable booklet for every member of staff, some people also need specific printouts:

Who needs it? Why?	What do they need?
Subject Leaders / Heads of Department • Need to locate members of their department • Need to know when their specialist rooms are free	• Staff timetable for the department eg. all the Maths dept. • Room timetable for the department eg. for the Technology rooms
Science technicians / other technicians • Need to know which lab a teacher is in • Need to know when labs are empty	• Room timetable for the Science labs, and other specialist rooms
Heads of Year / Year Leaders • Need to locate members of their team • Need to locate students in their year	• Staff timetable eg. of all Year 10 tutors • Class timetable eg. of all the Year 10 classes
Head of Learning Support • Need to locate members of the team	• Staff timetable for everyone who does learning support
Daily Cover Organiser • Need to know who is free to do Cover • May need to move a class from a specialist room to an empty room	• 'Free staff' timetable • 'Free Rooms' timetable If they are using 'StaffCover' software then all this will be known by the program – but give them paper copies for when they are away from their office
Examinations Secretary • For organising exam timetable cover / location	• 'Free Rooms' timetable • 'Free Staff' timetable • Year 11 / Year 13 timetables
Caretaker / Site Manager • Needs to know when rooms are empty for maintenance jobs	• 'Free Rooms' timetable • Perhaps a 'master' Room timetable
Reception / Office Staff	Ask them. It depends on what software they have available in order to locate a teacher or student.

The printouts can vary in size from compact 'wallet-size' sheets (with a small font) to large posters for the staffroom wall, in black-and-white or with the lessons in subject-colours.

If you make all the different versions available as web-pages on the school intranet, then not all these paper copies may be needed.

With timetabler software you can design the timetable printouts that you want:

11.16 Printing out timetables

Using timetabler software allows you to full control.

You can to choose to:

- print out different sizes, with different fonts,
- design the layout for each cell of the grid ie. decide the position of the teacher's name, class name, subject, room, set number, block label, etc.

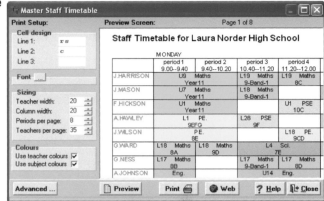

A 'master' Staff Timetable : Design Screen

- add subject or faculty colours for clarity,
- print out on paper, or as HTML web-pages for emailing or for your web-site.

11.17 How do you know when the school timetable is becoming close to impossible?

As timetabler you rarely know how much flexibility you have, or how close you are to the limit. Each year, Subject Leaders ask for new features, you supply these new features, and the following year staff expect to keep the old features and any new ones that they ask for. Or the school's Curriculum Working Party, perhaps looking at the latest initiatives proposed by the government, ask for new features, new demands on your skills.

The timetable tends to spiral upwards towards some invisible ceiling of possibility, and as timetabler you don't know how close you are to this limit.

So it's important to evaluate the timetable regularly (see section 11.19).

If you are close to the limit there are some symptoms that begin to appear. For example, you will be making more and bigger compromises, such as:

- Requested double-lessons appearing as two singles (and vice-versa).
- Requested single lessons appearing as two on the same day.
- Split classes: teaching-groups that were intended to have one teacher for all their lessons now have two or more teachers during the cycle.
- The Combing Charts of several departments start to overflow the desired range (see section 7.7).
- If you have a 'Sixth Form', an increasing number of lessons appear 'out of block', during minority time or at lunch-time or as twilight extra lessons.

11.18 Alternative timetable structures

Some aspects of different timetable cycles have already been discussed in sections 2.21 and 2.22.
And in section 7.8 we looked at a non-rectangular week as a way of releasing resources (particularly specialist rooms).

A modification of the same idea leads some schools to adopt a **staggered lunch break**. In a 6-period day, this might require half the school to work a 4-lunch-2 day while the other half operates a 3-lunch-3 day, like this:

	Monday						Tuesday
Year 11					lunch		
10					lunch		
9				lunch			
8				lunch			
7				lunch			

In this arrangement a 6-lesson day is treated as a 7-period timetable structure. It allows Years 10-11 to use valuable lab space etc while Years 7-8-9 are eating, and vice-versa. It may help with misbehaviour during lunch-time, and relieve pressure on dining facilities.
Note that Years 7-8-9 now have a 3-3 day which has fewer double-periods in it which may be a problem for fitting Technology etc (see also section 7.8).

A rather different idea is that of a '**Modular**' or 'Grid' or 'Granular' timetable. This is based on the idea of a module of time, say 15 minutes.
French might request 2-module lessons (= 30 minutes), Maths might want 3-module lessons (= 45 minutes), while Science and Technology might want 5-module lessons. Break might be 1-module; lunch 3-modules, etc.
An alternative structure is based on 20-minute modules.

A problem arises in fitting in compatible units of time; this is partly solved by having staggered breaks as well as staggered lunches for each class, though the resulting noise from those classes having break isn't helpful to those classes still in lessons. Similarly with the noise of (some) classes moving every 15 minutes.
In constructing the schedule you'll find that having lessons of 1-, 2-, 3-, 4-, 5-modules makes it more difficult to find 'musical-chairs' moves, especially if the length of the morning or afternoon session is not compatible with the modules you want to fit. If you have a 24-module day it is probably best thought of as 8:8:8.

If you are thinking of changing your structure then you are strongly advised to do some 'What if...?' experiments first. Timetabler software allows you to try out many experiments quite quickly and easily.

11.19 Evaluating your timetable

Many timetablers are easily tempted to ignore this topic, partly because it is a difficult thing to do satisfactorily. However, it ought to be attempted, preferably during the first half-term of its operation. Inevitably the result will be a matter of opinion.

You'll need to decide who to ask and how to ask them. The boxes (on this page and opposite) show some possibilities:

Among the criteria that you might consider are essential for a quality timetable are the following:

1. The timetable should enable, support and project the school's educational philosophy. It should comply fully with the required setting and option structures. All constraints imposed by part-time teachers and fixed points (e.g. linked courses) should be observed absolutely.

2. There should be a good distribution, rhythm and pattern of subjects throughout the school week. Students should have a good balance of staff (age, expertise, gender, teaching style). Each day should have a balance of types of activity, and academic subjects should not appear consistently late in the day. No class should have two teachers for the same subject unless this was planned.

3. Staff timetables and individual teaching loads should be as close as possible to those requested by the Head of Department, in terms of classes, period-breakdown and rooms requested. Each teacher's timetable should be well distributed, with a good pattern of 'PPA' or free time. Part-timers should not have unpaid 'trapped time'.

4. There should be optimal use of the school's resources, particularly specialist rooms. Travel, and particularly hurried movement, should be kept to a minimum.

See also the list in section 11.17.

You mean that merely because the Head of Science can't be in two places at once, you want me to change all this?

Evaluation methods:

1. You could give all the staff a questionnaire, though this may inadvertently raise expectations for next year.

2. Keep your ears open in the staffroom.

3. Raise it casually with individual Subject Leaders, particularly those that are well aware of their colleagues and are also analytical and not unreasonably demanding.

4. Analyse (with the clarity of hindsight) the printed timetable, looking at bad (and good) patterns (eg. only 2 lessons for a teaching group with both of them in the afternoon).

5. Analyse the patterns of PPA time and 'free' periods.

6. Analyse traffic patterns between lessons if yours is a school with widely separated teaching areas.

7. Analyse commuting patterns if yours is a split-site school.

8. Use some shoe-leather to walk the corridors, both during lesson-change-over times and during lesson-times, observing the timetable in action.

9. Where there are restricting structures on the timetable (eg. setting in French in Year 7) investigate whether your colleagues are actually using the possibilities of this structure ...if not, then before next year's timetable you can discuss abandoning that structure in order to implement someone else's request for something new.

10. At a meeting of Subject Leaders in the Autumn Term, have an agenda item 'Good things about this year's timetable'.

11. Ask some Heads of Year to have a look at the timetable from a student's point of view (maybe talking to a few students) to get their perspective.

12. Ask the School Bursar / Admin Officer to conduct a survey of all non-teaching staff, to see how the timetable impacts on their work.

Did you know that if you read this backwards it says something quite rude about the Head?

11.20 Summary

One of the most important factors in developing a good quality timetable is the choice of a good model — be it manual or using timetabler software — one which suits you and is **flexible** in use.

Although guides to rules and tactics have been given in this chapter, it is practice which gives a timetabler the skill and fluency in manoeuvring the 'jig-saw' pieces to get a solution.

However, quality is what really matters and this can only be obtained by a timetabler who, in addition to having the skill, also knows well the teachers (and their preferences and strengths, foibles and failings) and knows the school and regularly observes every part of it in action.

According to Simpson's timetable, he's got himself teaching one lesson of PE every three weeks!

Now if you could just agree to be in two places at once, it would help me enormously...

12 Scheduling 'Sixth Forms'

By a 'Sixth Form' we mean Years/Grades 12-13 (the older term of 'Sixth Form' is still often used).

Most of what has been discussed in previous chapters applies to the Sixth Form as well, but there are two main differences that affect our scheduling in Years 12 – 13.

- It is customary for Sixth Form students (aged 16–19) to have non-teaching ('free' or 'study') periods.
  ie. they do not have a teacher for every period of the cycle, which gives some freedom and flexibility to the timetabler.

- It is customary for teaching-groups to have shared teaching ('split classes') by design. For example, the students have 5 periods of Maths: 3 periods with Mr Smith and 2 periods with Mrs Jones.
  Although this may have arisen from the desire to give more teachers some Sixth Form experience, it is very helpful to the timetabler as it gives more flexibility. Timetabler software can take good advantage of this flexibility to give you more solutions.

It is often thought that schools with Sixth Forms are more difficult to schedule, but this is usually not true. There may be more data to handle than in an 11–16 school, but there is usually more flexibility as well.

Because of this misconception timetablers often feel that they must start by scheduling the Sixth Form, but often it is better to schedule Years 11 and 10 first — the main criterion is the size of the teacher-team, see section 11.10.

12.2 Curricular structures in the Sixth Form

	A	B	C	D	E
Year 13	Bio	BSt	Che	Gg	Art
	Lit	ThSt	FMa	Ger	PE
	Fre	Ma	D&T	Psy	Re
	Phy	Mus	Sp	His	Soc

For larger Sixth Forms (>100 students) the common format is 4 or 5 blocks of subjects (eg. at AS or A2 level), from which the students choose up to 4 or 5 subjects to study.
For smaller Sixth Forms, see section 12.9.

These options blocks are heterogeneous (see section 3.3).
They are usually changed from year to year to accommodate the wishes of the particular population of students, and are usually designed using options software (see chapter 3 and the CD at the back of the book).

Each block typically occupies around 16–20% of the timetable cycle.
There may be an extra column for whole-year Games, or for Tutorials (PSHE).

12.3 Minority time

	A	B	C	D	E
Year 13	Bio	BSt	Che	Art	KeySkills: Maths
	Lit	ThSt	FMa	Gg	KeySkills: English
					General Studies
	Fre	Ma	D&T	Psy	Maths units
					ASDAN
	Phy	Mus	Sp	His	Careers/PSHE

In this model the 'Minority' studies are all in one block, so as to be accessible to all students.
The timetabler will often use the last block's time to schedule subjects from the main blocks that otherwise won't fit (see section 12.10).
An alternative model, giving more flexibility is discussed in section 12.6.

In all these digrams it would be helpful to the timetabler if the blocks filled only 95% of the timetable cycle. The 5% spare would prove invaluable during the scheduling stage, and would get filled by lessons which were impossible to fit in the blocks because of other parts of the school. See also section 12.10.

12.4 Shared minority time

	A	B	C	D	E
Year 13	Bio Lit Fre Phy	B St Th St Ma Mus	Che F Ma D&T Sp	Art Gg Psy His	Minority Subjects KeySkills: Maths KeySkills: English General Studies Maths units ASDAN Careers / PSHE
	P	**Q**	**R**	**S**	
Year 12	Art Sp Ma Lit	Psy B St F Ma Bio	Gg Che Mus Fre	Phy Th St D&T His	

In this model, block E is common to both years.

The other blocks may or may not be linked. ie. in some schools Block P must co-exist with Block A; Block Q with BlockB, etc., to give more choice to the students.

12.5 Courses spanning option blocks

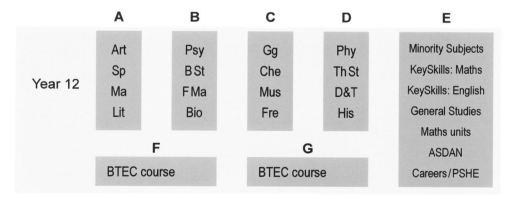

	A	B	C	D	E
Year 12	Art Sp Ma Lit	Psy B St F Ma Bio	Gg Che Mus Fre	Phy Th St D&T His	Minority Subjects KeySkills: Maths KeySkills: English General Studies Maths units ASDAN Careers / PSHE

In this model the Block F for longer courses (eg. BTEC certificate) spans two (or more) AS/A2 blocks. In principle students could study F + C + D + E. Schools may also have IB (International Baccalaureate) blocks in parallel with the AS/A2 blocks.

12.6 The idea of 'spread'

Consider this simplified diagram, with the 'Minority' subjects kept in their own block:

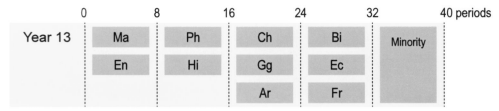

In this school the 'Minority' subjects are given the same priority as the subjects in the main blocks, but this may not be an accurate reflection of the school's objectives. If, instead, the 'Minority' subjects are left until later in the scheduling process, to be fitted in where they can, then this allows the main blocks to **spread**, like this:

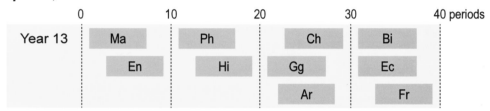

The 'minority' subjects will now be timetabled (later) into the gaps between the main blocks giving you more flexibility (but of course not all minority subjects will be available to all students, unless you duplicate subjects).

This policy allows the subjects in each block to spread over a greater number of periods (10 periods for each 8-period subject in the diagram).

This has two timetabling advantages:

1 It will be easier to fit this scheme against the Year 11 and Year 10 teacher teams (on average, fewer resources are needed in each period).

2 It allows subjects within the same block to have different period-breakdowns. In this example, if required,
Ch could be scheduled as [a Triple + 2 Doubles + 1 Single],
while Gg is scheduled as [3 Doubles + 2 Singles],
while Art is scheduled as [4 Doubles], like this:

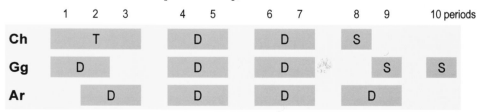

It is possible to vary the amount of spread allowed. This is an advantage if some pools are more difficult to schedule than others. For example: two 'easy' pools kept to 8 periods each and two other 'difficult' pools allowed to spread over 12 periods each.

Other permutations are possible. For example: two of the option pools allowed to spread over 10 periods each, two pools kept to only 8 periods each, leaving 4 periods for common activities (eg. General Studies, Games).

Of course, the decision about the importance of minority subjects should be taken as a matter of policy (bearing in mind the advantages to the Sixth Form and to the main school), rather than merely as a matter of scheduling expediency.

12.7 Aligning the blocks

This suggestion (from the Qualifications & Curriculum Authority, QCA) argues that Sixth Form blocks should:
(i) have fixed subjects (unchanging from year to year), and
(ii) be aligned in a consistent pattern.
The claimed advantage is that students could see the combinations that are available to them over the two years.

For example (with a common Block E, and each block having a Double and 2 Singles):

period:	Monday 1	2	3	4	Tuesday 1	2	3	4	Wednesday 1	2	3	4	Thursday 1	2	3	4	Friday 1	2	3	4
Year 13	A	A	E	D	B	B	C	D	C	C	A	E	D	D	B	C	E	E	A	B
Year 12	C	C	E	B	D	D	A	B	A	A	C	E	B	B	D	A	E	E	C	D

In this example, if each AS/A2 subject in Years 12–13 had 4 periods per week (20%) and each GCSE subject in Years 10–11 had 2 lessons per week (10%) then QCA further argue that it might be possible to align the Sixth Form blocks with blocks in Years 11 and 10, like this:

period:	Monday 1	2	3	4	Tuesday 1	2	3	4	Wednesday 1	2	3	4	Thursday 1	2	3	4	Friday 1	2	3	4
Year 13	A	A							A								A			
12	C	C							C								C			
11	Sc	B							Sc								B			
10	D	DT							D								DT			

This is a 'block timetable', see also chapter 13.

Of course the more year-groups that join in this alignment, the less flexibility for scheduling the rest of the school, making it less likely that you can provide setting in lower school. It is a question of where your priorities lie.

12.8 Looking for more flexibility in the Sixth Form

Two ideas currently being proposed are:

- The 'flexible day'
  This is a variation on the 'non-rectangular week' (see section 7.8), whereby the Sixth Form is scheduled in 'twilight time'. For example, the main school has a 6-period day and the Sixth Form has a 7-period day.
  This has to be carefully negotiated with staff, students and parents.

- The 'Fifth Hour' project
  This uses the notion of extra time to encourage staff to re-think the relationship between taught lessons and independent learning. For example, each A-level subject is taught for 4 hours per week; an extra (fifth) hour is scheduled for the students but no teacher is scheduled. The students go to the room at the specified time and undertake activities specified by the teacher, but without the teacher being present. The teacher has to think in terms of preparing students' learning, not their own teaching.
  An increasing number of schools are using this scheme and it is likely that this system will permeate lower down the school in future.

Shared teaching

Each of those ideas can give the timetabler more flexibility for scheduling the Sixth Form, but probably the biggest boon to the timetabler is the shared teaching of subjects (see the introduction to this chapter).

The more this happens in the Sixth Form, the more inherent flexibility there is for scheduling.

For example, suppose Block A is staffed like this:

Some students have 5 periods of Maths, 2 with AB and 3 with CD.
Other students have 5 periods of History, 3 with RR and 2 with JC, etc.

Year 12	Block A	
Maths:	AB_2	CD_3
History:	RR_3	JC_2
Physics:	KJ_2	BP_3
French:	DK_4	JW_1

When you are looking for times when Block A can be scheduled, you can use times when the following teams are free:

	AB + RR + KJ + DK
or	CD + JC + BP + JW
or	AB + JC + KJ + JW
or	AB + JC + BP + DK
	etc, etc.

You can use any of these permutations, as long as all the lessons stay within the container block.

There is a lot of flexibility here. It is not so easy for the human eye to see the best choices, but timetabler software is particularly good at finding these solutions.

12.9   Schools with small Sixth Forms

If your school has a small Sixth Form (eg. less than 80–100 students) then a blocked timetable as discussed in sections 12.2–12.8 may not suit your students. There are two reasons:

- You will probably be very keen to hold on to these students, even if they wish to choose very unusual combinations of subjects.
- Because they are fewer in number, they are unlikely to have chosen all the possible permutations of subjects. This means you may be able to schedule the Sixth Form timetable by ignoring blocks entirely, and just looking at the students' clashes.

There are two ways of doing this:

1.   Using computer software

If you are using software, just specify what you want.
For example, using *TimeTabler* software you can enter:

12A	DSSS	KJo **jsm** otw nni dco ...
12B	DSS	MWa abe **jsm** cde ...
12C	DSSS	PMu ghi mno stu ...

The first line is saying that we need to schedule Year 12 Art (12A), for a Double-period and 3 Singles (DSSS), with teacher KJo teaching students John Smith (**jsm**), Oliver Twist (otw), Nicholas Nickleby (nni), David Copperfield (dco), etc.

Similarly for Year 12 Biology (12B) with teacher MWa and some students.

However, because student **jsm** is common to both Art (12A) and Biology (12B) these two groups will never be scheduled at the same time. **jsm** cannot be in two places at the same time.

On the other hand 12C (Chemistry) can be scheduled at the same time as either 12Art or 12Biology because they have no resources in common.

The software takes care of all this for you. It will produce a timetable where sometimes 12Chemistry is at the same time as 12Art and sometimes at the same time as 12Biology, or at the same time as any other subject with no clashes. The resulting timetable does not have any kind of block/column structure, but does satisfy the requirements of the students.

This method is also useful for scheduling students in special schools, with individual learning programmes.

2.   Working manually

If you are timetabling manually then you'll need to draw a Clash table (as in chapter 3), either manually or using options software.
For example, see the diagram on the next page.

As before, the Clash Table is symmetrical about a diagonal. The crosses on the diagram show where there is a clash for this particular group of students.

Clash Table for Year 12 (L6)

	Ma	En	Ph	Hi	Ch	Gg	Ar	Bi	Ec	Fr
Ma	X		X		X			X	X	
En		X		X		X	X	X	X	X
Ph	X		X		X	X		X	X	
Hi		X		X			X	X		X
Ch	X		X		X			X		
Gg		X	X			X			X	X
Ar		X		X			X	X		
Bi	X	X	X	X	X		X	X		
Ec	X	X	X			X			X	
Fr		X		X		X				X

In this simple example the option blocks in Year 12 were:

> Ma *or* En
> Ph *or* Hi
> Ch *or* Gg *or* Ar
> Bi *or* Ec *or* Fr

Inspection of the Clash Table shows that the grouping of subjects could be changed (for some or all of the scheduled periods) if the change would help to schedule other classes in the school.

For example, from the Clash Table shown above:

with	Ma *or* Hi Ph *or* En
or, with	Ma *or* Gg *or* Ar Ch *or* En
Alternatively, with	Ch *or* Ar *or* Ec *or* Fr Gg *or* Bi etc.

Having some flexibility in these Sixth Form option blocks allows the timetabler to put a lower priority on the scheduling of the Sixth Form, and so give a better quality to the scheduling of the main school.

This method is also valuable even if you have a block structure in Year 12. The chances are, even in big Sixth Forms, that not all the possible permutations were actually chosen in Year 12 (and some students may have left). So when you come to schedule **next year's** Year 13 there may well be some flexibility. A Clash table like the one above will show you where this flexibility is.

Timetabling

12.10 When something will not fit, what do I do?

Please see section 11.6 for a number of solutions. See also section 12.8.

When an activity in the Sixth Form will not fit because the teacher is unavailable there is an additional set of solutions. The usual way is to schedule the rest of the activity (block) with this teacher missing, and then find another time when the teacher and that specific group of students are free together.

There are several possibilities:

1. Can the subject be fitted into another Option Block? i.e. will any of the students have a clash of subjects? – a Clash Table will tell you, see the end of section 12.9.

2. Can the subject be fitted into a space where no lessons are scheduled for that year-group? If so, this lesson then becomes a 'reserve slot' for any other subjects from that same option block.

3. Can the students involved miss out on some 'general' provision to fit in the lesson? Can they miss P.E., Games, General Studies, Tutorial work, 'Minority' time, etc.

4. Can the lesson be run over lunchtime? (with a protected free being given to the teacher in lieu).

5. Can the lesson be run during registration and assembly? (may need a slightly earlier start for those students).

6. Can the lesson be run as a 'twilight' session? (with a protected free being given to the teacher in lieu). See section 12.7.

7. Can the lesson be run with two half-groups of students? (If some are free for one period and others are free for another period - with a protected free being given to the teacher in lieu).

8. Can the students be taught for one lesson with the other part of the Sixth Form? (i.e. a combined Years 12–13 Lesson). This is easier in some subjects (eg. Art, History) than in others (eg. 'linear' subjects like Maths, French).

9. Can the idea of the 'Fifth Hour' be applied to this subject (see section 12.7).

Some of the above actions can be carried out by the timetabler and some are left to the teacher/Subject Leader to deal with at the start of term, depending upon size of group and other circumstances.

All these additional potential solutions suggest that the Sixth Form should not be the starting point for your schedule. Instead the starting point should usually be (i) Fixed Points and then (ii) large teacher-teams (see section 11.10).

12.11 Summary

Although most considerations from earlier chapters apply here, scheduling the Sixth Form has a slightly different flavour because of its different characteristics, which provide additional flexibility to the timetabler.

13 Block timetabling

'Block timetabling' is an ambiguous term. In some schools it just refers to a timetable which has some blocks in it (eg. a block of 4 Maths sets in Year 9).

In the United States of America it refers to a timetable with larger blocks of time than was traditionally the case. For example, a common pattern in the US now is '4 x 4' scheduling where the students study in four 90-minute blocks of time each day of an 18-week semester.

The 'Block' timetabling or 'Faculty' timetabling or 'Consistent Blocking' that is discussed in this chapter is an attractive idea, and commonly used in universities though rarely in secondary schools, for good reasons.

In essence the school timetabler decides the basic structure of the timetable but the details of the schedule are left to individual faculties. An example was shown in section 12.7.

This method is in contrast with the method that has been taken in this book from chapter 6 onwards. We assumed in those chapters that Subject Leaders 'pre-staff' the Curriculum Diagram by specifying in advance who should teach each group, before we start to build the schedule. In Block timetabling the reverse is used.

What do you mean, you don't want to teach Classical Studies
— What kind of Dinner-lady are you?

13.2 Simple 'consistent blocking'

The 'Consistent Blocking' method is feasible only where the school is organized into true faculties or where it is easy to form natural ad hoc 'faculties' for the purpose of timetabling. It enjoyed a brief popularity in some schools in England in the 1980s. The schools divided their teaching staff into 5 curricular areas. For example a school in Oxfordshire had the following 5 teams of staff:

A	B		D	E
English & Expressive Arts	Community Studies	Science & Technology	Mathematics	Recreation

From this a blocked timetable structure can be compiled very easily.
For example:

	Monday					Tuesday
	1	2	3	4	5	
Year 11	A	B	C	D	E	....
10	B	C	D	E	A	....
9	C	D	E	A	B	....
8	D	E	A	B	C	....
7	E	A	B	C	D	....

This timetable structure was then given to Heads of the 5 teams, to decide the actual staff teaching each group.

This sounds delightfully simple. However the model assumes (i) that no staff teach in more than one area and (ii) that all 5 areas have an equal allocation of time!

While (i) can be dealt with by negotiation between the relevant Team Leaders, and (ii) can be solved by adjustments to the grid above, nevertheless the resulting timetables often had poor quality, with a large number of '**split classes**'. For example, class 7A is due to have 4 periods per week of English but it is impossible to arrange for the *same* English teacher for all 4 lessons.

13.3 Another consistent blocking model

Another variation on the last model is to pair departments consistently. The blocking is consistent in the sense that Maths and Science (grading pupils by similar criteria) are paired together for a year group. Similarly English and Humanities are usually paired together.

The result of this blocking may show, for example, that on Monday period 1 (a 60-minute period) the Maths and Science 'faculties' each have half of Year 7 and half of Year 8. (See the diagram on the next page.)

This information is then passed to the faculty timetabler (or to a faculty meeting) to decide the details of which teacher will take which group in which room.

If they wished, the Maths and Science faculties could agree to exchange the two halves of Year 7 after 30 minutes on Monday morning so that the pupils have a shorter period of each subject.

	Monday	
	1	2
Year 8 Band A	Ma + Sc team	
8 Band B		
Year 7 Band A	Ma + Sc team	
7 Band B		

Among advantages claimed for this method are: the teachers at the chalkface can have a greater say in determining the timetable that rules their days; the faculty can decide whether to employ mixed-ability teaching, team-teaching or setting by ability; departmental meetings are more easily arranged; cover for absent staff becomes a responsibility of the faculty.

The arrangement makes it easier to 'accelerate' gifted and talented students. In the diagram a Year 7 student can join Year 8 lessons. See also section 2.17.

13.4   Block scheduling in Scotland

Traditionally a different variation of Block scheduling has been used in Scotland. In this Scottish method the timetabler looks for *triplets* of columns. That is, a column for the S3 yeargroup, one for S4, and one for S5/6, that are compatible. The subjects in a column may be written on strips of paper (or in a spreadsheet) and the strips are moved against each other until a viable arrangement is found.
See the diagram on the next page.

In practice S3 and S4 may each have up to 11 columns and S5/6 may have 5. Subjects and option columns may be 'cross-set' as shown in the diagram for Ma and En in S3 columns E and F.

In the diagram, the triplet shown would need 3 Art teachers and 3 Business Studies (BS) teachers to service it, and the timetabler can easily decide if this is feasible (by the number of teachers and number of specialist rooms).

If (typically) the S5/6 subjects have 5 periods, and the S3, S4 subjects have only 3 periods, then you need at least two compatible triplets to service the S5/6 requirement. For example 5A+4B+3F for 3 periods and 5A+4C+3B for 2 periods, with the remaining periods for 4C and 3B used elsewhere.

Once the timetabler has a viable pattern of triplets then:
(i)   The 'schematic' can be given to Heads of Departments, for them to assign the specific staff to each group, and
(ii)   Vertical slices of the schematic can be cut up and assigned to particular time-slots of the timetabling cycle.

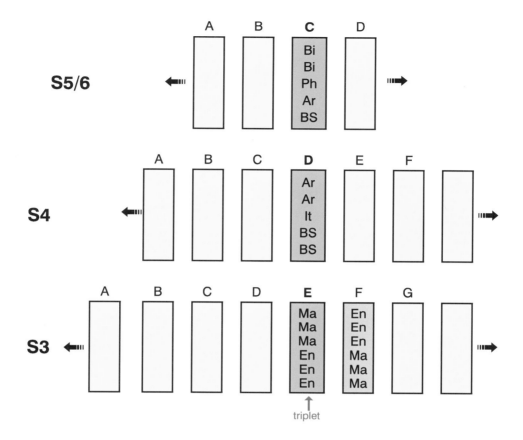

Although it looks simple at first sight, it requires a lot of skill by the timetabler to end up with wholly viable triplets.

As before the significant disadvantage of this blocking method is the resultant number of 'split classes' and their effect on the pupils' learning.

It also relies heavily on Heads of Departments having sufficient expertise to assign their staff efficiently in order to minimize the number of 'split classes'.

13.5 Summary

Although these ideas may seem attractive, in practice there are difficulties.

Consistent blocking may be impossible to implement because of the difficulties in forming natural 'faculties', either because of staffing or more often because of specialist accommodation, and it is particularly difficult if any of the option pools are heterogeneous.

Block scheduling of triplets has been traditional in Scotland but there is now a distinct movement towards the 'pre-staffed' timetable described from chapter 6 onwards.

14   Scheduling in Primary Schools

14.1   introduction
14.2   The balance of subjects
14.3   The structure of the timetable
14.4   Timing of subjects
14.5   Fixed points
14.6   An example
14.7   Summary

Timetabling in primary schools is usually a simpler affair than in secondary schools and takes less time.
Consideration of quality and rhythm are just as important, but because the structures are less complex, it is normally easier to find a good solution quickly.

Although there is less need for timetabling software, using a computer program can still bring clear benefits, not least because of the professional printouts and the ease of updating any changes during the course of the year. For example, if there are staff changes, or if some subjects are taught in bigger blocks of time but for one term only.

This short chapter gives an overview of the main considerations when timetabling for Key Stage 1 and Key Stage 2.

14.2 The balance of subjects

In England the government has recommended a minimum of 21 teaching hours per week for children in Key Stage 1 (ages 5 – 7) and a minimum of 23½ teaching hours per week for children in Key Stage 2 (ages 7 – 11).

These hours are *teaching* hours, exclusive of registration, breaks, lunch, and collective worship.

Within these hours, the government's Qualifications and Curriculum Authority (QCA) has suggested the following subject times as 'starting points', for schools to add to if they wish.

Key Stage 2

Subject	hours (h) minutes (m) (approx average per week)	Total hours/year (36 weeks)	%
En	5h — 7½h	180 – 270	21 – 32%
Ma	4¼h — 5h	150 – 180	18 – 21%
Sc	2h	72	9%
D&T	55m	33	4%
ICT	55m	33	4%
Hi	55m	33	4%
Gg	55m	33	4%
Art	55m	33	4%
Mu	55m	33	4%
PE	1¼h	45	5%
RE	1¼h	45	5%
Totals	19¼ — 22½h	690 – 810h	82 – 96%*

* leaving some slack for individual schools to bias their curriculum.
Figures for Key Stage 1 are similar.

Within these guidelines, schools need to decide which subjects will be taught separately and which will be integrated, at each age.

The school will also need to decide which subjects are to be taught daily (eg. Literacy, Numeracy) and which are to be taught weekly (eg. PE, Science?). Other subjects may sometimes be grouped into bigger bundles of time, and alternated each half term. For example, a double-period of History one half term, and a double-period of Geography the next half term.

Where a subject is taught as a separate subject, either daily or weekly, then it is easy to check that the total number of hours per year falls within the desired range. However with multi-dimensional project work or topics this is more difficult.

14.3   The structure of the timetable

Most primary schools use a 'rectangular week', with the structure for each day identical. There is usually not the same need to free up specialist rooms and resources as in a secondary school, see section 7.8.

But even if you use a rectangular week, the lessons in a day do not have to be equal in length (see below).

Most primary schools now have 3 periods in the morning (with a break) and usually only two in the afternoon (with a break if it is an infants school).

Lesson length : In practice lessons vary in length from 20 – 60 minutes, or even 75 minutes at Key Stage 2. When deciding the lesson-length for a subject you need to consider that lessons involving sustained writing, or un/dressing time (PE) or clearing-up time (eg. D&T) all need longer times.

If you use longer times for other subjects you will need to consider whether your staff can make effective use of the longer time.

14.4   Timing of subjects

Often Literacy and Numeracy lessons are placed in the morning, though not necessarily in the same sequence every day.

A problem that arises is that resources that are shared across the school (eg. the Hall for PE, or an ICT room) cannot be used effectively because the Literacy and Maths lessons may prevent these resources being used in the morning. This is exacerbated if the Hall is used for lunch and so cannot be used for PE immediately before or after lunch. Putting some of the Literacy and Maths lesson in the afternoon can help, and gives the children some variety.

Some schools discuss and adopt as policy some outline rules, such as:
- Most of the Literacy & Maths lessons should be in the morning, but not all.
- Every morning session should include a non-core subject.
- Longer lessons (double-periods) should only be in the afternoon.

This system can give a pattern such as:

	1	2	3	4	5	
Mon	Lit	Ma				....
Tues	Ma		Sc	Lit		....
Wed	Lit	Ma				....
Thurs	Ma		Sc	Lit		....
Fri	Lit	Ma				....

When adding the other subjects, and thinking of the rhythm and pattern of the week, you will need to consider if a child's day is likely to be balanced, by considering how the subjects are likely to affect the balance between:
- practical work and 'paper' learning,
- whole class, group, and individual work.

14.5   Fixed points

When you start the schedule, the first items to be placed will be the 'fixed points'. For example:

● Assemblies
● Fixed points such as the use of a Sports Hall at a local secondary school, or the availability of a pool for swimming, or the timing of an internet video-conference with children in another country.
● PE, to make effective use of the Hall. Similarly with any other specialist learning-space (eg. an ICT room).
● Any vertical grouping with older/younger children; and any horizontal grouping with another class of the same age, to ensure the times coincide.
● Part-timers, or job-share teachers, especially if they are the only ones to offer some specialism (eg. French) or if they are Support Teachers and you wish their support to be offered during the Literacy and Maths lessons.
● Any fixed times for staff exchanges or 'bridging' courses with the local secondary school.

14.6   An example

Finally, here is an annotated example of part of a primary school timetable:

Monday

Registration	ASSEMBLY	Literacy	break	Maths	Science	LUNCH	Registration	Daily French	RE	Music
10	15	60	15	50	50	60	5	10	55	55 minutes
	①	②						③	④	⑤

①   Some schools have Assembly at the end of the morning or in the afternoon.
②   In this sample day, Literacy & Maths are shown in the morning but they can well be in the afternoon on some days.
③   Some schools have a short spell at a fixed time of day for quiet Maths, or reading, or in this case a daily dose of French.
④   In this sample there are two lessons (RE, Music) in the afternoon, but some days the whole afternoon can be given over to History, or Art & Design, or project work.
⑤   Schools with children at Foundation Stage and Key Stage 1 are likely to have a break in the afternoon.

14.7   Summary

Primary school timetables are neither as rigid nor as complex as those of a secondary school, but they still need careful attention if the school is to benefit from a timetable with the right rhythm, pattern and quality.

15 Timetabling by Computer

15.1 Introduction
15.2 An electronic computer v. the human 'computer'
15.3 What to look for in a timetabling program
15.4 The 4 steps in timetabling software
15.5 Computer timetabling compared with manual timetabling
15.6 What can timetabler software do for you?
15.7 Exporting the completed timetable to your MIS
15.8 Summary

There has been a huge change in timetabling practice over the last thirty years because of the computer.
In the 1970s a few people timetabled using enormous mainframe computers. There is an apocryphal story about a Deputy Head who spent a whole day typing his timetable data into a mainframe computer terminal.
The computer whirred and flashed its lights and eventually typed out, as its solution, the single word 'No'.
'No what?' typed the Deputy Head in a fit of rage at the idiot machine.
The machine hesitated and then slowly typed out 'No *Sir*'.

The key to progress has been the availability of fast personal machines and the design of software which allows the machine and the human timetabler to be complementary to each other, and to have a 'symbiotic relationship' as a biologist would say. This is explored in more detail in this chapter.

In earlier days, to ask a timetabler to do more than one (manual) timetable in a year would likely have caused a nervous breakdown. Today, you can a run a 'What if...?' experimental timetable and have the answer before you have finished your cup of coffee.
In earlier days, a timetabler might puzzle for two hours trying to solve a 4-step 'musical-chairs' move. Today with a computer you can have 16-step moves at the click of a mouse.

There are a number of timetabling programs on the market, including *TimeTabler*, Nova-T, gp-Untis and others that are more ephemeral. Try typing 'school computer timetabling' into Google to see what is available at present. (Note: 'school' is needed or you may see a lot of pricey university programs.)

Inevitably most of the illustrations in this chapter are from the ***TimeTabler*** program, because this is the software that we know best. There is a Tutorial copy of ***TimeTabler*** on the CD at the back of this book, together with a PDF of its step-by-step Tutorial Booklet.

15.2 An electronic computer v. the human 'computer'

The electronic computer and the computer 'between your ears' have different advantages and disadvantages when using them for timetabling.

A modern computer is extremely fast. It can do in one minute what would take you over a century! It doesn't forget what it's told, and it doesn't get tired like we do.

By contrast you are good at making judgements of quality, and you know a lot about your school (all the things that you don't know that you know, until you find yourself using them).

So the ideal is to work in *partnership*, with the electronic computer doing all the donkey-work, at high speed, while *you* make the quality judgements about the human factors.

electronic computer	human 'computer'
• fast	• slower
• accurate	• can overlook or forget things
• does not forget	
• meticulous	
• never bored or tired	• easily bored
so	but
• it can do what you can't do,	• you know a lot about the school and human factors, and you can make quality judgements,
but	
• it only knows what it is told.	
	so
	• you can do what a computer can't.

so we need partnership, task-sharing ('symbiosis')

For this to work well you need to choose a software program that works with you. It's a bit like buying a car : any car will get you from A to B, but some have a style or features that suit you better, and get you there faster, more easily.

15.3 What to look for in a timetabling program

On the CD there is a PDF with a comprehensive CheckList of features that you ought to expect in the timetabling program of your choice.

It is also worthwhile asking around to see if you can find someone who has used two or more different programs.

Timetablers who have only ever used one program are often unaware of the range of features that a good program has.

The full CheckList is on the CD:

What to look for in a timetabling program
The program should:
Screens:
 • be intuitive ✔
 • have friendly screens ✔
etc, etc

Help & Support
 • have a Help button on each screen ✔
 • have a fully-illustrated manual ✔

Scheduling
 • be designed by experienced timetablers ✔
 • emulate manual timetabling models ✔
etc, etc

Printing & Exporting
 • have fully-customisable printouts ✔
 • export to SIMS .net, RM, Phoenix, etc ✔
 • produce web pages for your web-site ✔

15.4 The 4 steps in timetabler software

In using any timetabler software there are basically 4 steps:

Step 1 is to tell the program the names of your teachers, subjects, rooms, etc. Usually you can import this data from your MIS if you wish.

1.	Enter the Basic Data
2.	Enter your Activities
3.	Schedule the timetable
4.	Print, Publish & Export it

Step 2 is to enter details of the activities you wish to schedule on this timetable (usually in bundles or batches, perhaps one Year group at a time).

Here are 3 examples (in *TimeTabler*):

Example 1

7A   SSS   KJo

means that you want to schedule class 7A with teacher KJo for 3 Single periods (on 3 different days).

Example 2

7A   DD   MWa

means teacher MWa for 2 Double-periods (on different days) for the class 7A. (The teacher's subject and room-preferences have been entered earlier.)

Example 3

8ABC   DSS   KJo MWa CJo

means that you want the program to schedule all of 8A+8B+8C for a Double and 2 Singles with 3 teachers (KJo, MWa, CJo) teaching at the same time, in parallel. ie. 8ABC students will be divided between these 3 teachers (so it could be 3 Maths sets, or it could be 3 Technology groups on a termly rota, or it could be an option block of 3 subjects ...all 3 scenarios are basically the same scheduling requirement).

Step 3 is the actual scheduling stage, when the activities that you entered in step 2 are now scheduled to particular times of the week.
This can happen in any of 3 ways:

- **Interactively**
  The computer does the donkey-work, leaving any decisions to you.
  This is ideal for the final timetable that you actually use.

- **Semi-automatically**
  In this mode the computer takes some decisions for you, but leaves the important decisions to you.
  This method is often useful when doing the later stages of a timetable (eg. the lower school) when it is often 'hard to see the wood for the trees'.

The Main Menu in *TimeTabler* follows the same 4 steps.

Sub-steps give you extra features,
for example:

Availability for dealing with the availability of part-timers, non-rectangular weeks, etc.

Check & Validate for automatically drawing a Combing Chart, a Curriculum Diagram, Zarraga's Rule, etc.

Check & Tidy gives you tools for polishing your completed timetable.

Export allows you to export the completed timetable to SIMS .net, Facility, RM, Phoenix, PASS, iSAMS, SchoolBase, and other MIS systems.

The on-line SupportCentre contains a large Knowledge-Base with Help and articles about timetabling.

- **Fully-automatically**
  This is especially useful for doing 'What if...?' trials and experiments. 'What if...?' we provide more setting in Year 8 next year? Or 'What if...?' we introduce more diplomas next year, etc. The speed of a modern computer means you can have a 'solution' within a few minutes ...but of course it won't have the quality that you get using the 'interactive' method.

Any time that you hit a problem (a 'kickout'), you will probably need a musical-chairs move like the ones shown in section 11.5. The software will give you musical-chairs moves (up to 16-step moves) at the click of your mouse, and divided into 3 different levels of quality so that the best one can be used.

The algorithms used by the software are a mixture of mathematical ones (based on timetabling theory) and heuristic algorithms (based on many years of timetabling experience).

Step 4 is to Print and Export your timetable.
The printouts come in a wide variety of styles (see sections 11.14 and 11.15) and they can be customised to the style and size that you want.
They can be printed on paper, or as HTML web-pages (which you can email to colleagues, and put on your school's web-site).
The completed timetable can also be exported to your school's admin system or 'MIS' (see section 15.7).

15.5 Computer timetabling v. Manual timetabling

If you've been timetabling manually, you may be wondering why experienced timetablers think that using computer software is better.

Here are 10 reasons for you to consider:

1. Computers don't forget what you tell them.
   A timetabler's worst nightmare is forgetting that Mrs Jones (a part-timer) doesn't work on Fridays, and accidentally using her on Friday ...and then not finding out until the first Friday of the new term!

   If you tell timetabler software that a teacher is not available at particular times, it does not forget.

2. Another timetabling nightmare is accidentally double-booking a teacher (or a class) ...so that Mr Smith has to be in two places at once!

   Timetabler software won't allow you to double-book a teacher, or a class (or a room unless you tell it to).

3. Computer programs are meticulous, and don't get bored or weary.
   They are excellent at following specific rules and checking your data.

   If a timetable works in *TimeTabler** then it is guaranteed to work on the first day of term.
   No more anxious fears during the summer holidays and at the start of term.

4. But computer programs are not as clever as 'the computer between your ears'. And a computer program can never know all that you know about your school and your colleagues!

   The ideal relationship between an electronic computer and your brain is a symbiotic one:
   -- the electronic computer works at incredibly high speed, finding solutions for you to look at,
   -- while you use your personal judgement, and all that you know, to decide which solution to use.
      eg. the computer might suggest as one solution that Mrs Murray can teach 9Z on Friday afternoon
      ...but you know instinctively that this would not work well, so you choose a different solution from the list.

   TimeTabler* has a very friendly & intuitive interface, so that the electronic computer and the 'computer between your ears' work well together.

   You are in charge; but the computer does the donkey-work.
   You are not so tired. You are more likely to get a quality timetable ...this is good for you, good for your colleagues, and good for your students.

5. The Visual Builder Screen in *TimeTabler** (see section 15.6) is constantly prioritising your timetable data, and suggesting which lesson you should place next (though of course the choice is yours).

   *TimeTabler** guides your way through the timetabling process, all the way.

6. If you get stuck, and can't immediately see a solution, then the **FIT** button in *TimeTabler** will do millions of 'musical-chairs' moves and give you a list of possible solutions, for you to choose from.

   *TimeTabler** software can find timetabling solutions a million times faster than you can.

7. Are you introducing Diplomas? Joining a consortium? Vertical grouping? Or introducing 'primary' features into Year 7?
   Or changing the options blocks?   What effect will these changes have?
   Doing experiments to see 'What if...?' is almost impossible if you work manually.

   With *TimeTabler** you can easily do 'What if...?' investigations when changes to the curriculum are proposed.

8. And when you've finished your timetable, how do you print it and publish it?

   With *TimeTabler** you just click a button to get a printout.

   You have control over the shape & size & style of the printouts ...for teacher timetables, for class timetables, for room timetables.

   In glorious technicolour if you wish.
   And you can send timetables to colleagues by email. And you can publish them on the school web-site.

   And you can **export** the completed timetable electronically into your school admin MIS, such as SIMS .net, Serco-CMIS-Facility, RM Integris, Phoenix, WCBS/PASS, iSAMS, SchoolBase, Bromcom, etc., etc.

9. Someone going on maternity leave? Or leaving part-way through the year? And their replacement can't take exactly the same classes?

   With *TimeTabler** it is easy to re-jig the timetable when it is necessary.

10. Needing help with a tricky part of the timetable?

    *TimeTabler** is fully supported by experienced & expert timetablers.

    The software has Help buttons throughout, HelpMovies, a printed Manual with dozens of Worked Examples, and a 24/7 fully-searchable KnowledgeBase on the dedicated Help & Support Centre.

*   The parts marked * may not apply to other timetabling software — you will need to check this.

15.6 What can timetabler software do for you?

Different timetabling programs have different features and different screens, but here is an example, from **TimeTabler** (see the CD).

It is called the **Visual Builder Screen**. It helps you to build up your timetable interactively, in a very visual and intuitive way.

In the example below, the activity about to be placed is: **10B   S   LM AJ AT HI**
ie. a **S**ingle-period lesson, for Class **10B**,
with 4 Teaching-Groups (teachers **LM**, **MJ**, **AT HI**),
and it is about to be placed on Tuesday-period-1.

Follow boxes 1 to 12 to see how it works:

4. Just drag the lesson (with your mouse) to where you want it to be, and let go.

You can **only** place it in green positions, where the class is free **and** the teachers are free.

TimeTabler will **not** let you make a mistake.

As simple as that. So easy!

1. The list at the left hand side shows the 'top-ten' Priority List.

TimeTabler has calculated these for you, by looking ahead and using complex algorithms.

Each row shows a lesson, in priority order.

Click with your mouse to select any of them. It turns yellow to show you it has been selected.

Here the User has decided to place item no. 7, even though it is not top of the Priority List.

You choose, you decide.

3. Fuller details of the selected (yellow) lesson are shown in this top area.

2. When you select a lesson to place, a Class Timetable Strip (upper) and a Staff Timetable Strip (lower) are displayed.

These show the Class and the Staff needed **for the lesson that you have selected.**

Interlinking classes are also shown for you. The relevant Class row is highlighted in yellow.

You can see who is free, and when.

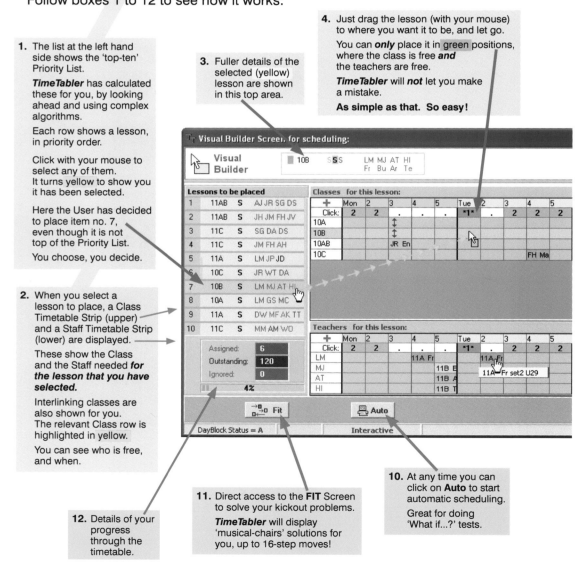

12. Details of your progress through the timetable.

11. Direct access to the **FIT** Screen to solve your kickout problems.

TimeTabler will display 'musical-chairs' solutions for you, up to 16-step moves!

10. At any time you can click on **Auto** to start automatic scheduling.

Great for doing 'What if...?' tests.

This particular screen is used when you are working interactively, but you can switch to semi-automatic or fully-automatic working at the click of your mouse.

Like every other screen it has a Help button to give you immediate Help about that screen.

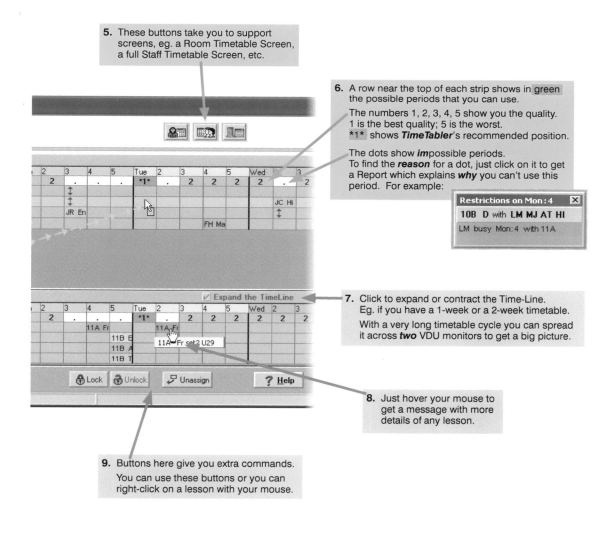

5. These buttons take you to support screens, eg. a Room Timetable Screen, a full Staff Timetable Screen, etc.

6. A row near the top of each strip shows in green the possible periods that you can use.

The numbers 1, 2, 3, 4, 5 show you the quality. 1 is the best quality; 5 is the worst.
1 shows *TimeTabler*'s recommended position.

The dots show *im*possible periods.
To find the **reason** for a dot, just click on it to get a Report which explains **why** you can't use this period. For example:

Restrictions on Mon:4   ☒
10B D with **LM MJ AT HI**
LM busy Mon:4 with 11A

7. Click to expand or contract the Time-Line. Eg. if you have a 1-week or a 2-week timetable.

With a very long timetable cycle you can spread it across *two* VDU monitors to get a big picture.

8. Just hover your mouse to get a message with more details of any lesson.

9. Buttons here give you extra commands.
You can use these buttons or you can right-click on a lesson with your mouse.

15.7   Exporting the completed timetable to your MIS

Of course once your timetable is completed you usually want to export it into the school's MIS (admin system).

The export will transfer all your timetable data into the MIS, so that all parts of the MIS can use the timetable information.

Ideally, the export will also transfer the curricular structure of your timetable. The reason for this is that the timetabler software knows the 'eligibility rules' for your curricular structure. ie. it can give information to the MIS about which teaching groups a student is eligible to be placed in, or at least allow the MIS to provide your office staff with only valid choices when they are assigning students to particular Maths sets or to particular option groups in Year 10.

In the past not all timetabling software could transfer data to all MIS. This has been changing slowly, but with the advent of SIF it should be accomplished more easily.

SIF (formerly **S**chools **I**nteroperability **F**ramework, now renamed **S**ystems **I**nteroperability **F**ramework to reflect its wider role), is a government-backed system that transfers the data in one school system into another school system. This allows timetabler software to talk to any MIS system.

15.8   Summary

Timetabler software can help you to produce higher quality timetables, more quickly, by doing the donkey-work for you and releasing you to consider the human judgements that are the basis of all good quality timetables.

Free period!?
But you had one of
those last year!

16 Doing the daily Cover for absent staff

16.1 Introduction
16.2 Using Cover software
16.3 Summary

As soon as your masterpiece of a timetable is printed and published it is almost immediately damaged!
It can be 'damaged' in three ways:

- During the first fortnight of term your colleagues are likely to make some 'private' room-swaps. You need to ensure that such swaps are reported to you so that you can update the 'master' timetable.

- Events may take place that need an alteration to the daily timetable.
  eg. suspending the timetable for 'project days' or for examinations.

- Some of your colleagues are absent and so are not available in school in order to fulfil the requirements of your timetable.

There are many reasons for teachers being absent.
They may be ill at home, or visiting the doctor or dentist or the hospital. There may be family illness or bereavement. They may be doing jury service or magistrate's duty, or attending an exam meeting.

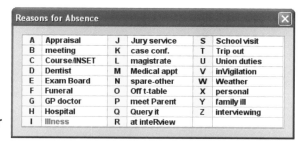

Reasons for Absence						☒
A	Appraisal	J	Jury service	S	School visit	
B	meeting	K	case conf.	T	Trip out	
C	Course/INSET	L	magistrate	U	Union duties	
D	Dentist	M	Medical appt	V	inVigilation	
E	Exam Board	N	spare-other	W	Weather	
F	Funeral	O	Off t-table	X	personal	
G	GP doctor	P	meet Parent	Y	family ill	
H	Hospital	Q	Query it	Z	interviewing	
I	Illness	R	at inteRview			

Often they will be attending courses for continuing professional development (CPD) or inservice training (INSET).
Many of these absences will be known in advance and planned for — but often you will find out only at the last minute as the school day starts!

At one time it was universally accepted that the assigning of staff to Cover for absent colleagues was a task requiring the attention of the Timetabler.
However these days, with the use of Cover software, it is commonly seen as an administrative task, not necessarily requiring a teacher.

He's late for his free period!

16.2   Using Cover software

As you would expect, the Cover software gets its data from the timetabler program, so that it knows who is normally teaching each class and in which room.

The Cover software will allow you to quickly tell it about:

- Any planned absences (eg. for CPD/INSET), or events (eg. examinations). These can be entered at any time in the days/weeks/months before the event.
- Any last-minute absences (eg. due to illness, bad weather, traffic, etc).

As soon as the Cover program knows who is absent, and for which periods, it has all the information to decide which classes need to be covered and who is free to do the Cover.

It will display its suggestions.

Cover TimeTable					
	Reg	1	Break	2	3
JAr	-	8J	-	7N	13C
	_	S1	_	S1	_
LBa	8P	8C	-	7P	7J
		SCh	-	LAt	S1

L Baker
Absent due to **Illness**
Periods abs this year: **20**
Lessons abs this year: **11**

S Chalcraft
Free period (pp: 2)
Year done / limit: **0** / –
Week done / limit: **0** / –
Cover loading: **20**
Main subject: **MA**

H French
Supply Teac

StaffCover software

The program takes into account many subtleties.

Some examples:

- If a Science teacher is absent, do you want the Cover program to recommend a Science teacher to do the Cover, for Health & Safety reasons in the laboratory?
- If a female PE teacher is absent, do you want the software to recommend a female teacher to do the Cover, in case she has to enter the changing rooms?
- If a teacher has been used recently to do Cover, then they should have a lower likelihood of doing Cover today (depending on the number of absentees today). But at what point do the first two scenarios over-ride this?

You can customize the program to take into account these and other factors. And you can quickly swap teachers if you wish.

Obviously the Cover software will balance out the amount of Cover done by each teacher, taking into account their teaching load, their other responsibilities and their 'free' periods, as well as any existing workforce agreements.

It will keep a full record of absences, and of Cover done (both by permanent staff and by temporary 'supply' staff). These statistics are always availble for listing or displaying graphically.

The software will also allow you to quickly locate classes and staff, including staff who are doing Cover in the current period.

The program will print timetables and messages in various forms, including:

- A 'master' Cover timetable, showing all the Cover for today (eg. for posting on the Staffroom Noticeboard).
  And an email version of this is sent to named senior staff.

- Individual cover-slips, to be given to staff who are being asked to do cover, with details of which class, where to go, whether work has been set, etc.

  And email versions of these, so that colleagues can get the details via their laptops.

Laura Norder High School   7 May
To: Mr S Chalcraft
Please cover the following lesson:
Period 1 8C Maths in room 7 (for L Baker) Work has been left with the Technician
Thank you Keith Johnson Deputy Head

For more details, see 'What to look for in a Cover program', on the CD.

There is a copy of the Tutorial version of the **StaffCover** software on the CD at the back of the book.

16.3 Summary

Although it is a daily chore, doing the Cover efficiently is important.
For the benefit of the students, and especially for the good morale of the staff it it is vital that the Cover is seen to be managed fairly, and that it is well-tuned to the classes being covered.

Wadya mean, you're going to be ill a week next Friday!

Appendix 1

The Timetabler's Year — A timetable of timetabling

September — October   (if the school year begins in September)
Transfer the data from your timetabler software to your Cover software (if not already done).
Evaluate the new timetable; observe it in action; listen to colleagues' comments.
If colleagues make minor room-swaps etc, make the changes in your MIS and/or timetabler software and/or Cover software.

November — December
Begin discussions on changes for next year.
Aim for complete agreement by New Year on any major changes (eg. in the number of periods per week, or the subjects in the options blocks/ columns/electives), to allow time for 'What if ...?' experiments with your timetabler software.
After any major changes, or routinely every year, re-calculate the contact ratio and the distribution of curriculum bonuses, and check the rooming fraction, and compare them with earlier years (see Chapter 5).
Review and revise the Curriculum Diagram (see Chapter 2).

January — March
Finalise the optional subjects to be offered to Year 9 (and Year 11) students for next year's Year 10 (and Year 12).
Arrange Careers Evenings and other options advice; issue proformas of the choices to students/parents (see Chapter 3).
Collect in and vet the students' choices, and use Options software to analyse and arrange an efficient pattern of option subjects/electives.
Involve Year-Tutors, Subject Leaders, students, parents as necessary.
Counsel any students who do not fit the pattern, until all are catered for.

March — April
Produce a revised Curriculum Diagram (see Chapter 2).

Re-check that it can be covered by existing staff expertise, or is expected to be covered by appointments that are due to be made.
Ask Heads of Department/Subject Leaders to nominate staff for each group, on a proforma sheet. See Chapter 6.
Do you expect Subject Leaders to draw up a Combing Chart for their own department? See Chapter 7.

April — May
Check the Subject Leaders' replies to ensure that all the curriculum is covered, with no omissions or duplications. See Chapter 6.
Check the loading for each teacher, with due allowance for other responsibilities (Year-Tutors, etc).

Apply the pre-scheduling checks, eg. Combing Chart (Chapter 7), Conflict Matrix (Chapter 8), Zarraga's Rule (Chapter 10), on paper or within your timetabler software, especially to suspect areas of the curriculum.
Or just do some automatic 'What if ...?' runs in the timetabler software.

Distribute a final version of the Curriculum Diagram, with the staffing marked on it, for final approval by Subject Leaders.

May — June
Enter the data into your timetabler software and begin scheduling.

Print and publish drafts for consultation (on paper or email), especially if you are using a block timetable. Adjust the schedule as necessary.

June — July
Print and publish the timetable (see Chapter 11), including:
- a 'master' staff timetable for the staffroom/office,
- individual staff timetables for colleagues,
- class timetables for tutor-group noticeboards, etc.

Transfer the timetable data,
- from your timetabler software to Options software, and/or
- from your timetabler software to the school Admin System (MIS)

in order to print out
- Individual Student Timetables, and/or
- Group Lists for colleagues,

to distribute either now, or on the first day of the new term.

Transfer the timetable data from your timetabler software to your Cover software, ready for next term.

September
Begin the cycle again !
Observe your timetable in action ...and feel proud of an amazing achievement ...a timetable that works !

Appendix 2

A flowchart for curriculum planning and timetabling

Bold frame boxes = policy decisions for the Head or Senior Leadership Group
Other boxes = calculations, operations for Director of Studies, Timetabler

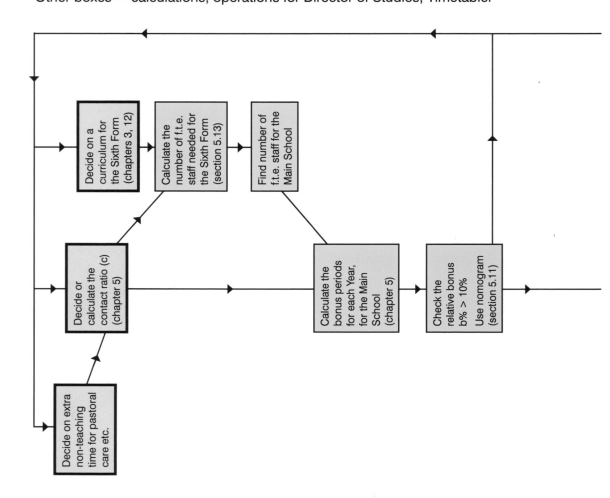

The events on these two pages might not not take place every year –
perhaps in alternate years, or when there is a major change in the
curriculum, intake, or staffing.

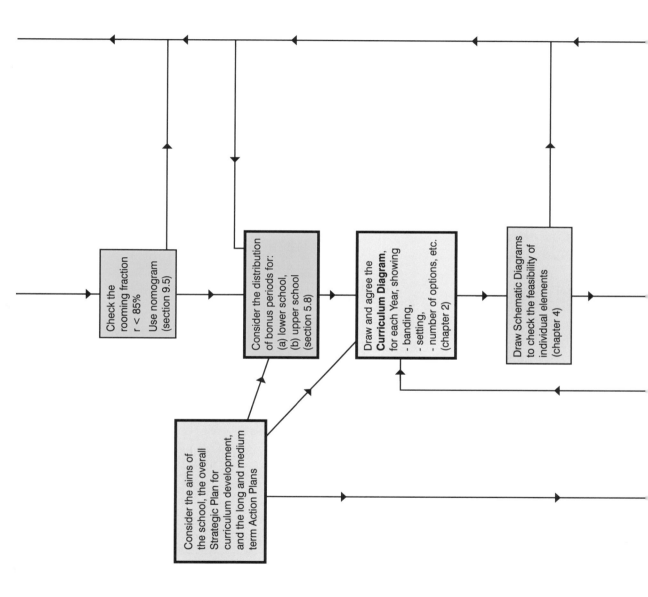

Check the
rooming fraction
r < 85%

Use nomogram
(section 9.5)

Consider the distribution
of bonus periods for:
(a) lower school,
(b) upper school
(section 5.8)

Draw and agree the
Curriculum Diagram,
for each Year, showing
- banding,
- setting,
- number of options, etc.
(chapter 2)

Draw Schematic Diagrams
to check the feasibility of
individual elements
(chapter 4)

Consider the aims of
the school, the overall
Strategic Plan for
curriculum development,
and the long and medium
term Action Plans

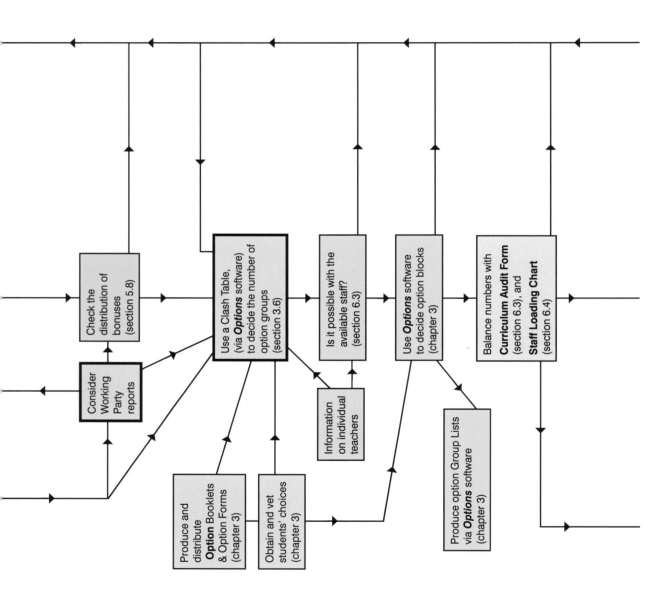

Check the distribution of bonuses (section 5.8)

Consider Working Party reports

Use a Clash Table, (via **Options** software) to decide the number of option groups (section 3.6)

Is it possible with the available staff? (section 6.3)

Use **Options** software to decide option blocks (chapter 3)

Balance numbers with **Curriculum Audit Form** (section 6.3), and **Staff Loading Chart** (section 6.4)

Information on individual teachers

Produce and distribute **Option** Booklets & Option Forms (chapter 3)

Obtain and vet students' choices (chapter 3)

Produce option Group Lists via **Options** software (chapter 3)

Spring Term

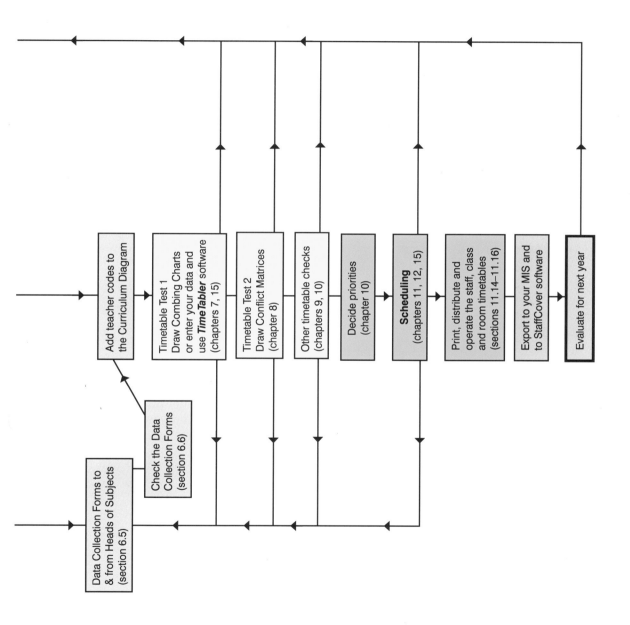

Summer Term

Appendix 3   *Who* should do the timetable?

There are some Heads and governors who seem to believe that the construction of a Secondary School timetable is an administrative task. Those who may be inclined to agree are almost certainly those who have never been closely involved with the construction of a timetable for a school.

Schools exist above all to deliver a curriculum. Teachers, quite rightly, spend a great deal of time reviewing and modifying the curriculum in their schools. In order to deliver this they need an effective and enabling timetable.

Traditionally, the construction has been by a very experienced teacher who not only shares the vision of the school in terms of the curriculum, but also has an intimate knowledge of subjects of the curriculum and their requirements as well as a detailed knowledge of the staff, their capabilities and their aspirations. The Timetabler will also need to have a good professional working relationship with all those who have a responsibility for any part of that curriculum.
He or she will also have monitored the previous timetable, noting any feedback.

In most secondary schools, every year, parts of the curriculum are modified. The Timetabler needs to play an active role in any discussions about possible changes. It is the Timetabler who can point out the implications (and perhaps impossibilities) of any changes.
What is changed in one year or department will have implications on other years or departments. The Timetabler is best placed to guide the group making such changes when costs and benefits are being considered.

During the Spring Term, pupils in Year 9 are working through the process of selecting which subjects to study in Key Stage 4. The Timetabler is normally closely involved in this process as the way choices are made will have a significant impact on the use of staff and the use of specialist accommodation. The Timetabler is often a key person in the discussions that take place about viability of small groups in certain subjects. This is not usually a straightforward 'yes or no' decision but takes into account a range of curriculum and staffing issues as well as taking note of the overall direction in which the school intends to move in terms of its curriculum.

In those institutions with Sixth Forms a similar process takes place, with the Timetabler again playing a key role.

In the late Spring, when the curriculum plan has been finalised, it will be the Timetabler who will begin to look at how this new curriculum will be delivered. Who will teach which subject and how much of each subject will they teach? It is the Timetabler who will work with the Head to ensure that any future vacancies are filled with a view to future demands of the timetable.

At this stage the Timetabler (and the Head) will use their knowledge of staff to guide certain teachers in certain directions in order to both facilitate the delivery of the curriculum but also to enhance the careers of the teachers concerned.

When Subject Leaders allocate staff to teaching groups they will do so within the constraints laid down by the Timetabler. This of course might well be a contentious issue if the Timetabler were not a senior colleague from the teaching staff team.

Once these allocations have been made the Timetabler will test the data to check out the feasibility of the allocations. With any problem, the Timetabler will go back to the Subject Leader with suggestions of changes, which could be made to remedy the situation. To originate such suggestions assumes on the part of the Timetabler some knowledge of the subject, a detailed knowledge of the staff involved and an established working relationship with the Subject Leader. On occasions some Timetablers encounter an 'uncooperative' Subject Leader. At such times, if the Timetabler's status is not at least equivalent to a Subject Leader, unsatisfactory outcomes can be expected!

After all of these departmental tests have been completed, the Timetabler does further feasibility checks and at this stage perhaps identifies problems that are not specifically within one department. At this point the Timetabler may need to convene a meeting between (say) three Subject Leaders in order to resolve an issue involving them all. If the Timetabler is part of the Leadership Group and chairs the meeting the dynamics are accepted as normal.
If however, the Timetabler is not part of the teaching staff of the school, then such a meeting is likely to have a strange 'feel' for those involved.

During the construction phase, problems are likely to arise which will require delicate negotiation with individuals or groups of people.
It is difficult to imagine how these will take place satisfactorily if the Timetabler is not an established member of the school's teaching team.

A small part of the timetabling process may well be correctly described as an administrative task. If a school uses a computer system in order to construct the timetable then the entry of the data into the computer may be just an administrative or even secretarial process. This however assumes that a considerable amount of work has been done by a senior member of the teaching staff in converting the school's curriculum plans into a practical working document. At the end of the construction process there is also some administrative work involved in printing out the various extracts that will be useful to staff at the beginning of the Autumn Term.

Transferring the completed timetable from a manual model or from timetabling software to the school's MIS will involve administrative tasks, though it will also need the involvement and interpretation of the Timetabler.

All of the rest of the task of constructing the timetable is far from being administrative and needs to be handled by a teacher with considerable experience. It needs a member of the leadership group who has a detailed knowledge of the process by which the curriculum is delivered.

Appendix 4

21 Curriculum Formulae

Symbols used in this appendix:

N = number of pupils ⎤
T = number of f.t.e. teaching staff   these are determined by external factors, eg. funding
R = number of rooms / teaching spaces ⎦

c = contact ratio (as a decimal fraction) ⎤
r = rooming fraction
p = number of teaching periods in the curriculum   these are determined by the school
$b\%$ = relative bonus
W = number of periods in the timetable cycle ⎦

These formulae apply to the main school only (see Chapter 5); if you have a 'Sixth Form' or other years that are not taught for all the periods of the cycle, see section 5.13.

A.   Following T. I. Davies (1969):

Since p teaching periods are provided for N pupils, each of whom studies W periods:

the average group size = $\dfrac{W}{p}$ of N = $\dfrac{WN}{p}$ (1)

If a class has a zero bonus, then the average group size is 27 ('mean sea level', as laid down by Davies, as a reference level, see Chapter 5).

Then from (1): $\dfrac{WN}{p} = 27$

Since this class has zero bonus, therefore: Basic periods (p) = $\dfrac{NW}{27}$

Also, since the effective number of Teachers is cT, for N pupils, we can say:

the average group size = $\dfrac{N}{cT}$ (2)

Equating (1) and (2) and eliminating N, we get the **Staffing Equation** or 'First Law':

$p = cTW$ (3)

The number of bonuses = actual – basic = $p - \dfrac{NW}{27} = cTW - \dfrac{NW}{27}$ (4)

The relative bonus $b\% = \dfrac{\text{bonus}}{\text{basic}} \times 100\% = \dfrac{\text{actual provision} - \text{basic}}{\text{basic}} \times 100\%$

$$= \frac{p - NW/27}{NW/27} \times 100\% = \frac{27p - NW}{NW} \times 100\% \qquad (5)$$

From (4) and (5): number of bonuses $= \dfrac{b\% \times NW}{2700} \qquad (6)$

From (3) and (5): $b = \dfrac{27cTW - NW}{NW} \times 100 \qquad$

Rearranging we get: $\dfrac{N}{T} = \dfrac{2700c}{(100+b)} \qquad (7)$

This is the equation used in drawing up the nomogram (for the top labels).

B.   I. B. Butterworth (1975) proposed:

rooming fraction, $r = \dfrac{\text{average number of teaching spaces in use } (cT)}{\text{total number of teaching spaces } (R)}$

That is: $r = \dfrac{cT}{R} \qquad (8)$

Eliminating c from equations (7) and (8), we get:

$$\frac{N}{R} = \frac{2700\,r}{100 + b} \qquad (9)$$

C.   However we can take the ideas of Davies and Butterworth several steps further, as follows:

Eliminating T from (3) and (8) we get the **Rooming Equation** or 'Second Law':

$$\boxed{p = rRW} \qquad (10)$$

From (3) and (10), it is sometimes useful to think of the timetable as requiring:

average number of staff teaching at any time		average number of classes taught at any time		average number of rooms used at any time	(11)
cT	$=$	p/W	$=$	rR	

For **curricular** flexibility, b should not be less than $\sim 10\%$ (see section 5.9).

From (5) : $\quad \dfrac{27p - NW}{NW} \times 100\% \geqslant 10\%$

hence: $\hspace{4cm} p \geqslant 0.0407 \, NW$ $\hspace{3cm}$ (12)

This gives the minimum number of teaching periods required for a main school of N pupils (ie. not including any 'sixth form').

From (3) and (12) : $\quad cTW \geqslant 0.0407 \, NW$

therefore $\hspace{3cm} c \geqslant 0.0407 \, \dfrac{N}{T}$ $\hspace{3cm}$ (13)

This gives a minimum value of c once the staffing ratio N/T has been decided. ie. c cannot continue to decrease indefinitely unless the staff ratio improves.

For **scheduling** flexibility, r should not be greater than ~ 0.85 (see Chapter 9).

From (10) : $\quad \dfrac{p}{RW} \leqslant 0.85$

Therefore: $\hspace{2cm} p \leqslant 0.85 \, RW$ $\hspace{3.5cm}$ (14)

This gives a preferred maximum value for the number of teaching periods in the school or in a department requiring specialist rooms.

From (3) and (14) : $\quad cTW \leqslant 0.85 \, RW$

therefore: $\hspace{3cm} c \leqslant 0.85 \, \dfrac{R}{T}$ $\hspace{3cm}$ (15)

This gives a preferred maximum value for the contact ratio.

Changing the subject to T : $\quad T \leqslant \dfrac{0.85 \, R}{c}$ $\hspace{3cm}$ (16)

This can be used to calculate the 'maximum' size of a specialist department.

For both curricular and scheduling flexibility, we combine (12) and (14):

$$0.0407\,NW \leqslant p \leqslant 0.85\,RW \tag{17}$$

This gives the range of values which p can take.

Also, from (13) and (15):

$$0.0407\,\frac{N}{T} \leqslant c \leqslant 0.85\,\frac{R}{T} \tag{18}$$

This gives the range of values which c can take.

Equating the upper and lower limits in either (17) or (18), we get Johnson's rule of thumb:

$$\frac{N}{R} < 21 \tag{19}$$

If the number of students divided by the number of teaching spaces is greater than 21, then the school has lost curricular flexibility ($b < 10\%$) or scheduling flexibility ($r > 0.85$) or both.

If a 9-13 middle school or the lower school of a split-site complex has a simple curricular structure which is only a 'basic' provision of $NW/27$, then from (14) we get, for that building :

$$\frac{N}{R} < 23 \tag{20}$$

This implies a correspondingly lower value of N/R for the upper school building.

Finally, though it is not very useful, we can combine N, R, T, c, r, b into one equation. The best version, from (7) and (8) is:

$$\frac{NR}{T^2} = \frac{2700\,c^2}{r\,(100+b)} \tag{21}$$

The left-hand side of this equation is determined by external factors (eg. funding); the variables in the right-hand side are determined by the school. The value of each side of the equation is usually in the range 16 ± 2.

Ah-ha ...I was wondering when someone would spot the deliberate mistake!

A Glossary of timetabling terms

Activity
A set of timetabling resources.
eg. 7A for 3 periods of Science with Mr Johnson.
eg. All Year 11 with 14 teachers for 2 Double periods of Option Block B.

Band
A sub-division of a year-group (ie. a Year or a Grade), representing a population of students with a common curriculum. Bands may be ability-bands (eg. Upper-band, Lower-band).
eg. in Year 9 there are 6 classes 9A, 9B, 9C, 9D, 9E, 9F, and 9AB form a band.
A band may be a 'half-year-group' (eg. 9DEF in this example).

Basic Data
The basic resources used in timetabling, including: Classes (of students), Teachers, Rooms, Subjects. See also Resource.

Block
A group of activities timetabled at the same time ('in parallel').
The activities may be 'setted', or may be 'option choices' ('electives'), or may be part of a 'circus' or 'rota', or may be parallel groups divided on the basis of sex (eg. for PE.)
The diagrams in chapter 2 show a variety of curricular models with different blocking arrangements.

Block timetabling
Sometimes called 'Faculty timetabling'. See chapter 13.
An overall Block Timetable is sketched out by a senior member of staff, and then the responsibility for staffing the activities is devolved to each faculty.

Circus, or rota, or carousel
A blocking arrangement on the timetable which allows students to rotate to different groups during the course of the year.
eg. suppose 7AB is timetabled with 3 Technology teachers in parallel, so the students in 7AB are divided into 3 thirds. After a term (semester) the students rotate so that students who were doing Food Technology change to the Textiles teacher, while the group which was doing Textiles moves to the Design Technology teacher, etc.

Clash Table
A clash table of Subjects chosen by students for their Options (Electives). For more details see the free Tutorial Booklet for the *Options* program, available from www.timetabler.com
Note: this is different from another clash table called a 'Conflict Matrix' (below).

Class
This can be an ambiguous word for a population of students. 'Class' can mean:
i)   A Registration Group (or Tutor Group, Form Group).   eg. class 7A
     This is the normal meaning used in *TimeTabler*.
ii) A group of students brought together for the teaching of a particular subject.
     eg. 7A-French The more correct name for this is 'Teaching Group'.

Columns   See Option Blocks.

Combing Chart
A useful graphical method for checking whether a set of teachers (eg. a department) will fit into the timetable cycle. See chapter 7 of 'Timetabling'.
TimeTabler software will draw a Combing Chart for you automatically.

Common Core

The part of the curriculum (usually in Upper School) which is compulsory for all students (as distinct from the optional or elective part).

Composite class

When 2 or more classes (forms, registration groups, tutor groups) combine to form a band. For example, 7ABC is a composite class (of 7A, 7B, 7C). Compare with 'pure class'.

Compromise

A change (a relaxation) in the original data in order to make progress with the timetable. Timetabling has been described as the art of (acceptable) compromise.

Conflict

Activities with common resources are in conflict.
The conflicting requirements mean that they can't be timetabled simultaneously.
eg. Mrs Jones cannot teach both 7A and 8B on Monday-period-1.

Conflict Matrix

A clash table for analysing the conflicts between 2 sets of teacher-teams. Not to be confused with a Clash Table. See chapter 8.
TimeTabler will draw a Conflict Matrix for you automatically.

Consistent setting

When a number of subject departments agree to group students consistently, to facilitate scheduling the subjects in a block.
See the diagrams in sections 2.10–2.12 of this book.

Contact Ratio

This is equal to the average teaching load of the staff (in periods) divided by the number of periods in a full timetabling cycle.
A typical value in the UK is in the range 0.70 – 0.84 (70% – 84%).
See chapter 5.

Container Blocks

A block of curriculum time into which a number of activities (with classes, teachers, rooms, subjects) must fit, without breaking out of the block of time. In the UK this can include blocks involving:

- Coordinated Science sets (with Physics, Chemistry, Biology taught by 3 teachers in consistent groups), or

- 'Consistent setting' blocks (eg. with History and Geography to be taught in the same setted groups as English, see chapter 2), or

- Option Blocks, particularly in Years 12/13, with split-teaching (eg. the History group is taught by 2 teachers at different times, while the Physics group is taught by 2 teachers at different times, with any permutation of a History teacher plus a Physics teacher to be allowed), etc.

TimeTabler allows you to specify Container Blocks while retaining the flexibility of movement (using 'musical chairs' moves) within the block.

Cross-setting

A method of mixing two subjects in a block when you don't have enough teachers for the entire block. See chapter 2.

Curriculum

The courses of study arranged by the school, to be staffed and timetabled.

Curriculum Analysis   See Staff Deployment Analysis.

Curriculum bonus

A measure of the amount of curriculum time allocated to a class (or student population) in excess of a notional basic provision.

Curriculum Diagram

A concise and accepted method of showing the structure of a curriculum.
Sometimes called a Curriculum Plan or Curriculum Notation. See chapter 2.
An essential tool and the starting point of the timetabling process.
See also http://www.timetabler.com/SupportCentre/CurriculumDiagram.xls

Cycle

The Curriculum Cycle, or Timetable Cycle, is the period of time after which the timetable repeats itself.
The most common types currently are : 25-period 5-day week, 50-period 10-day fortnight, 30-period 5-day week, or 60-period 10-day fortnight.
Sometimes 6-day cycles are used, both the fixed type (eg. Mon-Sat) and the 'rolling 6-day' type (eg. Day1 is on Monday the first week, on Tuesday the second week, etc.)

Day-Blocking

The intention that similar activities should not be scheduled on the same day.
For example, *TimeTabler* will automatically ensure that 5 single periods of French are placed on 5 different days.
P.E. and Games will often be DayBlocked.

Degrees of Freedom

A measure of how much flexibility exists for the placing of an activity. This in turn has implications for the best sequence of scheduling the activities.
TimeTabler automatically displays a Priority List for you, based on the number of degrees of freedom and many other criteria.

Disjoint teams

Non-over-lapping teams. ie. with no teachers/resources in common.
The idea also applies to class-combinations and room-combinations.
See also the Principle of Compatibility and the Combing Chart.
More details in chapter 8.

Electives   See Option Blocks.

f.t.e.

This stands for Full-Time-Equivalent when talking about the number of teachers.
eg. a school might have a f.t.e of 61.5 staff.
A part-time teacher who is paid for 2 full days (only) in a 5-day week would have a f.t.e. of 0.4.

FIT

A very powerful feature in *TimeTabler*, which finds 'musical-chairs' moves of up to 16 steps.

Fixed points

The parts of the timetable which are at pre-determined times and locked in place.
eg. "Year 11 always have Games on Wednesday afternoon."
eg. "All classes have PSE on Thursday period 1."

Free choice

A system of Option Blocks (or Pools, or Electives, or Columns) where the students can choose a specified number of subjects from a list, without any restriction on their choice.
The Blocks are then constructed so as to maximise the student satisfaction, while minimising the staffing cost, using a program like *Options*.

Form-entry (f.e.)
A unit used for indicating the size of a school's intake of students, normally based on the number 30. For example, 4 f.e. = 120 students in the year-group.

Grid timetable
A timetable cycle based on a small unit of time, with lessons taking multiple units. For example, a 20-minute grid, with lessons taking 2 units (40-minutes), 3 units (60-minutes), etc. Also called a 'modular' or 'granular' timetable. See chapter 11.
More common in colleges than schools.

Guided choice
A system of Options where 'choice' subjects are arranged in Blocks (or Pools, or Electives, or Columns) and students choose one subject from each Block.
A program like *Options* will check group-sizes and look for swaps to balance the groups.

Heterogeneous option
Where the subjects in an Option Block are from different areas of the curriculum.

Homogeneous option
Where the subjects in an Option Block are basically from one curriculum area.
eg. a Science Block. See chapter 3.

Key Stage
A description of the stages of education in the UK, where: KS1 = ages 5–7. KS2 = ages 7–11. KS3 = ages 11–14. KS4 = ages 14–16. KS5 = 16–19.

MIS   Management Information System
An administration system for the school or college. Examples include Capita SIMS.net, Serco Facility, Phoenix e1, RM Integris, WCBS/PASS, iSAMS, SchoolBase, etc.
(*TimeTabler* can export the completed timetable to each one.)

Multiple periods
Consecutive periods of the same activity. eg. doubles (D), triples (T), quadruples (Q), etc.

Musical chairs
An essential scheduling tactic. An interchange of activities on the timetable in order to allow another activity to be scheduled. Moves can be 2-step, 3-step, 4-step, etc., as illustrated in chapter 11.
TimeTabler software will easily find and use moves of up to 16-steps for you.

Non-class activity, non-teaching activity, non-contact activity
A scheduled activity involving staff but not students. eg. a timetabled departmental meeting.

Non-rectangular week
When the days are of different length. eg. 6 periods on each day except Friday which has only 5 periods.

Option Blocks
Also called Option 'Pools', or 'Electives', or 'Columns'.
Areas of the (Upper School) curriculum where 'choice' subjects are grouped into Blocks for simultaneous teaching, and allowing students a choice of curriculum.
For more details of how to organise efficient Option Blocks, see the free download of the Options Tutorial Booklet, and the free *TimeTabler* Tutorial Booklet, at www.timetabler.com

Parallel activity
Linking of two or more classes for an activity. eg. if you want class 7A and 7B to be together for a **D**ouble and two **S**ingle periods with both teachers PQ and RS, then in *TimeTabler* you would enter : 7AB   DSS   PQ RS

Period spread or breakdown
The way in which all the periods of an activity are to be placed across the school week (timetable cycle). eg. 2 Doubles (DD), or 5 Singles (SSSSS) on 5 different days.

Pre-assignments   See Fixed Points.

Principle of Compatibility
An important timetabling rule. When dividing a larger set of resources into smaller sets, the sub-sets should ideally be disjoint.
It applies mainly to teachers and to classes. See chapter 7.

Pure class
A single class with one teacher. eg. 7A-History with teacher KJo.
Most common for lower-school activities. Sometimes (in SIMS only) called a 'linear group'.
Compare this with the entry for 'composite class'.

Resource
The fundamental data: Classes, Teachers, Time, Rooms, (Subjects). See also Basic Data.

Rooming fraction
The ratio of the average usage of rooms (in periods) divided by the number of periods in the timetable cycle. A value of more than 0.85 (85%) will cause increasing difficulties.
More details in chapter 9.

Scheduling
The actual constructing of the timetable, assigning the activities to specific time-slots.
By contrast the word 'timetabling' is typically used for the entire process, from curriculum planning to final publication of the printouts.

Schematic diagram
A diagram (of classes v. time) for checking the theoretical fit into the timetable cycle of one (or more) year-groups, without taking account of period-breakdown. See chapter 4.

Set or setted activity or ability set
Where teaching groups for the same subject are taught in parallel, with students allocated to groups according to their attainment level or ability in that subject.
This allows a student to be taught in the top set for Maths and in the bottom set for English if this is appropriate to his/her level of attainment.
In some countries (eg. France) this method is never used.

A more modern terminology is 'grouping according to prior attainment'.
In some MIS, 'Set' is sometimes wrongly used to mean any Teaching Group.

In *TimeTabler*, 4 Maths sets (with teachers Ma1, Ma2, Ma3, Ma4) across classes 7A, 7B, 7C, for 3 Single periods, would be entered as: 7ABC   SSS   Ma1 Ma2 Ma3 Ma4

SIFA   Systems (Schools) Interoperability Framework Association.
An organisation originating in the USA (but now in the UK and Australia) for software that allows the transfer of data between different MIS and other programs such as *TimeTabler*.

Split-class, split-teaching
An adverse feature of a poor timetable when a teaching group unintentionally has different teachers for some of their lessons.
eg. 7A has 4 periods of Maths; three with Mr Smith and one (unintended) with Mrs Jones.

Split-site
Where a school is organised on two (or more) sites, usually with the older students on one site and the younger students on the other. The timetabler has to allow time for staff to commute between the sites.

Staggered lunch
When different year-groups have a lunch-break scheduled at different times (to facilitate better use of resources). See chapter 11.

Staff Deployment Analysis
A method of analysing the usage of staffing resources, so as to compare schools or to compare year-groups (grades) within a school.
(It is sometimes, wrongly, called Curriculum Analysis.)
It analyses the distribution of teaching time to different parts of the school, by calculating curriculum bonuses or bonus periods for year-groups (or bands, or classes).
This is done for you in *TimeTabler*. See chapter 5.

Staffing ratio eg. 1 : 16
The ratio of the total number of (full-time-equivalent) teachers to the total number of students.
PTR (pupil-teacher ratio) is the same quantity inverted (eg. 16 : 1).

Staff Loading Chart
A table used to check:
i) that each teacher will have a suitable teaching load (contact time), and
ii) that the entire curriculum is covered by teaching staff. See chapter 11.

Sub-band
Where a population is divided differently at different times of the cycle.
eg. Year 9 is divided into sub-bands **a** and **b** for English/Humanities and sub-bands **x** and **y** for Maths/Science. See chapter 2.

Teacher-team
There are 2 possible meanings:
i)   A team of teachers teaching in parallel, at the same time.
     eg. 4 Maths teachers teaching 4 Maths 'sets' at the same time. eg. several teachers teaching the subjects in an option block. This is the usual meaning.
ii) A team of teachers that teach a class at different times of the week.
     eg. the group of teachers that teach class 7A for different subjects.

Teaching Group
A group of students brought together for the teaching of a particular subject. eg. 7A-French. In some admin systems (MIS) a Teaching Group is sometimes ambiguously called a 'Set' or a 'Set Group'. See 'Set'.
Teaching Group information can be transferred from *TimeTabler* to an MIS.

Time-slot
A time (period) during the timetable cycle, to which a lesson can be assigned (scheduled).

Time-frame
The timetable cycle (school week/fortnight), divided by periods, breaks, days, etc.

Trapped time
A feature of a poor timetable when a part-time teacher has unpaid periods trapped between paid periods, rather than grouped together.

Zarraga's Rule
This states that: "as far as possible, teachers who are members of the same teacher team in one part of the school should be allocated to different classes for pure-class activities in another part of the school". The reasons are explained in chapter 8.
TimeTabler software will automatically do this analysis for you.

About the Authors

Keith Johnson was born in Darlington and went to Manchester University before beginning his teaching career in schools in Manchester. He was Physics teacher, Head of Physics, Deputy Head, Timetabler, and Acting Head before becoming Science Inspector/Adviser for the City of Manchester.

He is the author of the best-selling *GCSE Physics for You* which for many years was the most widely-used Physics textbook in the UK. He is co-author of the *Spotlight Science* series for Key Stage 3 and *Advanced Physics for You* and many other books. He has won awards for directing 16mm films.

He has been timetabling and running timetabling courses for over 30 years and was one of the first teachers to write software for timetabling.

Keith and his wife Ann, a painter, have two children and three grandchildren. They live in Manchester and in the Pyrenees. Keith enjoys playing his guitars and riding off-road on his 600cc trail bike ...which he often falls off by riding too slowly!

Web-sites : www.timetabler.com   www.physics4u.co.uk

Mervyn Wakefield is a consultant and a leading UK expert in curriculum organisation and timetabling.

He taught in secondary schools in the UK and in Asia for 16 years before becoming an LA inspector in Cumbria. He also had 10 years' experience as an Ofsted inspector. Mervyn began timetabling 30 years ago and has been running timetabling courses for over 20 years. As a consultant he is often called into schools as a trouble-shooter in timetabling.

Mervyn and his wife Anne (both originally from Norfolk) have three children and enjoy living in the Lake District.

Mervyn is a qualified CAA Air-Ground Operator and for a number of years he ran the Control Tower at his local airport at the weekends – no room for conflicts there!

Website :   www.education-management-services.co.uk

Chris Johnson was exposed to timetabling at a tender age – his earliest memories are watching his father poring over hundreds of pieces of coloured card. Despite this early brainwashing, Chris started his career as a Nuclear Physicist. However, he was gradually lured back to timetabling and has spent the last 10 years developing the *TimeTabler* software.

Chris spends his family-time practising at being a good husband and father, to Rachel and their 3 children. He spends his spare time writing poetry and marvelling at how many different ways Man City can conspire to lose a football match. His goals in life are to see *TimeTabler* used by every UK school and to see Man City win something!

Web-site :   www.timetabler.com

Bibliography

Brooks, J.E., Dixon, C., and Zarraga, M.N., *The Mechanics of School Timetabling*, School Timetabling Applications Group, 1975
A concise straightforward introduction to the principle of compatibility, conflict matrices and schematic diagrams.

Brookes, J.E., *Timetable Planning*, Heinemann, 1980, ISBN 0-435-80150-3
Includes detailed descriptions of conflict matrices, schematic diagrams, schematic matrices and solution space diagrams.

Davies, T.I., *School Organisation*, Pergamon, 1969, ISBN 08-013419-X
The original statement on staff deployment analysis, but difficult to read.

Delacour, A.W., *Logical timetabling*, Pulin Publishing, 1971
A wordy book, covers the timetabling process but short on details.

Hottenstein, D.S., *Intensive Scheduling*, Corwin Press, 1998, ISBN 0-8039-6654-7.
A look at block scheduling in America.

Knight, B., *Managing School Time*, Longman, 1989, ISBN 0-582-03085-4
An interesting look at timetabling and the school day, worldwide.

Lawrie, N., Veitch, H., *Timetabling and Organisation in Secondary Schools,* NFER, 1975.
With a survey of the sequences in which timetablers tackled scheduling in the 1970s.

Lewis, C.R., *The School Timetabler*, Cambridge University Press, 1961
A readable book, but based on simple grammar school curricula of the time.

Salt, F.B., *Timetabling Models for Secondary Schools,* NFER, 1978
A look at consistent blocking.

Shearer, G., Vacher, K., Hargreaves, D.H., *System Redesign-3, Curriculum Redesign,* Specialist Schools & Academies Trust, 2007, ISBN 1-905150-93-8
A look at vertical grouping and new school structures, short on detail.

Simper, R., *A Practical Guide to Timetabling,* Ward Lock, 1980, ISBN 0-7062-4064-2
A concise coverage of the timetabling process.

Walton, J., (ed), *The Secondary School Timetable,* Ward Lock, 1972
A desultory treatment of timetabling; one good chapter on block timetabling.

Yes, I'm sure I'll have it done in no time at all

Index

A

B

C